Catastrophe and Survival

Catastrophe and Survival
Walter Benjamin and Psychoanalysis

Elizabeth Stewart

continuum

NEW YORK • LONDON

The Continuum International Publishing Group Inc
80 Maiden Lane, New York, NY 10038

The Continuum International Publishing Group Ltd
The Tower Building, 11 York Road, London SE1 7NX

www.continuumbooks.com

Library of Congress Cataloging-in-Publication Data
A catalog record for this book is available from the Library of Congress.

ISBN: 978-1-4411-9632-3 (hardcover)

Typeset by Newgen Imaging Systems Pvt Ltd, Chennai, India
Printed in the United States of America

For Charles

Contents

ACKNOWLEDGMENTS

I am greatly indebted to Adam Zachary Newton, my friend and colleague, for his thorough readings of and always productive questions about my manuscript, to my friends, colleagues, and readers Chris McGahan and Allison Smith, to Luke Thurston for use of his translation of Lacan's Seminar on the *sinthome,* to Hunter College Art Galleries and Mary Ann Caws for use of her wonderful translation of Bonnefoy's essay on Mallarmé's "Igitur," to Michael Steinberg for having invited me to the German Studies Association's panel on "Walter Benjamin and Martyrdom" in Milwaukee in 2005 that got the ball rolling, to Dr. Judy Eekhoff for long-distance and face-to-face conversations about Bion, feedback on much of Chapter 5, and for getting me to the "Bion and Catastrophic Change" conference in Seattle, to Jules Simon for a wonderful ISSEI panel on Benjamin and Arendt in Malta and for his feedback on my work-in-progress. Many thanks also to my student assistants Benzion Chinn, Mordechai Shinefield, Michael Silverstein, and Meir Areman.

Profound, affectionate thanks go to Harold Bloom, "big bear" and *Doktorvater,* for years of teaching and friendship.

Many thanks to the Deans Office of Yeshiva College (in particular, Deans Srolovitz and Sugarman) and the Office of the Provost of Yeshiva University for their financial support.

Last but not least, deep thanks to Haaris Naqvi at Continuum Books for believing in the project and for his gentle leadership.

Ingrid, Asher, and Binyamin made it possible.

INTRODUCTION

[T]he artistic expression of the miracle . . . is what dominates [art and architecture] in the period after the counter-reformation . . . the impression of supernatural forces is supposed to be aroused in the powerfully projecting and apparently self-supporting structures precisely in the upper regions . . . With the sole purpose of intensifying the impression, the reality of these laws is, on the other hand—in the lower regions—recalled in an exaggerated fashion. What else can be the purpose of the constant references to the violence of the supporting and supported forces, the enormous pedestals, the doubly and triply augmented projecting columns and pilasters, the strengthening and reinforcement of their interconnecting elements . . . What other function have they than to emphasize the soaring miracle above, by drawing attention to the difficulties of supporting it from below?

(Benjamin 1928/1998, 234–5)

It is said that the basic idea of *The Origin of German Tragic Drama* came to Walter Benjamin while he was looking at a king in a puppet theater whose hat sat crookedly on his head (Szondi 2006, 27). *The Origin of German Tragic Drama* (1928/1998) is a treatise on the catastrophic demise of the subject of faith, an event that Benjamin situates in the seventeenth century and that he says found its expression in the obscure genre of the disaster-ridden German *Trauerspiel* ("mourning play"). However, Benjamin's book is also a response to the *Souveränitätslehre* ("doctrine of sovereignty") presented in Carl Schmitt's book *Political Theology* (1922/2005). Schmitt was the German jurist and political theorist whose work and thought, among other things, theorized and legitimated Hitler's four times repeated suspension of the Weimar Constitution. Benjamin's book is dedicated to him.[1]

Writing during the Weimar Republic, Schmitt defines the sovereign as he who decides on the state of emergency. The state of emergency beckons to what Schmitt thinks is a necessary dictatorial element within a (democratic) state's constitution which enables this state, embodied in its leader, to act decisively and authoritatively. Such a leader is freed from all legal ("normative") restraints so that he may act and make a decision toward a new constitution. Sovereignty thus includes the power to decide on a radical and absolute break in and suspension of the normative. This *Stillstand* (standstill) allows for the emergence of an act within and upon "bare life," life as such, hovering in a limbo of *anomie*, unprotected by law.

Schmitt envisions a "miracle": the enactment of a new law that imposes, immediately, a new order and a new untroubled and decisive identity. The result is the modern subject (of the state), who is newly constituted at that same moment and who mirrors himself in the *Führer* of a new law. This modern form of sovereignty, which is given the power to act decisively in order to create new law and "life," so Agamben notes, can also under certain circumstances transform the state into a "killing machine" (Agamben 2005, 86).

The fact that Benjamin dedicated his *Trauerspiel* book to Carl Schmitt can be explained by a fascination the two men shared with theological deterritorialization (secularization, suspension of the normative) and with the emergence of a disturbingly vulnerable "bare life," both of which, in Benjamin's view, come to characterize modern human existence. This shared fascination, which in these same years also finds an echo in the increasingly thanatically-oriented preoccupations of psychoanalysis, is the constellation that underlies my book. An urgent need to imagine alternatives to the Schmittian miracle for a subjectivity whose traditional moorings in modern times are unraveling pervades Benjamin's work. His preoccupations lie with the various violences and spell-binding encroachments occurring on the individual's psychophysical fields of experience. They are echoed in various corners of psychoanalytic theory in these same years and in other related cultural productions—related, whether Benjamin was aware of them or not. The psychoanalytic strands I engage here originate both in the most uncanny heart of Freud's thought, and, after Freud, are often judged "esoteric" enough to be pushed to the margins of—sometimes even be banished from—orthodox psychoanalytic theory.

Both of the two discourses I bring together here hover, like Benjamin's Angel of History, above the threat of totalitarian "solutions"—welcomed by Schmitt and parried by Benjamin—to modern *anomie*, and both offer implicit and explicit suggestions for imagining other than "miraculous" models for the modern individual's mental topography. These suggestions are linked by what the Benjaminian and the psychoanalytic thinkers I present here agree are the necessary conditions by which a non-totalitarian subject capable of experience could appear: first, a new relationship to the body and materiality, and second, a wholly new and hugely expanded conception of "writing" and "reading" and the role they can play in everyday human life. The results are a very particular and newly psychoanalytic reading of the mimetic and "creaturely" Benjamin, on the one hand, and on the other of trends in psychoanalysis (Freud, Lacan, Klein, Bion, and Milner) that are literary and political in a new and intimately Benjaminian sense.

Regarding "the creaturely": with Hanssen (2000) I define it as corporeal, anti-systematic contingency that, by introducing a different kind of knowledge which makes the other proximate in anxiety-provoking ways, explodes self-obsessed, omnipotent subjectivity. In my opinion, the "creaturely" involves an expression of the death drive, even as it also provides a modality for "survival" and preservation of the self-within-the-other and vice versa. What Hanssen calls "openness to the natural" within the notion of the creaturely, I call openness to death: faithfulness to transience means faithfulness to absolute discontinuity (and infinite divisibility [Fenves 2001]) as the only truth. While Santner (2006) sees the "creature" as bent and set upon, in need of redemption through "straightening out," I read the turn toward the creaturely itself as the way toward redemption and not as the start of an escape from the state of the creaturely; this involves an immersion into the body—more specifically, into the symptom (what Hanssen calls "fate"). For Santner Benjamin's messiah will come to flatten out the kinks, to unfold and un-cramp an abject rigidified existence. I believe, however, that total "release" from creaturely life is an impossibility to begin with, and that for Benjamin transcendence is precisely what is not available. Thus, conceiving of a formerly crouched creature that has been straightened out crosses a line that Benjamin never crosses.

In much of his work Benjamin wishes to counter Schmitt and the totalitarian theory he represents. His wish becomes increasingly more urgent in the early 1930s with the rise of Nazism and culminates in his esoteric short works about mimesis in 1932–33. Why mimesis? I argue that this work is still necessarily and profoundly related to—in fact, offers answers to—the questions Benjamin begins to ask in his *Trauerspiel* book regarding the possible mental topographies of the individual in the context of legal, political, and psychological states of emergency. How can the encroached-upon individual evade and survive "miraculous" powers of psychic fortressing? And exactly how can she re-collect and reconfigure her new relationship to the material world, which Benjamin describes the seventeenth-century subject as encountering in a wholly new way, a way invaded by the creaturely? How is the subject to be configured if she is to escape those modes of subject-object relations that become dominant in the modern Western world: authoritarian, psychically crushing, and equally predicated on unilateral "miraculous" decision and determination?

The indirect answers that I argue Benjamin provides take us through the disorienting, unstable, even uncanny field of mimesis. Some less traditional definitions of mimesis, in particular those from which I see Benjamin forging his own, are paradoxically predicated in one way or another on instances of catastrophic shattering, disarray, and dissociation.

Countering Schmitt, Benjamin suggests that it is precisely in the "disaster" itself, inside the catastrophe,[2] in the emergency of "bare life" and in *anomie*, that "salvation [is] hidden," rather than in the sovereignty-bestowing "miracle." While mimesis would become Benjamin's major preoccupation in the early 1930s, it is already latently present in the morbid *Trauerspiel* phenomena among which Benjamin lingers at such length and so insistently. Mimesis is also powerfully present in what in the 1920s Freud was to define as the most primitive and originary—that is, pre-historical, pre-verbal, pre-oedipal—recesses of the psyche.[3] These conjunctions come together to formulate the fundamental questions constituting my book: what constitutes the modern subject with whom Benjamin attempts to counter Schmitt's "miraculous," totalitarian subject? And, given some of these conjunctions, how can the praxis of psychoanalysis contribute to concretizing and putting into practice Benjamin's often esoteric statements concerning a subject whose "experience," whose modes of perception and thought, have not succumbed to the enchantments of apotheosis and "miracle"?

Accepting such a Benjamin-psychoanalysis conjunction implies assuming the validity of the claim that there is a meaningful connection between individual life, body, and history and collective life, bodies, and history. Benjamin thinks of individual and collective history and memory as analogous in structure. His concepts of "phantasmagoria," "dream," and "awakening" make that clear, as does his idea that collective structures of experience shape individual perceptual possibilities. Benjamin's essays "The Mimetic Faculty" and "Doctrine of the Similar," both of 1933, are permeated with the basic assumption that phylogeny and ontogeny, micro- and macrocosm, stand in an oscillating and mimetic relationship to one another. The stance that a historical materialist and an individual who is truly alive take toward the past is analogous, too, in Benjamin's thought: both read history critically and against-the-grain; both blast open the narratives of a "historicism" (official, academic history) that have become rigid and exclusive, both retrieve the excluded by way of complex mimetic operations, and both re-construct, re-read, and re-write history in constellations. One may think of what happens in the face-to-face of the psychoanalytic realm in this way, too.

For Benjamin the distinction between collective and individual history is false. Surrealism, for instance, shows how in modernity the individual body has been invaded by modern technology, potentially setting free bodily innervations that could "become revolutionary discharge" (1929*a*/1999, 218). Thus, "[t]he [. . . Surrealists] exchange, to a man, the play of human features for the face of an alarm clock that in each moment rings for sixty seconds" (218). One of the drawings produced by Susan, whose case

I present in Chapter 6, functions as a similar dialectical image. It is entitled "Geometric Head":

> the eyes are widely staring, almost horror-struck [; it is] made of concentric circles; the nose is also made of circles, and the mouth a double circle, with bars in the middle—it looks like a sort of gag. Everything as usual is nailed up, and on the head, as well as the butterfly phallus, is a sort of square dial with numbers, so that the whole head looks mechanized. At the top is a magnet-like shape, as if there to draw out nails. (Milner 1969, 225–36)

The drawing (its actual production a "bodily innervation") lends shape to the effects on individual perception of modern psychiatric technology: the "gag," part of ECT (Electric Convulsive Therapy) equipment and process, finds its response, so to speak, in the "eyes . . . widely staring, almost horror-struck," which recall the "eyes widely staring" of the Angel of History in Benjamin's Thesis IX on the "Concept of History."

FIGURE 1 Paul Klee, Angelus Novus (1920?). *Source:* Retrieved from http://www. google.com/imgres?imgurl=http://www.omm.de/veranstaltungen/festspiele 2005/bilder/RUHR-shadowtime-angelus-novus.jpg&imgrefurl=http://www. johncoulthart.com/feuilleton/2006/12/18/angels-1-the-angel-of-history-and-sensual-metaphysics&h=743&w=581&sz=61&tbnid=I1GKdaN4G68Q8M:& tbnh=141&tbnw=110&prev=/images%3Fq%3Dklee%2Bangel&hl=en&usg =__2-ZHwflkwWeArWy5RVGYT6T8sRw=&ei=6QVaSsaLO8ODtgemhcTdCg sa=X&oi=image_result&resnum=5&ct=image

While much psychoanalytic theory is silent on the relationship between individual and collective history, those trends that underlie my book—the Freud of *Civilization and Its Discontents* (1930), *Group Psychology and the Analysis of the Ego* (1921), "Why War?" (1933), as well as the work of Bion and many instances in Lacan's thought—follow Benjamin's thinking in this. Still, while a psychoanalytic reading of Benjamin has the advantage of throwing light on Benjamin's often mystical, possibly obfuscating, vocabulary ("redemption," "messiah"), reading psychoanalysis through a Benjaminian lens allows psychoanalysis to become conscious of its own historical determinations by a specifically modern European context.

In the chapters that follow I make the case, then, that it is through nuanced psychoanalytic readings of Benjamin and through Benjaminian readings of psychoanalysis that Benjamin's answers to the ethics of subjectivity can and must be formulated. Benjamin claims that the effects of modern experience—the incursions of modern *anomie*, commodification, and violence—are inscribed onto the most monadic levels of an individual's psychophysical life. Like psychoanalysis, Benjamin argues that the individual's psychically and materially determined body and the subject's language are inextricably linked. Both discourses do nothing less than to imagine—and also realize—forms of individual "redemption" (the Benjaminian term) of body-language and body-mind through transformative constellations of thought, corporeality, and language. Imagining such a "re-written" and "re-read" subject involves imagining a radically new configuration of a coherent *Lebenswelt* for a subject that rests on new ontological foundations of the real. This is how I understand the "coming" thought that Benjamin attempted to project in his 1918 "On the Program of the Coming Philosophy."

The overarching thought that emerges from my reading of *The Origin of German Tragic Drama* is that a sine qua non of the survival of the individual's health and resistance to various forms of tyranny is the ability to engage with the enormous psychological challenges posed by theological deterritorialization: not only the ruptures that define modernity but also the leakage of materiality and corporeality that appears symptomatically, swelling up and leaking out of language and psychophysical experience in general. These ruptures and leakages define modernity for Benjamin, according to his reading of the baroque *Trauerspiel*. The latter, for Benjamin, is a symptom of this historical moment.

While Benjamin projects this defining historical moment approximately two centuries into the past, in 1920 Freud changed the course of psychoanalysis by performing an analogous philosophical and psychological operation when he formulated the death drive in *Beyond the Pleasure Principle*.

But instead of, like Benjamin, linking this catastrophic upheaval to the ori gins of modernity, he universalized it: his "origin" is nothing less than the origin of life in death, the origin of mind in the most biological of facts. Nevertheless, unintentionally perhaps, Freud in fact does link it to modernity, to its obvious signpost: World War I. It was from within the symptoms exhibited by shell-shocked soldiers, the repetition compulsion, that the "catastrophe" of the death drive emerged—through the stuttering repetitions, the fascinations, the tics and other mimetic enchantments of the "traumatic neuroses." Benjamin's work echoes (mimetically) Freud's thanatic work. His descriptions of a number of psychological states, stances, and acts in the Baroque—catastrophe, martyrdom, melancholia, mourning, allegory, and writing—all of which, I argue, have anti-tyrannical political ramifications, are here given concrete shape and, more impor- tantly, realizable praxis in psychoanalysis, as I describe it in the following chapters.

Before I outline those chapters, one more note. I understand Benjamin's "coming philosophy," the various psychoanalytic theories and practices, as well as the other discourses infused with "catastrophic" forms of mimesis that I call upon to help contextualize both Benjamin and psychoanalysis, as forms of what Benjamin, in his correspondence with Florens Christian Rang, termed "agon." He was referring to Rang's assertion that "agon" lies at the heart of Greek tragedy. "Agon" is the protagonist's "run" from his "sealed fate" by escaping (whether literally, metaphorically or both) from the sacrificial altar always at the center of the tragic stage: he runs from his "destiny as a sacrifice." Agon represents "humanity's consciousness of victory over hieratic petrification," a "redemptive run," a "race run by the soul to reach the god of redemption." It is "a contest between those fleeing and those pursuing; but it becomes this completely only if it results in the possibility of freedom, if its conduct is predicated on the possibility of freedom" (Benjamin 1994, 233–4, letter of January 28, 1924), Rang writes to Benjamin. Benjamin and the discourses with which I associate him run the agon against the petrifying sacrificial fate that makes its comeback in modernity in the form of the Schmittian "miracle," for one, as well as in the phantasmagorias of a modern anaesthetized experience, in the cocoons provided by a totally administered but unexperienced life—as well as in the disappearance and disposal of that "bare life" deemed unworthy and unable to assimilate to it.

Part 1, "Psychoanalytic Benjamin," forms the first part of my dialectic: Chapter 1 reveals "martyrdom," which pervades Benjamin's presentation of the *Trauerspiel*, to be lying at the center of his largely implicit ideas for a modern subject. The martyr-figure who learns to mourn loss is Benjamin's way of intimating a subject who may render himself useless to the authoritarian solution to the catastrophic *anomie* characterizing modern conditions. Constituted by rupture and re-collection in the midst of a decaying tradition, the martyr-allegorist constructs himself in bits and pieces of contingent signifiers that have fallen outside of symbolic structures. Here, through a language that in modernity becomes increasingly more corporeal, Benjamin transforms metaphysics into a theologically inflected materialism. It necessarily sets up the innovative readings of Chapter 2.

This site of "martyrdom" acts as gateway into my psychoanalytic way of reading Benjamin here and in the chapters that follow. While Benjamin's *Trauerspiel* as I present it in Chapter 1 opens the modern subject up, like a body lying on an operating table, Chapter 2 juxtaposes the martyr-allegorist with the Lacanian *sinthome*. The *sinthome* describes a mental topography and a modern and "heretical" (as Lacan puts it) subject that, post-oedipal and post-traditional, in a way that is uncannily close to Benjamin, *writes* itself into being. In the *sinthome*—Lacan's explicit example of *sinthomatic* subjectivity is Joyce—paternal signifiers and authorities are undone, and the new subject (as "supreme artificer") re-configures itself through a language that in its materiality distances itself from merely communicative language and that lays paternal signifiers to waste. Within this Benjamin-Lacan-Joyce conjunction it is possible to see how language can become redemptive-therapeutic in a way that concretely reflects both Benjamin's and Lacan's philosophies of language. *Sinthomatic* and martyr-allegorical forms of reading and writing in this Lacan-Benjamin conjunction transform eschatology into profane praxis. A psychoanalytic understanding of this language provides a praxis for an often abstract Benjamin and is a major theme of the remaining chapters. Lacanian "half-truth" and Benjaminian residual fragment—unfinished, open-ended, and non-transcendental conceptions of self and historical reality—stand as alternatives to the Schmittian and Counter-reformational "miracle," to (delusional) omnipotent subjectivity and dictatorial assumptions of power.

Part 2, the second part of the dialectic, focuses on mimesis and immersion as the profound link between Benjamin's thought of the late 1920s and early 1930s and some of the origins and "heresies" of psychoanalysis. Chapter 3 looks at the specifically European modernist fascinations with mimesis and their representations of mimicry as disappearance, assimilation, even schizophrenia; thinkers such as Ferenczi, Caillois, Mallarmé, and Warburg link it to the experience of modern shock, psychic death, and the death drive. Benjamin, on the other hand, also recognizes mimesis as the secret antidote to petrification and disappearance. An archaic mimetic faculty survives in hidden pockets in language, in children's play and art for Benjamin, and I show that its best-kept secret hiding place is psycho-analysis. Chapter 4 focuses on Benjamin's mimesis essays, and Chapter 5 on the hidden presence of mimesis in the psychoanalytic theories of Klein and Bion. It is a "catastrophic" mimesis with far-reaching affinities with the psychophysical topographies of Benjamin's Baroque. Reading Klein through a Benjaminian lens opens her work and reveries up in unexpected ways. These affinities throw light on what Benjamin meant by the "creaturely" and with it on redemptive models of subjectivity.

Part 3, "Benjaminian Psychoanalysis," brings all of the preceding discussions together in a concrete Benjaminian graphological reading of the drawings in Marion Milner's psychoanalytic case history of "Susan." Benjamin's theory of graphology is mimetic, "catastrophic," and "messianic." In this case history the "creaturely" expresses itself in the reading and writing of embodied language where *Schriftbilder* become *Denkbilder*. With their projections of a post-catastrophic subjectivity a new non-pernicious aura framing the self's relationship with others and with its "material community" comes into being and survives.

Trauerspiel

The importance of Benjamin's *Origin of German Tragic Drama* as a genealogy of modernity and its correlated theory of allegory are well known.[4] The Baroque, as a time and place of drastic experiential and political transformation, is signaled for Benjamin by the collapse of the theocratic state and the rise of absolutist monarchy (Benjamin 1928/1998, 65). The central idea of the *Trauerspiel* is lament for the loss of the human world's unmediated relationship with the Heavens and thus of a whole and harmonic image of origins and history. In the Baroque, "something new arose: an empty world" (138). The *Trauerspiel* puts on display the unhinging of the collective sense of reality and the fragmentation of experience that defines modernity. Everything within creation seems to have suffered an indelible catastrophic rupture; even the "religious man of the baroque clings so tightly to the world because of the feeling that he is being driven along to a cataract with it" (6). The reactions to this world experience are varied. We see the rise of the absolutist state, the imposition of iron-fisted, secular rule onto a world profoundly shaken in its transcendental framing; but we also see a baroque obsession with experiences of physical and psychological rupture, accompanied by excessive passion, suffering, and violence. Both are embodied in the dialectical figure of the "tyrant-martyr" in the *Trauerspiel*, the shaken sovereign who is one moment "martyr" and "tyrant" the next. Benjamin suggests that the ubiquity of martyrdom and suffering is at least partially symptomatic of the tensions between the religious feeling and absolutist secular power. Martyrdom, as the ostentatious presentation of the body in pain, emerges when metaphysical energy displaces and distorts itself into the physical realm, resulting in extreme and excessive interest in the corporeal, the body subject to transience and decay. In the *Trauerspiel* the monarch has two faces: robbed of the transcendental basis of his sovereignty, on the one hand, he displays his worldly power with excess; on the other, as the suffering king of creatures and as creature himself, he is—in reality—far from sovereign and subject to his own creaturely state. The *Trauerspiel* dramatizes this suddenly precarious idea of sovereignty defensively, in ostentatious and often violent displays of power, while the split-off "transcendental impulse" is, as libidinal energy, displaced and, like the puppet king's crown that Benjamin witnessed, slips into the realm of the creaturely.

For my purposes, the most significant points Benjamin makes regarding the Northern German *Trauerspiel* have to do with the plays' treatment of both individual protagonist and history as strangely arrested, reduced to utter materiality, and fragmented. They show that in modernity both human life and human history, with the waning of the subject of faith, are pervaded by a profound anxiety about having become "creaturely." History, as Benjamin never tires of repeating, spreads out in space, in materiality. He shows how, for baroque man, the barred transcendental impulse does not simply evaporate. Instead, it returns in the baroque *Lebenswelt* in the guise of an often morbid fascination with concrete, physical existence, and in the form of ostentatious displays of creaturely suffering, decay, and death. History becomes petrified, fragmented, broken—and corporeal. Underlying "all the provocatively worldly accents of the baroque," he writes, is the "over-strained transcendental impulse" (1928/1998, 65–6), now barred in its upward direction and transformed, almost as if in a backward alchemy, into the basely material. What is denied metaphysical expression finds it in the physical. Julia Reinhard Lupton refers to these traumatic and psychically fraying transformations in baroque experience as the "passion of secularization" (1996, xx). The pervasiveness of martyrdom is correlated with this. Kings as martyrs go mad with the recognition forced on them that they too are creatures:

> When Hallmann's Antiochus is driven mad by the sudden terror awoken in him by the sight of a fish's head at the table; or when Hunold introduces his Nebuchadnezzar in the shape of a beast . . . this reflects the conviction that in the ruler, the supreme creature, the beast can re-emerge with unsuspected power. (Benjamin 1928/1998, 86)

The "unsuspected" character of this "power" that re-emerges suggests both that it has repressed its origins and that a traumatic unbinding has taken place. It is here too that we see the relationship of martyr to melancholiac. A general cultural mode and mood of melancholy pervades the baroque *Trauerspiel*. The closing off of the route to the beyond and the exaggerated weight of secular power, on the one hand (primarily in the southern variant), and the uncanny emergence of the natural creature world on the other (the Protestant variant), engendered scenes of martyrdom in both cases. It is the Northern variety that is of interest to me for imagining a Benjaminian post-catastrophic subject.

Intimately related, in my opinion, to this fundamental theme of the *Trauerspiel* is a methodological consequence for Benjamin: throughout the *Trauerspielbuch* Benjamin's presentation and thinking are monadic. In other words, he suggests that collective historical transformations—how culture encounters and interacts with the object world of modernity—are experienced at the same time by the individual on the micro-levels of his psychophysical life. Individuals register historical developments both psychically and corporeally, and their individual sensoria and symptomatologies can function almost as historical documents. Thus, in the Baroque, history transforms primarily into collective, but also into individualized, pain.

Throughout his treatise Benjamin registers these changes taking place as catastrophic, which does not mean, however, that he thought that they should be evaded and defended against. The important phenomenon for Benjamin is the *caesura*, even the violence, implied in the baroque experiential catastrophe, insofar as it blasts open reactionary defenses against modern fragmented experience. The *Trauerspiel* presents a wholly new sort of violence and destructiveness. On the one hand it makes manifest some of the lethal ingredients of modernity, most obviously, the empiricization and thus heightened expendability of human life. But violence as destructiveness is one of the most ambiguous terms in Benjamin's work and is crucial to a full understanding of his link to psychoanalysis. In his "Critique of Violence" Benjamin had made the case for a form of violence that lies absolutely outside the bounds of the law and that could "shatter the dialectic between law-making violence and law-preserving violence . . . The proper characteristic of this violence is that it neither makes nor preserves law but deposes it . . . and thus inaugurates a new historical epoch" (Agamben 2005, 70). "Pure," "divine," or "revolutionary" violence, violence that momentarily shatters paralyzing and falsifying narratives and myths, is to be distinguished from "mythic" violence, the force behind the law. The latter predictably typifies the figure of the tyrant in the *Trauerspiel*. It also characterizes the aesthetics of the dramatic works of the Counter-Reformation, where Baroque religious aspirations meld with a celebration of secular Absolutism and find formal resolution and apotheosis. Catastrophic violence as "pure" violence or *caesura*, on the other hand, the martyr's passion, opens up the space of the "creaturely." It does so by a reversion toward what Benjamin calls "origin": *Ursprung* or *Ur-sprung* ("primal leap").

Origin

"Origin" and "the creaturely" are spaces opened up by modern *anomie* and form the substratum and the question of my book, insofar as they constitute the main points of connection between Benjaminian and psychoanalytic thought and thus also the possibility of imagining something like an everyday Benjaminian praxis.

Benjamin's definition of "origin" appears in the "Epistemo-Critical Prologue" to his *Trauerspiel* book:

> Origin [*Ursprung*], although an entirely historical category, has, nevertheless, nothing to do with genesis [*Entstehung*]. The term origin is not intended to describe the process by which the existent came into being, but rather to describe that which emerges from the process of becoming and disappearance. Origin is an eddy in the stream of becoming, and in its current swallows the material involved in the process of genesis. That which is original is never revealed in the naked and manifest existence of the factual; its rhythm is apparent only to a dual insight. On the one hand it needs to be recognized as a process of restoration and reestablishment, but, on the other hand, and precisely because of this, as something imperfect and incomplete. There takes place in every original phenomenon a determination of the form in which an idea will constantly confront the historical world, until it is revealed fulfilled, in the totality of its history. Origin is not, therefore, discovered by the examination of actual findings, but it is related to their history and their subsequent development. The principles of philosophical contemplation are recorded in the dialectic which is inherent in origin. (45)

Origin thus underlies the existence of the factual. It emerges when normative structures break open. The idea of "origin" permeates Benjamin's treatment and analysis of the German *Trauerspiel*—mainly because he considers the *Trauerspiel* itself to be an acute approximation and adumbration of "origin." Origin constitutes a glimpse at both the material basis of history, primarily the mortified nature of things, as well as at the most basic principle of the historical: transience in dialectical relationship with the human desire to make restitution and to make whole. The *Trauerspiel* is made up of "original phenomena" that share the structural principles of destruction ("disappearance") and restoration, the latter occurring simultaneously with its re-construction. Further "restorations" are transformations, translations of the originary phenomena; the latter "exist" only insofar as they "themselves" are put under erasure ("the process of becoming and disappearance").[5] Pizer's (1987) and Weber's (1991) interpretations of origin represent two major fields in Benjamin scholarship: the Romantic-messianic on the one hand and the deconstructive on the other. While I find Weber's understanding of origin to be most helpful, there are some elements in Pizer's that need to be retained as well.

To begin with, the pull of "origin" takes the shape either of a reaching for origin that returns only with originary fragments in hand or of an uncanny return on the part of something original, something that knocks on the door but presents only fragments that are infused with powerful, if opaque, significance. Pizer places origin primarily in the aesthetic context, as the unidentifiable eddy-like origin of works of art that have a strong truth content and in which the truth content is identical with the truth of the form: its fragmentedness and transience, both of which refer to human history as inherently catastrophic. The catastrophe, however, always already contains the kernels of the messianic. Origin becomes identifiable only in the context of the pre- and post-history of a work; the work opens up virtual reference to origin (Pizer 1987, 75). Since "on the one hand [origin] needs to be recognized as a process of restoration and reestablishment, but, on the other hand, and precisely because of this, as something imperfect and incomplete," the work as origin offers both a "restoration" of something forgotten or repressed that has historically been "disappeared" (this "restoration" is the work's "post-history") *and,* because it remains forever unfulfilled, is an idea that can be evoked only by fragmentary phenomena, the ruins (this is its "pre-history"). "Origin" is both the basis of existence and its fragmentary historical manifestations, its approximations in these reappearances. It is not difficult to understand Benjamin's origin as playing the role on the philosophical and theological levels that Lacan's *objet a* plays on the psychic level, of which more in Chapter 2. The *objet a,* briefly, is the material remnant of the original object, no longer available, but active in shaping the individual's history.

Samuel Weber emphasizes the elements of transformation and dislocation of the original (truth) in the origin's historical "reappearances," that is, its tropological and historical dimensions. Psychoanalytically, the transformativeness of origin corresponds to the ubiquity of repetition and displacement. Origin is never available as such in its entirety. The return to origin is logically mimetic—it always enacts similarity, not identity. Understanding works of art as "original" means reading them in the register of "typology," as they can be the conduits for the (always transformed) reappearance of certain "truths" within history. In fact, Osborne's English translation of Benjamin's text in the passage from the Prologue I have quoted is not entirely accurate in this sense: instead of saying, "it needs to be recognized," Benjamin actually says, "it wishes to be recognized as, etc." ("*Sie will als Restauration, als Wiederherstellung einerseits, als eben darin Unvollendetes, Unabgeschlossenes andererseits erkannt sein*" [1974, 226].) This is important because Osborne's looser translation suppresses the element of wish, even illusion, on the part of origin inherent in its restorative function.

Weber's readings honor more than Pizer's do Benjamin's insistence that "origin" is a fundamentally historical idea: "Indeed it [origin] could be said to define and *name* the essence of the Historical, not just in the *Origin of the Mourning Play*, but for Benjamin's writing in general" (Weber 1991, 468). Origin is the "offspring (*Entspringendes*) of coming-to-be and going-away, *Werden und Vergehen*." This "offspring" is not an idea that came into being some time in the past, but something that leaps out "from the alternation of becoming and passing-away, of coming and going. Origin, the original leap, as it were, thereby emerges as a kind of cast-off: an Ent-springendes, an abrupt jump" (Weber 1991, 468). This cast-off, I will argue, is the Lacanian "little piece of the real," the *objet a*. Although it is unclear whether Weber sees this "cast-off" as an object or as the reflection of a cast off "*Ur-*," this is what Weber means by the "essence of the Historical." In other words, the "Historical" is both absolutely material and unavailable as such, a recollection of history's substratum. The materialist historian constructs history in constellations of original leaps of truth, of messianic flashes, that emerge from and disappear back into this substratum of history. Benjamin will also come to refer to "*Ursprung*" as the "expressionless," "*das Ausdruckslose*," what is unavailable. The historical originary leap is entirely analogous to the leap from divine into human, fallen language in Benjamin's philosophy of language (Benjamin 1916/ 1996), just as the recovery of original "names," instead of conceptual name-tags for creatures and phenomena, constitutes for Benjamin an act of recovery that would explode the slick shell ("historicism") of a fallen history (history as the litany of "once upon a time"). Returns of "origin" in works of art break this historicism open by inserting the seed of something forgotten as origin, something made manifest in an idea's pre- and post-histories. The originary leap is thus like the original Word that bursts out of concealment when one language is translated into another (Benjamin 1921–23/1996). Because of this identification between language and history, the Benjaminian critic is always also a historiographer, and the work of art always also a recovery of true history.

Let us assume that "*Ursprung*," however impossible to grasp, is the clos est we get to "pure" or divine language. Originary moments, repeatedly emerging and disappearing,[6] are moments that have "nothing to do with taking a stand, going upright, with acquiring a certain stature, status or stability" (Weber 1991, 468). They are momentary releases of material that is *entbunden,* uncontained, born. In addition, insofar as origin consists of the rhythm of two moments—the restorative and backward-looking, and the never-finished messianic—it is also characterized by singularity and repetition at the same time. It is irretrievably linked to destruction and catastrophe and its most basic structure is the "eddy." In Benjamin's reading of the *Trauerspiel,* the idea of the ruin is an origin insofar as it recovers the idea of broken wholeness (the fall into material history); it is also messianic in that negatively it invokes messianic restoration.

It is the task of both the critic and the historian to recognize these flashes of originary moments and to bring them into a constellation with other emergences of origin, all appearing only as fragments. This task is recuper- ative and un-assimilating at the same time. Historicism—the lie of the single, authoritative narrative of historical progress—has "forgotten" about origin and holds the mythical narrative up as true. The materialist historian breaks open such imaginary, petrified, and repressive shells of historiography in order to release moments of originary truth. Reference to the originary-but-vanished and to the unfinished in human history is what the more truthful—and faithful—historian offers. According to Pizer, because of the dual movement required for a non-falsifying contemplation and reading of "origin"—namely the restorative moment which, however, can always only be fragmentary, open-ended, and material—for Benjamin truth is what

> blocks all attempts at closure. Fragmentary forms resist closure, as they
> motivate a contemplation characterized by a ceaseless breath-catching, an
> irregular rhythm, a continuous pausing for reflection. Only such forms—
> Benjamin cites the mosaic and the treatise as examples—subvert the inten-
> tionality of knowledge and allow noumenal truth to emerge. Contemplative
> representation is coterminous with a "prosaische Nüchternheit," the only
> manner of writing proper to the representation of ideas. From the dance
> of these represented ideas, truth is recollected ("vergegenwärtigt"). (Pizer
> 1987, 75)

As treatise, Benjamin's book itself is a work that respects origin, as it is open-ended and works to get at the truth of the *Trauerspiel* by collecting its most insistent, repeated, and extreme phenomena which are evoked in fragmentary form; it is both monadic and repetitious. This "breath-like" modality may in part account for its difficulty. Benjamin's reasons for turning to the *Trauerspiel* are at least twofold: on the one hand, in its presentations of primitive phenomena, the *Trauerspiel* presents an "*erstarrte Urlandschaft*" ("a petrified ur-landscape"), an anxious being-stuck in a landscape of fragmentation and violence and despairing attempts at salvation. The genre's lack of cohesiveness, its emphatic fragmentariness and repetitiveness, its emphasis on the contemplation of debris, loss, transience, and evanescence, mark it as particularly "originary," and thus filled to the bursting point with "originary" truth, the truth about history. Its "ideas" emerge repetitively and fragmentarily: these are the ideas of catastrophe, disappearance and retrieval, violence, and the truth of materiality.

But Benjamin also turns to the *Trauerspiel* because he detects a mimetic relationship between the Baroque and his own Weimar. At key moments, his treatise illuminates the usefulness of an understanding of the Baroque for his own historical moment, the collapse of democracy, that is, and the rise of totalitarianism. The *Trauerspiel* is thus originary for Benjamin's own historical and cultural context, and, though it would hardly seem so at first glance, the work is entirely relevant to understanding the rise of fascism: the German *Trauerspiel* arose just prior to the rise and establishment of Absolutism. Benjamin acknowledges that looking again at the *Trauerspiel* throws light on what he considers to be an instance of repetition, a return-and-dislocation of baroque sensibility: Expressionism. Both the baroque *Trauerspiel* and Expressionism for Benjamin secretly dramatize the psychology and phenomenology of the rise of tyranny. Both want to find a way out of the crisis, but remain impotent. "Expressionism" and "Baroque" are the names for a specific constellation of historical, psychological, and aesthetic phenomena that refer obsessively and urgently to "*Ursprung,*" the dialectic of catastrophe and restoration. Both are thus also informed by the dialectic of *anomie*: each involves a return to *Ur*-phenomena, in themselves unavailable and destructive, brought about by crumbling of traditional structures and authorities. And each contains within itself, as it were, the possibility of seeking refuge in a new authoritarianism. Southern Counter-reformation drama took that route, while the Northern *Trauerspiel* remained stuck in broken melancholy, in the "*erstarrte Urlanschaft.*" Implicitly Benjamin is asking, how can the modern fragmented individual escape authoritarian-tending melancholy? Modernity thus emerges from a primal scene of catastrophe and origin. Given their unconscious insight into "origin," the symptoms of *Trauerspiel* and Expressionism both are available to a reading that can provide answers regarding the post-catastrophic and anti-authoritarian subject.

This notion of "originary truth," however, those fragments and ruins of the Baroque, like the strangled scream of Expressionism, may still seem nebulous, confusing. What exactly is this thing that the work of art contains that the critic must rescue from confusion with a work's superficial content? Pensky suggests it is the discovery of the emptiness of the modern world, and with it the discovery of the creaturely (Pensky 2001). Pizer points to "the word of God," the originary, creative word—in Benjamin's terms, "pure language." Along these lines, literary and world history have been histories of the containments, repressions, preservations, and recollections of the divine logos, and ought to be the fragmentary re-collections of what perforce falls out of human narrative (to put it positively) or mythic law (to put it negatively). Weber, in contrast, emphasizes the emptiness of origin. His interpretation of origin approximates the un-symbolized real in the Lacanian sense and the rhetorical figure. He also recommends a reading of the moments of "restoration" and "reinstatement" in the complex mechanism of origin in the key of (German Romantic) irony. Both make for a more literary understanding of origin. For Weber, Benjamin's subversion of plenitude and authenticity are intractable:

> The Ur-sprung is the irremediable split or crack that marks the movement of restoration and reinstatement by which singular beings seek to totalize themselves in their extremity. It is the irreparable fissure or crack that impairs the possibility of history ever being written or thought in a full and authentic manner. (Weber 1991, 473)

Recollection of *Ursprung* explodes ("*sprengt*") myth. Ultimately, Benjamin's historical and literary critical methods aim to rescue original phenomena by means of interruption, by a crucial hesitation in their naming and presentation. In this interruption they are allowed a more diversified space in which to unfold and "un-assimilate" from beneath the concept (or their "forgetting") such that they are loosened from the demiurgic containers of a monolithic narrative.

This "un-assimilating" from below the concept is also what defines Beatrice Hanssen's (1995) interpretation of the "creaturely." The combination of a deconstructive Weber and a more materialist Hanssen provides a persuasive and faithful reading of Benjamin. Between the primordial ground—the concrete material objects of history "as such"—and represented history lies a gap which is a primordial emptiness[7] that Weber suggests is a space of rhetoric. The merit of the deconstructive reading of Benjamin's strategic use of the concept of origin is that origin understood this way undermines and interrupts mythical closures. Origin repeats an interruption of myth that the former has always already enacted. It produces a space of critical thought, a space in which difference can be thought, experienced, and imagined.[8] Origin is an act of cutting, a divergence, a turn away and a distortion. It is a space of *anomie,* where all structures, laws, narratives, concepts, judgments are momentarily unbound. This is also the space of bare life, of the creature.

PART 1

Psychoanalytic Benjamin

Chapter 1

WALTER BENJAMIN AND MARTYRDOM: *TRAUERSPIEL*

Origin as breach and as destruction is at work in the repeated references in Benjamin's "Theses on the Philosophy of History" (1940/1969) to the historian's act of dynamiting a piece of experience out of the deadly continuum of historicism's empty time, whose repressive malaise and depressive inanity is matched in horror only by the threat it provokes: fascism's attempt to make history and politics "whole" by aestheticizing them and eventually bringing them to their apotheosis in war. An alternative stance to *anomie*, in a period readying itself for rule by emergency decree, is to subject traditional narratives themselves to *anomie* and to dissolution in order to rescue their singular ideas, images, works, and thoughts, all of which are being threatened with obliteration. A *caesura* into the empty time of historicism brings the possibility of change[1] and a different mode of relating to objects—a non-grandiose, non-omnipotent mode. Uncovering "origin" is a consequential "act."

The *Trauerspiel*'s presentation of human language and knowledge as fallen and of man as "creaturely" among his crumbling ontological and social structures[2] is such an "act." Even its own emergence as a specific genre is "original" in this sense: the *Trauerspiel* owes much of its origin to its breach with and difference from tragedy. The *Trauerspiel* book demonstrates at length that tragedy is no longer possible for historical reasons. At the same time, tragedy and the *Trauerspiel* are both *entsprungen* (emergent) from the origin of human history, similar to Benjamin's image the breach between pure (divine) and human language. The *Trauerspiel* returns to that origin of fallenness, thus breaking down the main historical idea of tragedy which is also its lie: the omnipotence of the individual. Benjamin's exposition of the historical relationship between Greek tragedy and the seventeenth-century *Trauerspiel* shows how a literary analysis of the latter can function as a covert genealogy of modernity by unlinking the modern subject from the classical individual.

1. From Hero to Saint: The Stirrings of Psychoanalysis in Trauerspiel

Greek tragedy in Benjamin's interpretation narrates and metaphorizes the birth of the individual in Western history. In modernity the *Trauerspiel*

veers away from tragedy. The primary symptoms of this veering away
are the pathological changes that take place in the *Trauerspiel*'s language.
Language has become increasingly empty throughout the course of history,
and classical tragedy could not tell that story. Thus Benjamin sees the
Trauerspiel's displacement of tragedy as a necessary historical event. Tragedy
had helped bring to life a human language appropriate to the emergence of
the classical individual that had organized communities of individuals
standing in defiance of fate and myth, thus generating the beginning of a
truly human history. This is a fundamentally Kantian narrative, a coming-
of-age story: *Mündigkeit*. Ironically, this originating moment of tragedy
had been figured there as the hero's silence, which he opposed to fate.
Nevertheless, the genre of tragedy marked, through the hero's self-sacrifice,
the establishment of a community ruled by human law. Tragedy is Oedipal
in every way; it sets up the Oedipus to begin with in the tragic hero who,
as son, emancipates himself and his brothers from parental (and divine)
fate. Benjamin suggests that the baroque *Trauerspiel* is, with the waning of
the stability of patriarchal structures, no longer governed by a linguistic
Oedipus,[3] even though, not understanding itself and not recognizing its
own post-Oedipal status, it appealed on its own behalf to Aristotle's
authority. Extrapolating from Benjamin's reading of the modern status of
the *Trauerspiel*, one must say that modernity and modernism are no longer
governed by a linguistic Oedipus either. Undoing it are traces of "original"
language, such as sound in the *Trauerspiel*, traces that provoke extreme
anxiety and even threaten a complete linguistic breakdown. These explosive traces, lying at the genre's origins, disturb the symbolic order of tragedy characterized by the individual male hero's self-sacrifice for the sake
of a community ruled by patriarchal law. Benjamin's analysis plants the
suggestion in his reader that the *Trauerspiel* signals the end of the solution
of classical tragedy because the oedipal order can no longer contain the
displacements generated by the end of the theocratic state, the breakdown
of traditional meaning structures, the emergence of an "empty world," and
a flooding by contingent materiality. Christianity had introduced the suffering body, the suffering creature, into individual and collective narratives
and these narratives remain partially active in the Baroque; with the end
of the theocratic state, however, the experience of corporeality and materiality had also either to find new symbolic containers or find refuge
elsewhere.

The end of tragedy is signaled in Benjamin's (as in Nietzsche's) mind
by Socrates, Socratic irony, and Socrates' parody of the tragic hero's self-
sacrifice. In fact, says Benjamin, Socrates' death marks the beginning of the
martyr-drama (Benjamin 1928/1998, 113). Socrates dies a sacrificial death,

but whereas the tragic hero had endowed his community with the word that broke the spell of myth silently, Socrates talks and talks, thus subverting tragic language. Whereas the tragic hero had as it were made possible the formalizations of the unities of place (the court), time (the court session), and action (the proceedings), thus establishing a human symbolic order, in the martyr-drama the word loses that genealogical and stabilizing stature. It is de-centered and supplanted by chaotic entanglements of intrigue, violence, and suffering that drown any stabilizing power the word could ever have had there. Language becomes increasingly contaminated with, even inundated by, real, non-symbolic elements such that the drama could even be acted out in pantomime, says Benjamin (1928/1998, 118). Extreme garrulousness does not point to an increase in stability, reason, and individuality, but to their unraveling.

The martyr-drama substitutes the saint for the tragic hero (Benjamin 1928/1998, 118). With the birth of Christianity, tragedy wanes, and in the martyr-drama, the drama of Christian history, what in tragedy had been tragic action and tragic death becomes a "repeatable act of ostentation" (119). Here we see the historical workings of "origin": "restoration" with its necessary concomitant—transformation.

In the *Trauerspiel* Christian notions of sacrifice, suffering, and passion combine with the symptoms of secularization: the dissociations, emptiness, abjection, and melancholia to which I have already referred. The *Trauerspiel*, naïvely thinking of itself as restoring tragedy, actually perverts and dislocates it: instead of a trial ending in a decision and sentencing as happens in tragedy, the *Trauerspiel* presents courts where no decision can be made because everyone and everything is equally fallen, equally guilty, equally doomed to a hollow grave. Instead of the decisive, oedipal action that characterizes tragedy, here we have mainly chaotic schemes, machinations, and deals. The court is not the stabilizing place it had been in tragedy. Law is in disarray. History, as Weber points out, which had earlier been enfolded in a coherent divine scheme, has, even within a Christian context, been secularized as nature, and is now a "collection of particulars, with no possibility of its ever forming a whole" (1991, 490). A self-conscious theatrical attitude pervades the plays on every level, as the genre attempts, unsuccessfully, to recover tragedy's stability, rendering the *Trauerspiel* genre itself tragic and pathetic (Weber 1991, 491). This psychologically motivated theatricality sows the seeds for the florescence of the allegorical mode in the Baroque. It is in this way that one must think of allegory as both despairing and playful.

Weber places emphasis on how the *Trauerspiel* "repeat[s], restore[s], and at the same time dislocate[s]" (493) tragedy. However, while he then goes on to discuss Benjamin's depiction and presentation of the figures of the allegorist and the intriguer as indicating the way to the *Trauerspiel*'s difference and perhaps even its potential political usefulness in the struggle against mythical law, I feel that it may be fruitful at this point to consider rather what happens within the space of the *Trauerspiel*'s very act of dislocation. In its detour—restoration coupled with incompleteness and difference—away from tragedy, the *Trauerspiel* enters a space of *anomie*: the traditional figures and their symbolic containments break open and leak something. This leakage originates in the scenes of suffering and martyrdom.

What sort of leakage is this? The best way to put it at this point would be to say that the *Trauerspiel* becomes neurotic and symptomatic and that it leaks unbound, non-signifying, and "suffering" language. To the extent that language is constitutive of subjectivity, in that locus in the *Trauerspiel* where the tragic individual in his unity and cohesiveness is no longer possible and transmissibility fails, subjectivity suffers a state of *anomie*. The modern subject, figured there in the crazed behavior and suffering of the tyrant-martyr and saint—which is simultaneously the site of the origin of the *Trauerspiel* itself—is invaded by the real in the Lacanian sense. The consequence is an irremediable breach away from the possibility of tragedy. This site of *anomie*, suffering, moaning, and ranting, comes also to signal a point where the symbolic universe is encroached upon not only by real, but also by primordial, pre-verbal, and pre-formed phenomena. It implies both a negation and a withdrawal of the founding word of tragedy;[4] it marks linguistic *anomie* and conceptual vacuum. One could also put this more positively: behind the suffering martyr appears the sound of the word of God, the *Ur*-language, which precedes the conceptual and fallen division into subject and object. Earlier, in his work on Goethe and Romanticism (Benjamin 1920; 1919–22), Benjamin may have thought of this non-place in terms of Goethe's *Urphänomene*, accessible by way of an immersion into and a sort of hovering attentiveness to the phenomena of experience. Martyrdom is one such form of immersion, as it is self-fragmenting and, through identification, dissolves the classical knowing self. Martyrdom smashes the classical sovereign self. It leads into a language of suffering and sound: lament. Yet, while seeming to lie outside of history, primitive and primordial, the psychophysical states exemplified by *Trauerspiel* martyrdom are in fact historical through and through: they emerge at particular moments of crisis *within* human history, and, when read correctly, they offer the possibility of exploding mythical History. In this sense, the stoppages in communication, transmissibility, and meaning produced by martyrdom and the entire landscape of suffering depicted in the *Trauerspiele*—the spatialization of history, the petrified landscapes and sovereigns, the imagery of decay and death—may contain sparks of redemption insofar as they, hoping against hope, may interrupt a catastrophic history for the last time for who can read these symptoms correctly. "Origin," then, means putting a stop to and exploding the narratives of history that no longer work, that have become petrified. It means beginning to read and write, to piece things together, anew and in new directions out of a state of *anomie* at the same time that it also means, for the reader of the Baroque and the baroque *Trauerspiel*, attempting to restore the lives of first things. As Benjamin says, "*Ursprung ist das Ziel*" ("Origin is the end"). We will see how Benjamin may make this impossible (because it is self-dissolving) site of *Ursprung* half-possible by way of the figure of the allegorist—the baroque reader and writer. But first we must turn to the obverse of martyrdom: tyranny.

2. The Tyrant

In its experience of secularization the *Trauerspiel* responds to its age by presenting a world that is full of things but empty of meaning and solid experience. Makropoulos (1989) describes it as "a limbo of the real which was experienced as the absence of necessity and of all substantive foundations of the real" (27, my translation): in other words, a generalized state of *anomie*. The psychic correlative of *anomie* would be dissociation, with symptoms of depersonalization, derealization, and psychogenic amnesia (American Psychiatric Association), characterized by fragmentary perception and experience. In dissociated experience, as in the *Trauerspiel*, frozen and spatial images take over from experience in time ("chronological movement is grasped and analysed in a spatial image" [Benjamin 1928/1998, 92]). This emptiness, consequent upon the de-ontologization (Makropoulos 1989, 20) of the secularized world, this loss of meaning in the Baroque, subverts the very foundations on which decisions could be made. Hence the *Trauerspiel* sovereign's indecisiveness. Psychic energy has neither clear direction nor aim. Moreover, an almost persecutory sense emanates from the fragmented structures of the increasingly naturalized settings of the *Trauerspiel* so that, as Weber says, "mythical ambiguity," a heavy sense of fate, which tragedy had historically overcome, is reinstated in the Baroque. In this way the Baroque unleashes a primal anxiety that is then channeled either into the force behind the power of the tyrant compensating for psychic destabilization with total domination—that is, into sadistic defense—or into the self-destruction of the martyr. In both cases there is anxiety (Weber 1991, 496).

It is in the sadistic and persecutory scenes of the *Trauerspiel* that similarities with Melanie Klein's aggressive and persecutory infantile dramas (see Chapters 4, 5, and 6) emerge. Attacks, attempts at domination, and self-destructiveness seem to be the choices for identification and action with which the Baroque is faced: hence Benjamin's combination-figure of the "tyrant-martyr." In general the Northern baroque *Trauerspiel* tends toward the "abject" "solution" of martyrdom (which is ultimately no maintainable solution), while the Southern Counter-Reformation drama chooses the solution of tyrant and closure.

The tyrant is he, says Benjamin, whose burden it is to prevent the state of emergency (thus practically quoting Schmitt): "The function of the tyrant is the restoration of order in the state of emergency: a dictatorship whose utopian goal will always be to replace the unpredictability of historical accident [understood by the Baroque as fallen, guilty humanity] with the iron constitution of the laws of nature" (1928/1998, 74). Calderón and "the drama of Spain" choose this solution, and throughout his book Benjamin associates it with the political reaction of the Counter-Reformation and secular Absolutism.

At first, this solution took the route of solving the problem of *anomie* and "historical accident" by way of a "kind of playful reduction, within the sphere of the court, whose king proves to be a secularized redemptive power" (Benjamin, 1928/1998, 81):

> The stretta of the third act, with its indirect inclusion of transcendence—as it were mirrored, crystallized, or in marionette-form—guarantees the drama of Calderón a conclusion which is superior to that of the German *Trauerspiel*. It cannot renounce its claim to touch on the subject of existence. But if the secular drama must stop short on the borders of transcendence, it seeks, nevertheless, to assure itself of this indirectly, in play. (81)

By "superior" Benjamin means that this genre concludes, decides, resolves, whereas the German play does not. The word "guarantee" alludes to the meaning-crisis of the Baroque insofar as the age is flailing in the wake of the loss of transcendental guarantees. While the solution of "play" may not seem particularly tyrannical, the marionette form itself suggests tyranny: history and human lives are reduced to manipulatable puppetry and subjected to total control.

The idea of the tyrant who must avert the state of emergency repeats Carl Schmitt's *Souveränitätslehre* (Schmitt 2005) which, as a political theology determined to overcome the state of emergency brought about by the crisis in sovereignty, replaces theocratic with "decisionistic" sovereignty. Benjamin's analysis of baroque political theory, however indirectly he alludes to it in this text, follows Schmitt's *Souveränitätslehre* up to a crucial point: throughout his book Benjamin has followed the unfolding of Schmitt's statement that "all significant concepts of the modern theory of the state are secularized theological concepts" (2005, 36). Schmitt, the "Crown Jurist of the Third Reich" (Stirk 2005), theorizes a "sovereign" who is to construct and mystify into something transcendental a "decision" that suspends the legal order for an indefinite period of time so as to replace it with a new one. Additionally, the sovereign's decision is to suspend the rule of contingency with the aim of abolishing the subordination of sovereignty to contingency in the modern world. But, as Benjamin shows throughout his analysis, the sovereign in the *Trauerspiel* is an extreme figuration of the modern subject of contingency and thus presents a massive contradiction were he the one expected to make the sovereign decision. In fact, Makropoulos points out, because the decision-making process that attempts to subdue contingency is itself contingent and produces more contingency, contingency itself grows exponentially (1989, 39). The tyrant-martyr in the German *Trauerspiel*, says Benjamin, suffers from a run-away indecisiveness. While the sign of him who would avert or decide for the state of emergency is the crown, in the *Trauerspiel* that crown slips, and the "unpredictability of historical accident" (Benjamin 1928/1998, 74), that is, contingency, takes over, and the tyrant is suddenly awash in martyrdom. In other words, Benjamin's *Trauerspiel* book deconstructs Schmitt's theory: "The sublime status of the Emperor on the one hand and the infamous futility of his conduct on the other create a fundamental uncertainty as to whether this is a drama of tyranny or a history of martyrdom . . . In these dramas the structure undermines the formal stereotype associated with the subject. . . . an element of martyr-drama lies hidden in every drama of tyranny" (Benjamin 1928/1998, 73). Traits associated with martyrdom, then, pop up within the drama of tyranny: fragmentation, dissociation, dissolution, and opaque contingency.

Language, too, suffers as it loses its communicative powers in the Baroque. Disarticulations of thought and language find their response and "solution" in the "restoration" of Calderón's and the Counter-Reformation's closed drama of fate and guilt, where power, authority, and stability are reestablished by way of closures and stoppages that stand at the other extreme of the fragmenting stoppages of the martyr. Fate in these dramas of reaction is not what hangs over everyone in the form of ambiguity, as it is in the *Trauerspiel*, but is rather embodied and controlled by the king:

> In the drama of the Spanish dramatist [Calderón] fate emerges as the elemental spirit of history, and it is logical that the king alone, the great restorer of the disturbed order of creation, is able to conciliate it. Cosmic fate—sovereign majesty; these are the two poles of Calderón's world. (Benjamin 1928/1998, 130)

The German *Trauerspiel*, on the other hand, is deeply steeped in the (Christian) abjection of martyrdom, which acts corrosively on the iron laws of fate. Benjamin seems to suggest that there are positive aspects to the martyr's immersion into his own broken indecisiveness, his identifications with the creaturely, his passion. Especially in light of Benjamin's philosophy of language, which I will look at below, there is a sense that, by way of what Weber calls "dislocation," the passionate entanglement with the creaturely and the objects of the world through and in language *could* be accompanied by the emergence of a new and redemptive relation to language and thus to objects. This redemptive relation paradoxically emerges together with the martyr's psychophysical abjection. Loss and suffering come to be enjoyed, and language comes to luxuriate in its sounds and feelings[5] rather than being used, as it had been in tragedy, primarily for its community-building properties, and in modernity, its instrumentality.

3. Toward a New Subject: Through Melancholy . . .

The most Benjaminian (i.e., paradoxically reparatory) move of all in the *Trauerspiel* book occurs when it becomes possible for the martyr's abjection, that "symptom," to turn into the allegorical mode. There is more to allegory than mechanistic—and sadistic—manipulation of language and omnipotent productions of meaning. The excesses of the martyr do not necessarily become useful to the allegorist's intention-ridden productiveness, but they do play a part in the partial retrievals of "origin" in a work of art, a genre, or a subject in the mode of self-reconstruction. Despite its inertia, baroque melancholy constitutes the first step in a subject's reconstruction.

Baroque contemplation of the ruins of history and self is said by Benjamin to be "passionate" and a "release" from the "satanic ensnarement of history" (1928/1998, 141–2), although it can also lead into "the abyss" of melancholy and, in "serious cases," to "violent insanity" (142). At first the melancholy tyrant-martyr contemplates astrology, in particular the influences of Saturn,

> which 'as the highest planet and the one farthest from everyday life, the origi-
> nator of all deep contemplation, calls the soul from externalities to the inner
> world, causes it to rise ever higher, finally endowing it with the utmost
> knowledge and with the gift of prophecy.' (149)

I want to suggest that Benjamin's analysis of this complex figure of baroque melancholy contains a crucial positive element which is necessary to the construction of the modern subject.[6] Benjamin associates the baroque melancholic's contemplations with "extremitas," the "uncanny," and with "manic ecstasy" (1928/1998, 149). The melancholic burrows down into an "immersion in the life of creaturely things; [he] hears nothing of the voice of revelation. Everything saturnine points down into the depths of the earth" (1928/1998, 152). In this way, he becomes attached with "a hopeless loyalty to the creaturely" (Andre 1998, 155).

He also becomes esoteric in his use of language and in his thinking. With the immersion into the creaturely and an interruption of intentional and meaningful language comes a new relationship to language altogether. It becomes "originary," reaching for a restorative paradise and able to grasp only fragments. But even as it grasps for a restorative paradise, Benjamin's theological conception of language remains, as Winfried Menninghaus puts it, "*weltimmanent*" (1980, 196): immanent to the world—historical, not transcendental. Menninghaus claims that Benjamin's originary language returns not to God, but to the "abyss" (1980, 199) in language, to Weber's "breach." This is the meaning of "origin" and the "messianic" in Benjamin: "capable of change," transformative. It is a Lacanian "abyss," as we will see in detail in the next chapter, an approach to the real that grasps for what has fallen out of symbolic structures and that returns uncannily. The historical conditions of the seventeenth century, here embodied in the *Trauerspiel*, thus lift certain historically conditioned repressions. This grasping for the truth of the not-yet symbolized is what a Benjaminian "attentiveness to the creaturely" means. It constitutes the main link between Benjamin's thought and psychoanalysis.

In order to understand better the psychological repercussions of the crises in language and meaning in the Baroque and the details of baroque experimentation with subjectivity, I now turn to Benjamin's 1916 essay, "On Language as Such and on the Language of Man" (1916). I will look at it in some detail as Benjamin's ideas concerning the "abyss" in language, resonant with Lacanian theory, are fundamental to his adumbrations of a post-catastrophic subjectivity.

4. . . . To "Pure," Human, and Incarnated Language in Benjamin and Psychoanalysis

Language, for Benjamin, is constitutive of reality as such. The world is language and vice versa, though for Benjamin the health of language changes throughout history. These changes incur varying degrees of what Benjamin calls "guilt," and Benjamin's baroque man seems to carry a heavy load of it. The 1916 essay, "On Language as Such and on the Language of Man," helps explain why: the language of intention and judgment into which human language has become ever more increasingly entangled, has alienated humans (who *are* their language) from the language of names and from name-giving, God's gift to humans. The human power to name lies in closest proximity to God's own creative Word. The language of judgment is a language perverted by the fetish of good and evil and other false dichotomies. Intention-driven language, turned by its users into a marionette,

> expels the first human beings from Paradise; they themselves have aroused it in accordance with the immutable law by which this judging word punishes . . . its own awakening as the sole and deepest guilt. In the Fall, since the eternal purity of names was violated, the sterner purity of the judging word arose. (Benjamin 1916/1996, 71)

The guilt—the Baroque has multiplied it exponentially and emblematized it in the figure of the allegorist—is for having increasingly failed the language of names and catastrophically turned it into a means and a heap of "*mere* sign[s]" (71). Language has become simply a parody of the divine word (71). Thought processes and character, too, have become perverted by dichotomous, instrumental, and judgmental attributes throughout history. In the Baroque, and then again in the early twentieth century, these developments take on extreme shape. On the one hand, they threaten to develop into their most extreme forms—that is, empty language and empty experience—so easily seduced by illusory promises of closure and eternity; on the other, driven to their extremes, they also have the potential to flip over into their opposite in the same way that, according to Freud, a civilization, driven to its highest heights opens itself up to barbarism (Freud 1930/1989). Benjamin opens up the possibility that the super-egoic language that he describes—judgmental, dichotomous, splitting—can explode into a language that in turn explodes the rigid dichotomies of judgment. But what is that original "name language"? In the broadest terms, language in general, not only verbal language, is and enacts communicability as such, basic establishment of relationship: "'All language communicates itself.' The language of this lamp, for example, communicates . . . the lamp in communication, the lamp in expression" (63).

Language, for Benjamin, has always already invaded objects and animates them. This trait leads to what Benjamin calls "the magic of language," its immediacy, in the sense that it opens up connections and relations between all existing entities, including human entities. Language places everything that exists into relationship (74). That language communicates itself means that each subject (lamp, human subject, animal) communicates itself to another subject as opposed to a subject communicating something *about* an inert and unaddressed object. All entities, however indirectly, always stand in a certain degree of proximity to revelation—the full, though un-encounterable, word of God. While the latter cannot be accessed, it can be approximated, albeit by way of a dislocation: translation provides that possibility ("naming" the lamp—we will see what that means), as do certain forms of contemplation. Surrealism will later provide pathways of "profane illumination," forms of profane revelation by way of reaching for the unconscious through language. All of these activities are instances of reaching for *Ursprung*. In this sense language is the most original of all phenomena, even though it "is" not origin. Man's particular language—and this is what sets him apart—is verbal, connected in some more proximate way to God's creative Word. Man was endowed by God with language and with the ability—and task—to name other things. This naming constitutes knowledge (*Erkenntnis*) and also art, just as it also constitutes human relationship with the material world (64). Naming allows man to communicate himself, as opposed to simply communicating about something else. To whom or what? Benjamin's answer to this question in this essay is, of course: God. But the essay also tells us that the original naming took place in Paradise, which we have lost and replaced with judgment and instrumental knowledge.

The original naming has already taken place, so naming in the full sense is no longer available to us. What did naming entail? What is it that we can attempt, however incompletely and by some form of dislocation, to restore and repeat when we name, to take back to its "origins"? The answer lies in the peculiarity of the name: it is a concatenation of sounds that may mean something but that is unavailable to becoming a means of communication. Names are monadic; they stand alone, whole and fragmentary simultaneously. Names are original:

> The name, in the realm of language, has as its sole purpose and its incomparably high meaning that it is the innermost nature of language itself.

> The name is that *through* which, and *in* which, language itself communicates itself absolutely. In the name, the mental entity that communicates itself is *language* . . . Only through the linguistic being of things can [man] get beyond himself and attain knowledge of them—in the name. (65)

Sound (constitutive of the name) seems to indicate a particular sort of regard for all of creation in an address to the Other:

> Things are denied the pure formal principle of language—namely, sound. They can communicate to one another only through a more or less material community. This community is immediate and infinite, like every linguistic communication; it is magical (for there is also a magic of matter). The incomparable feature of human language is that its magical community with things is immaterial and purely mental, and the symbol of this is sound. The Bible expresses this symbolic fact when it says that God breathes his breath into man: this is at once life and mind and language. (67)

Sound is thus what man can give to mute nature to include it into "God's breath," mental relationship. But sound, despite what Benjamin says here, also tends toward the material, the voice, in particular in lament. Through sound human language enmeshes itself also with the "material community" of things. Immersion into the creaturely in order to lend it our sound and breath was the original human task. Thus, quoting Hamann, Benjamin emends what he has just written:

> Everything that man heard in the beginning, saw with his eyes, and felt with his hands was the living word; for God was the word. With this word in his mouth and in his heart, the origin of language was as natural, as close, and as easy as a child's game . . .

But paradisal language is not historical language.

It is in this breach between paradisal and historical language, where language is both ethereal and strangely material, that Benjamin's philosophy of language encounters psychoanalytic theory most significantly. Willy Apollon, for instance, a Lacanian clinician and theoretician, describing the move from an original (real) attachment into the symbolic undergone by the young subject, writes about

> the relation of the subject . . . to the signifier as failing to symbolize the subject's truth. So the trauma, as a wound from the symbolic order, has no other representation than that primary fantasy where the subject is expelled from animal life, despoiled of the jouissance of animal satisfactions, and overwhelmed in the signifiers of the Other. That exile and that bewitchment constitute the subject as a ravished one in the site of the Other. (Apollon 2002a, 105)

In both cases this original scenario of exile from Paradise—which Benjamin goes on to bring to life in his reading of Genesis 1 and 2—is present only as a screen to represent the fundamental loss inhabiting human life, surrounded only by uncanny fragments of a lost meaning. A breach—a stop and an empty space—have come into being where, in the state of plenitude, God had been. This is fully the case for Benjamin by the 1928 *Trauerspiel* book.

The effects of those traces and fragments of a lost infinity do not go away—though they are usually ignored—and, for Benjamin, are the fount for possible renewal. This is the site of the remnant. Its status in psychoanalytic terms is analogous. I will go into considerably more detail in the next chapter to show the ways in which Lacan's *objet a* can explain Benjamin's more esoterically and theologically framed conceptions of language. Human language, for Benjamin, can only go so far as to "communicate itself" *in* language (which is itself a breach and "dislocation") and *to* an original abyss, the traces of the original word, as Weber puts it, and not to God, as Pizer has it (unless "God" is identified with the leap between human and divine language). The name, as language-matter, in Benjamin's hands acquires the status of the Lacanian *objet a*, the imaginary part-object which stands for the unattainable object of desire. For psychoanalysis and for Benjamin, subjectivity is structured by edges and cuts that are linguistic in origin. "God," in modernity, translates into loss and an anxiety that perpetuates itself through the sense of an increasingly less accessible original language for Benjamin. Such an understanding of subjectivity is also psychoanalytic.

5. *"Catastrophized" Language*

For psychoanalysis, the insightful human subject recognizes itself as being structured by loss. Similarly, in the course of history, in particular in the modernity that Benjamin describes in his *Trauerspiel* book, nature (the "material community") has, when it is not deliberately mute in a sort of protest against the increasingly failing human capacity to name it redemptively, achieved sound, but it is the sound of lament. In Paradise the muteness of nature had been "bliss, only of a lower degree," but

[n]ow begins its other muteness, which is what we mean by the "deep sadness of nature." It is a metaphysical truth that all nature would begin to lament if it were endowed with language . . . how . . . melancholy it is to be named not from the one blessed paradisiacal language of names, but from the hundred languages of man, in which name has already withered, yet

which, according to God's pronouncement, have knowledge of things. (Benjamin 1916/1996, 72–3)

In modernity language itself has suffered a catastrophe. This is the situation in which baroque man finds himself. Nature's lament, the sign of loss, is caused by what Benjamin in 1916 calls "overnaming" (the "hundred languages"), the single word that best sums up the physiognomy of the Baroque. In the Baroque, prompted by the excision of transcendence, man as martyr, suffering for what is lost, immerses himself in nature by way of mimetic identification with the residues of the divine creative word and by lending it a—however fragmentary—voice. Human language attempts again to sink itself into the "material community"—the ruin, remnant, *objet a* of God's unspoken word—in an "original" act. This act opens up the possibility of undoing the language of judgment and—in the midst of the din of the "hundred languages"—the language of "too much *din*," the kabbalistic term for judgment. The pun is intended: the "hundred languages" do make too much din and separate us from relatedness with others. As Menninghaus puts it, contemplating a mournful nature and brooding over the abyss of language—which is both loss and infinity at the same time--is a despairingly hopeful way of doing this (1980, 206).

Menninghaus also suggests that the actual letters, the material elements of words, the sounds, are experienced by this hopelessly hopeful man as containing the depths of God's secrets, so that revelation may seem to be promised by its material manifestations within human history: in the sounds and letters of language (1980, 211). This hope is implicit in Benjamin's language essay: that man join more and more with the "material community of things in their communication" (73). This should also be understood psychoanalytically: the "things" are the real leftovers, the remnants that lie outside of the tyranny-inclined Symbolic and which, in Benjamin's narrative, mourn their own exclusion. Benjamin's "man" can remain faithful to creation. In recognizing the creaturely and the things of the material world, he embodies and enacts Benjamin's early form of materialism.

This conception of man's relationship to the "material community" links Benjamin's thought to that of Lacan: the "little piece of the real" and the relationship between language and symptom. Mournful silence and bodily experiencing are instances of the material dimension of the signifier—the symptom, precisely the position of the martyr, and what Willy Apollon calls "the writing of jouissance in the symptom" (2002*a*, 103). In this sense, I understand Benjamin's notion of the "creaturely" as a communication in and through material signifiers, the mental communicativeness of human language enmeshed with the material world. The "letter," for instance, is, in Apollon's words, "any segment, mark or unit of that capture as an indefinable parcel of the body; a border, an opening, the outline of a hole, a stroke, or even a gesture or a glance as a referential mark. . . . " The "letter," the bridge between real and symbolic, symptom and law, "implies the parceling body underneath the ego that unifies it" (109). Play with and manipulation of it, as we will see, can become the vehicle by which subjectivity can survive the traumatic exposure to the emergence of "bare life" in modernity. Play with the letters of signifiers is not only the means toward creating new meanings, but also signals a new relationship between making meaning and the body. The letter as such does not signify; rather, it contains monadically the original intersection of word and matter, word and body. In this way it takes a critical position against communicative language.

In 1928 Benjamin suggests that in the German Baroque such a language rises to the surface: the "German lyric," he writes, quoting Harsdörffer, "was to 'grasp the language of nature, so to speak, in words and rhythms.' . . . it is God who is revealed in the rustling of the forest . . . and the roar of the storms" (1928/1998, 205). Such a fragmented language of sound is one of the manifestations of "martyrdom," in the sense that language no longer appears to be in man's sovereign possession. The sovereign's worldly power is undermined and dissolves into the "creaturely." It opens up potential passageways between man and the "material community": "In its individual parts fragmented language has ceased merely to serve the process of communication, and as a new-born object acquires a dignity equal to that of gods, rivers, virtues and similar forms which fuse into the allegorical" (Benjamin 1928/1998, 206).[7] The act of immersion leads into the creaturely, little bits of the real, and uncovers both "pure language" and *jouissance*.

Such immersions have ethical and political ramifications, even if they remain implicit in the *Trauerspiel* book.[8] From the Lacanian perspective, *objet a* gets desire moving again, and this is fundamental to the ethics of psychoanalysis. But there are implications for collective history as well. Bolz's interpretation of the way time turns into space in the *Trauerspiel*, a correlative of the materialization of language I am focusing on, is that it aids in breaking up, for him who immerses himself into the bits and pieces of history, linear temporality and narratives and myths of progress. The aim of Benjaminian historiography is "*den Weltlauf zu unterbrechen* ["to interrupt the course of the world"]" (Bolz 2002, 122) and the deep-sleep narrative of history. It creates the space for "the strait gate where the Messiah might enter" (Benjamin 1940/1969, 264). Redemption, Bolz claims, takes place not *in* but *from* history, though it originates there. A different knowledge lies hidden inside potentially messianic fragments: broken, petrified, and mute objects that might open up to "being named" and thus become communicable and release an energy that can be put to new use (Bolz 2002, 123). I want to emphasize the dialectical nature of the broken, petrified, and mute objects, which are both abject in that they have been abused as well as being the triggers for messianic transformation. The Baroque makes itself especially pregnant with such moments particularly because in it, as Benjamin says, history becomes material. Immersion in a fragmented history, in contrast to the controlled and synthetic narrative of progress of historicism, has a positive value.

Destruction and immersion appear again in the Angel of History's inexorably ambivalent relationship to both history and Paradise in Thesis IX on the concept of history:

> His face is turned toward the past. Where we perceive a chain of events, he sees one single catastrophe which keeps piling wreckage and hurls it in front of his feet. The angel would like to stay, awaken the dead, and make whole what has been smashed. But a storm is blowing in from Paradise; it has got caught in his wings with such a violence that the angel can no longer close them. The storm irresistibly propels him into the future to which his back is turned, while the pile of debris before him grows skyward. (Benjamin 1940/1969, 257–8)

The Angel is ambivalent toward Paradise precisely because returning there by a straight line would mean leaving behind the smashed "things," the "material community." But "immersiveness" into "things" carries a threat with it as well: that of remaining stuck in melancholy and passivity.

And there is an additional issue here: Martin Jay has called attention to a potentially dangerous nostalgia in this early Benjamin, in that he seems ultimately to demand an authoritarian "respect" before "objects" (Jay 2006, 323). My sense is that Benjamin felt compelled to disarm precisely that danger in his "attentiveness" to all there is. We can see this in the figures of the mourner and the allegorist.

6. *Mourning, Allegory, Writing*

A. *Mourning*

While baroque drama is dangerously entangled with both tyranny and melancholy, it is also true that something within it generates movement of a redemptive sort. It may be mourning that has the power to unlock the total stoppage—embodied in the martyr and "resolved" tyrannically by the

Counter-Reformation play of fate—and that differentiates the Northern *Trauerspiel* from Southern Counter-Reformation drama. I have argued that it is an attentiveness to what is "pathological"—because contingent, obsessive, and melancholy—in the *Trauerspiel* that according to Benjamin can be used against tyranny. This too has dangers associated with it, however. Mourning is the fundamental attitude of the allegorist, the key figure to emerge from the derailed sovereignty of authoritative meaning that defines modernity. It is, I believe, for Benjamin a coping mechanism. It begins an idiosyncratically baroque attempt to re-master and re-intend the world. In it the subject confronts loss by recollecting "reality" in bits and pieces and by re-building itself in constant dialogue with the objects that it must ultimately relinquish. Artifice and theatricality are associated with mourning, which

> is the state of mind in which feeling revives the empty world in the form of a mask, and derives an enigmatic satisfaction in contemplating it. . . . If the laws which govern the *Trauerspiel* are to be found, partly explicit, partly implicit, at the heart of mourning, the representation of these laws does not concern itself with the emotional condition of the poet or his public, but with a feeling which is released from any empirical subject and is intimately bound to the fullness of an object. (Benjamin 1928/1998, 139)

Mourning "release[s]" energy, newly liberated from the oppressive obsessions of melancholy, that the mourner uses in his acts of reconstruction. Insofar as mourning involves the beginning of new linguistic movement which is informed by loss and an "ego's" reconstructions of "world" through a "mask" (i.e. not the lost "real thing"), it is fuelled by "intimate" use made of the remnant of "fullness," the eternally fleeting transcendent now appearing in absolute immanence. This new "feeling" seems to occur in a newly opened up passageway between subject and object.

B. *The Allegorist, Lacan, and "Redemption"*

The figure of the allegorist is intimately tied to mourning. Constructing allegories, represented by the "mask," Benjamin seems to suggest, is an act of mourning. This activity differentiates the mourner-allegorist from the melancholy martyr who remains stuck. Allegory sets things going again, even as language still oozes a substance that has become associated with nature, matter, and corporeality. The allegorist is Benjamin's self-consciously modern user of language, the human being at a crossroads, having to re-negotiate his relationship to language and to the material world.

The allegorist chooses to use the empty shells of the language that has lost its metaphysical guarantees, a collection of arbitrary sign-systems without moorings in either divinity or nature, and to buy wholeheartedly into its own marionette-like nature. He chooses to re-master meaning, and he is defined by his artifice. He constructs his own master signifiers which, however, have hardly any staying power. The modality of allegory is temporality, evanescence, and transience, the characteristics that distinguish allegory from the totalizing, static, and eternal symbol, favored by totalizing modes of thought. This is the road "sovereignty" takes in the figure of the allegorist, who is both master of signification and subject to its transience. Allegory is in this sense also a manifestation of the death drive—hence Benjamin's identification of allegory with the death's head—which brings the allegorist into closer association again with the martyr.

The allegorist points, at least partially, to a non-totalitarian solution for modern subjectivity after the death of God. First, however, a word about the figure of the *Intrigant* ("intriguer"). Together with the allegorist the intriguer is a "third figure" who *could* perhaps offer a way out of the tyrant-martyr dead-end within the political context. The intriguer is discussed only minimally by Benjamin, but some critics[9] suggest that he offers resistance to both tyranny and the paralyzing passivity of the martyr. Zimnik (1997) goes so far as to say,

> As aesthetic form the allegory of the German Baroque has political implications, because it carries within itself the potential to conceive of a form of subjectivity that distinguishes itself ethically and structurally from that of the tyrant who is called into existence by the logic of the state of exception. It is the potential [hidden within] the intriguer that is thus capable of linking him to democracy and its form. (1997, 299, my translation)

While Benjamin's text does enact a search for an ethically viable new form of subjectivity, I am not sure that it is the intriguer who offers solutions; it is true that his pragmatic political abilities form a foil to the tyrant-martyr, though they would have to be modified somehow and combined with something else. The intriguer is the "organizer of [the *Trauerspiel*'s] plot," says Benjamin:

> He stands as a third type alongside the despot and the martyr. . . . The sovereign intriguer is all intellect and will-power. And as such he corresponds to an ideal which was first outlined by Machiavelli and which was energetically elaborated in the creative and theoretical literature of the seventeenth century before it degenerated into a cliché . . . [The German *Trauerspiel*] is dominated by the gloomy tone of intrigue. In *Leo Armenius* Michael Balbus laments: "Was ist der hof nunmehr als eine mördergruben,/ Als ein

verräther-platz, ein wohnhauss schlimmer buben?" ["What is the court but
a den of murderers, a place of treachery, a house of rogues and villains?"]
(1928/1998, 95)

I would suggest that insofar as the intriguer is connected to the realm of
the puppet theater, he cannot represent a redemptive model for the ethical
individual for Benjamin. He is closely associated with Calderón and the
Haupt-und Staatsaktionen, as well as the always latent potential of com-
edy (125–6). In the end, however, the "Lustspiel shrinks and is, so to speak,
absorbed into the *Trauerspiel*" (127)—that is, into the figure of the
allegorist.

The allegorist, demiurge of conventional meaning in the baroque, as
well as mourner, archivist, and writer, takes center stage in Benjamin's
book, and he becomes the master-manipulator not only in the context of
the transience and death-obsession that characterizes the Baroque, but also
in the context of knowledge. He becomes an architect of knowledge, but
this knowledge has no lasting power. All of this—his abstractions, his
architectonics of knowledge, and his strong consciousness of death—associate the figure of the allegorist with the field of the signifier and the symbolic order as it is defined by Lacan. He provides, so to speak, surveys of
conventional language, and he inhabits the world of linguistic convention—the world of Saussure. Thus Weber writes,

> Death is at work in allegory however not just as decline and decay, but more
> intimately, as that which separates each thing from itself: from its essence
> and from its name. In the world of allegory, the name, Benjamin writes, has
> become a mere "label" (Schild) with which a vulnerable physis seeks to shield
> and protect itself. The possibility that "each person, every thing, each rela-
> tion can signify any other, arbitrarily". . . pronounces a verdict upon the
> world that Benjamin describes as "annihilating, yet just: it is designated as a
> world in which details no longer matter very much." (1991, 498)

With the growing rule of arbitrariness and with the loss of a "gold stand-
ard" (1991, 498), as Weber puts it, knowledge becomes the most powerful
mode of being in the Baroque; however, it creates a sense of malaise because
it knows that it is ungrounded and constructed:

> If the object becomes allegorical when submitted to the glance of melan-
> choly, which drains the life from it, if it remains dead, albeit assured for all
> eternity, it is all the more at the mercy of the allegorist . . . It acquires the
> significance that the allegorist gives it. He lays it into it: this must be under-
> stood not psychologically, but ontologically. In his hand the things become
> something else . . . (Benjamin 1928/1998, 183–4)

So, what could make the allegorist relevant from the point of view of redemption? It is first of all that the allegorist's continuities with the baroque martyr have not been sufficiently emphasized: the allegorist is also still a "martyr" in that he immerses himself in contemplation into the things stripped of meaning and moves into death. Yet, differently from the martyr, he becomes active: he deadens the things entirely by bringing them into his own isolated gaze, and he infuses them, demiurgically, with his own meaning. He is thus (at least potentially) both masochistic and sadistic—the former in his self-dissolutions into the things, the latter in his omnipotent control of them. Benjamin often seems un-ambivalent about the allegorist's fallenness. In his theological conception of history, knowledge is a defensive reaction to the catastrophe of the Fall, but it is also the only possible replacement for naming. Nevertheless, allegorical knowledge makes language into a means; this occurs simultaneously with the rise of judgment and abstraction (Benjamin 1916/1996, 72).

The personal meanings the allegorist "lays into" the object, and the many possible meanings that now characterize the object, correspond both to the "hundred languages" of fallen history as well as to the thing's "over-naming," thus unleashing creation's lament and engaging the allegorist's other side, his identity as martyr. Benjamin insists on the allegorist's split nature, which is a weak version of the tyrant-martyr split.[10] The split as well as the allegorist's other—the martyr's—side become visible in a resulting tension between spoken and written language:

> The division between signifying written language and intoxicating spoken language opens up a gulf in the solid massif of verbal meaning and forces that gaze into the depths of language. . . . The spoken word, it might be said, is the ecstasy of the creature, it is exposure, rashness, powerlessness before God; the written word is the composure of the creature, dignity, superiority, omnipotence over the objects of the world. (Benjamin 1928/1998, 201)

With the written word, then, "the creature" enacts (sadistic) omnipotence. And yet, not even this stated dichotomy between written and spoken language holds, for written language, too, in the hands of the baroque martyr-allegorist, partakes of "the ecstasy of the creature," as we will see shortly. Benjamin's figure of the allegorist is finally irreducibly ambiguous: whether he is writing or speaking, the allegorist reaches into the depths, toward *Ursprung*, to redeem the forsaken things of this world in a way that neither martyr nor tyrant can. The former is unable to do so because he is in fact overwhelmed by the force of the originary, the latter cannot because he wishes to make *himself* all-powerful. And the problem with that allegorist who rests too heavily in omnipotence from the point of view of redemption

Is that too often he gives in to the temptation of sadistic mastery and control.

The allegorist, then, is complex and dialectical. He combines melancholy, mourning, and manipulation; passive despair and manic sense of omnipotence; originary digging and mechanistic constructivism and artifice. In the chapter "Allegory and *Trauerspiel*" Benjamin establishes immediately that allegory is its own mode of expression, "just as speech is expression and, indeed, just as writing is" (1928/1998, 162). Allegory and writing are nevertheless intimately related. Benjamin's main aim is to distinguish allegory from the symbol and to value it because it is faithful to transience, to singular objects (even if they are manipulated and emptied of their own concreteness) and to creaturely life. The symbol, on the other hand, like the Southern Counter-Reformation drama, wishes to totalize everything within itself. The allegorist is filled with a mania that is at the same time infused with the knowledge of death. Through artifice allegory restores movement, time, and a fragmented tradition from out of the self-destructive and melancholic stasis of the martyr. It creates a breathing-space.

The possible psychological responses to modernity that Benjamin presents in his *Trauerspiel* book—the martyr, the tyrant, the melancholiac, the allegorist, the intriguer—all relate differently to catastrophe, anxiety, and disappearance. They all also stand in a particular relationship to the peculiarly modern breaks and stoppages in meaning. Benjamin claims that the symbol, as opposed to allegory, decides on one meaning and puts a stop to further transformations in meaning; it creates a new and single-stranded myth. Allegory, on the other hand, engages in a complicated series of acts begun by the melancholy (and crazed) martyr who at first causes a "messianic cessation of happening" (Benjamin 1940/1969, 263) and then loses himself in the fragments of destroyed meaning and the demands of suddenly persecutory objects. A more positive outcome of exposure to the "bare life" produced by *anomie*—both externally and internally—is that it has the power both to interrupt the death, as it were, of an empty world and to resist the imposition of a new iron-clad myth, a "dictator's" intention. The symbol enchants and takes leave of the actual things of this world for the sake of phantasmagoria. Symbol and allegory present two main solutions: both involve a stoppage following the martyr's stoppage who is overwhelmed by the forces of the real unleashed when with the waning of faith and authority the symbolic order fractures. The martyr goes partially mad and disappears among the material ruin of the world. The martyr-allegorist, on the other hand, instigates a "cessation of happening" and becomes a master artificer within ad hoc systems of meaning. Always, however, he does so *only* by way of momentary regressions to the position of martyr, into moments of catastrophe and suffering. Even though allegory is highly conventional, it is defined by its immersion into the petrified face of decay and guilt in history, and into the creaturely subjected to death: the "disinterested self-sufficiency . . . of the sign" is broken open by the "allegorical depths"—melancholy consciousness of transience, death, and lament. "Significance" in allegory is directly proportional to the degree of "the subjection to death" (Benjamin 1928/1998, 166). Yet, "death" refers *both* to the creaturely real and the deathliness of convention. This double reference constitutes allegory's inherent dialectic of "overnaming" and the material ("material community") of creation.

Thus allegory is both conventional and originary, both mythical (though only transiently) and non-mythical. It consists of constantly changing mythemes or constellations determined by the individual, and it breaks open falsely totalizing representations of the world. Such totalizations, characteristic of the symbol, are lie and hubris generated by a delusional denial of the Fall, given that the symbol promises eternity, and correspond to the tyrant's dictatorial decision. So, while it is true that, as Steinberg (1996, 20) says, allegory strips the aura from the world and its representation, thus undermining the re-enchantments of the world typical of the totalitarian mentality, it is not necessarily the case that allegory is limited: it is and it is not, as it initiates both endless chains of signification and a potentially infinite and originary digging process.[11]

C. *Allegorical writing and subject-formation*

Rather than thinking of allegory as primarily omnipotent and sadistic, then, I endorse Heiner Weidmann's (1992) definition. The abyssal nature of language itself, which refuses a transcendental apotheosis and is only in this sense "limited"—bound to this world, that is—points to an "*Unbeschränkt-heit*" ["unlimitedness"] (Weidmann 1992, 24) out of the very negation of transcendence that allegory enacts. Allegory is thus itself an allegory for the human language predicament. Fallen language frames a lost language of names, which paradoxically finds expression only through the empty-and-dead-container language of allegorical convention (Benjamin 1928/1998, 175). In part what becomes expression in allegory is the despair of the undertaking itself. Additionally, though, allegory performs an act of recovery and preservation of the now scattered things of the world insofar as it allows them to re-emerge almost indiscriminately and dislocated in repeated acts of translation and transformation.

The antitheses of transience and "permanent immersion," of death and preservation, of convention and origin, of symbolic and real, of digging for life within death, find expression in the act of allegorical writing. Benjamin establishes a profound relationship between "acts" of allegory and writing. Both involve the body. In particular in his work on mimesis, graphology, and drawing in the 1930s Benjamin emphasizes the role played by the physical act of engraving letters and by the unconscious significances of lines and points in the relationship between writing and drawing, and their psychological effects on the individual writer.

The "digging" component in allegory and in writing in general tend to undermine myth and thus have, for Benjamin, a secret source of authority in their movements toward "origin"—an idea that I will pursue to a much greater extent in Chapter 6—just as they are linked by their association with forms of public authority. While the latter is an aspect of their conventionality, the former is located in the immersion in materiality that allegory and writing share:

> At the same time [allegory is] expression of authority, which is secret in accordance with the dignity of its origin, but public in accordance with the extent of its validity. And the very same antinomies take plastic form in the conflict between the cold, facile technique and the eruptive expression of allegorical interpretation. It lies in the essence of writing itself. (Benjamin 1928/1998, 175)

Allegorical writing wished to have its origin in hieroglyphic writing and thus participate in "[s]omething approaching a natural theology of writing" (Benjamin 1928/1998, 169) even though, as Benjamin says, alphabetical script is historical and non-hieratic. Nevertheless, hieroglyphic writing, bordering on drawing, though it is also "conventional," comes to contain what to Benjamin are unrepresentable depths. Thus, with sublime artifice as well as emphatic fragmentariness,

> [b]oth externally and stylistically—in the extreme character of the typographical arrangement and in the use of highly charged metaphors—the written word tends toward the visual. It is not possible to conceive of a starker opposite to the artistic symbol, the plastic symbol, the image of organic totality, than this amorphous fragment which is seen in the form of allegorical script. . . . [A]t one stroke the profound vision of allegory transforms things and works into stirring writing. (Benjamin 1928/1998, 75–6)

The baroque vision that transforms ideas of organic totality into "stirring writing" disturbs classical and even Romantic visions of wholeness and results in the mode of mourning, linking allegory, writing, and subject-reconstruction. The latter, which tends to lie concealed in Benjamin's texts, is nevertheless metaphorized in the "vision" attributed to Winckelmann:

> Winckelmann still has this penetration of vision in the *Beschreibung des Torso des Hercules in Belvedere zu Rom:* it is evident in the un-classical way he goes over it, part by part and limb by limb. It is no accident that the subject is a torso. In the field of allegorical intuition the image is a fragment, a rune. Its beauty as a symbol evaporates when the light of divine learning falls upon it. The false appearance of totality is extinguished. For the *eidos* disappears, the simile ceases to exist, and the cosmos it contains shrivels up. (Benjamin 1928/1998, 176)

Thus it is that, as Benjamin writes, "by virtue of a strange combination of nature and history . . . the allegorical mode of expression is born" (1928/1998, 167). The significance that baroque allegory inscribes into the petrified, primordial landscape of history is the significance of decay and death, but also of origin and truth. It undermines—literally loosens up—and transforms the symbol's mystical "*Nu*" into historical *Jetztzeit* in writing, the profane carrier of "origin":

> [T]he symbolic becomes distorted into the allegorical. The eternal is separated from the events of the story of salvation, and what is left is a living image open to all kinds of revision by the interpretive artist. . . . It is an unsurpassably spectacular gesture to place even Christ in the realm of the provisional, the everyday, the unreliable. (183)[12]

The contingent, that is. This last line may also be Benjamin's "unsurpassable" deconstruction not only of the symbol and the figure of the tyrant, but also of Schmitt's attempt to obviate contingency. He goes on:

> Where man is drawn towards the symbol, allegory emerges from the depths of being to intercept the intention, and to triumph over it. The same tendency is characteristic of baroque lyric. The poems have "no forward movement, but they swell up from within.". . . If it is to hold its own against the tendency to absorption, the allegorical must constantly unfold in new and surprising ways. The symbol, on the other hand, as the romantic mythologists have shown, remains persistently the same. (183)

It is precisely the "'swelling[ing] up from within'" and the "hold[ing] its own against the tendency to absorption" of the martyric element in allegory that links it to certain psychoanalytic conceptions of redemptive catastrophe. And yet, immediately following this passage, Benjamin reminds us once again that the allegorist is the great deadener through that melancholic gaze of his that empties the object in order to infuse it with new meaning: "That is to say, it is now quite incapable of emanating any meaning or significance of its own; such significance as it has, it acquires from the allegorist" (1928/1998, 184). Further, Benjamin refers to baroque writing as "a schema . . . at one and the same time a fixed image and a fixing sign" (184) as the allegorist's "knowledge" and his determination of "good and evil." Nevertheless, while the allegorist knows himself and his writing to be historical and fallen, if he is sufficiently driven by martyrdom, he also attempts to achieve a dialectical reversal, following the dissolutions of meanings and of self, where the writing may, however *via negativa*, come to remember "pure language" and to recollect it in its own image, fallen, fragmented, and mortifying. It can do so through its immersion into objects and the creaturely, the only remnants of the divine in this guilty world. The allegorist may share with the martyr a sudden openness to the sound of language, to the creaturely within convention. By thus attempting to participate in a "community of material things," even if they are dead, this act of preservation may release a hopeless hope for the objects' and, through them, the allegorist's own redemption.[13] The allegorist's writing, then, has an ethical potential whose mode is both a de-assimilation and a (re-)construction of history.

This complex and dialectical understanding of allegory reveals a significant link between Benjamin's latent theory of subjectivity and the complex dialectic of attack, guilt, mourning, and reparation in the formation of individual subjectivity as theorized by Melanie Klein and her followers, which I will examine in greater detail in Chapter 5. The "despair" that characterizes the baroque melancholiac, coupled with the partly manic and omnipotent "artifice" of the allegorist, this tense and always anxious combination of feelings and dispositions, goes to the heart of the psychoanalytic vision of the individual's struggles to construct herself: in both cases the subject who knows herself to be irretrievably constituted, sometimes also lacerated, by the Other is an ethical one capable of recognizing external reality as more "subject" than "object" and as separate from the self. Weidmann (1992) refers to the fragmenting nature of the construction and preservation dialectic that allegory performs as "*Rettung durch Zerstörung*" ["salvation by destruction"] (29). This is the condition of the modern subject, according to Benjamin. It is also the condition of the modern writer.

CHAPTER 2

BENJAMIN AND LACAN

I   The Saint and the *Saint Homme* (*Sinthome*)

Introduction

In this chapter I will show what sort of light Lacan's late theory of subjectivity and the *sinthome* can throw on the figures of the martyr and allegorist in Benjamin's *The Origin of German Tragic Drama*. My aim, ultimately,
is to make it possible to imagine a praxis emerging from this esoteric
Benjaminian work through psychoanalysis. Let us see where we are.

The martyr-allegorist, as I have extrapolated him from Benjamin's
The Origin of German Tragic Drama, immerses himself into the dead things
and the "creaturely." What does that mean, exactly? It means that with the
dispersal of both transcendental authority and sovereign meaning that
defines modernity, the subject's object world, language, and knowledge
suffer a crisis: they are emptied out. For Benjamin, however, this crisis has
the potential eventually to transform a metaphysical relation to the world
into a materialist one. At the beginning, however, the experience is one of
bottomless loss. The transformation first enters the phase of the *Grübler*,
the melancholiac, who contemplates the reified objects of the world and
who feels enmeshed in a language that has become abyssal, unable to find
a hold. The loss of a center, the loss of meaning structure—the baroque
meaning crisis, in other words, as the origin of modernity—sends the
subject on a search for truth that takes him further and further down into
the bowels of the material world as well as into the mysterious spaces of
his own body. Hence the frequent link between melancholia and psychoso-
matic disturbances of this period, as Benjamin describes them. In Lacanian
terms, Benjamin's *Grübler* reaches beyond symbolic configurations toward
the real, and in this same process language becomes inundated with real
and non-communicative elements. The baroque crisis—loss of metaphysical center and inundations by real elements in the shape of psychophysical
disturbances and transformed experience of the material world—has the
nachträglich effect of reawakening the wound of original loss that is suffered by all humans: the moment the signifier first moved in to symbolize
the subject's truth and, even while failing in this, nevertheless overwhelming

and bewitching the subject with the conventional system of signifiers—conventional, shared language. Benjamin's *Trauerspiel* book, I suggest, implies that the language crisis in modernity is lived specifically in the mode of martyrdom; this is so because the original wound inflicted on the individual by the conventional symbol is reawakened in a sort of secondary trauma. This trauma accompanies the deflation and delegitimation of traditional orders of meaning that occur when symbolic containment is breached and the real returns to rupture the symbolic.

I also want to show in this chapter how Benjamin's martyr-*allegorist* recapitulates, as it were, Lacan's idea of the mature, post-analytical subject's relation to language, truth, and knowledge. This subject, following the deflation and delegitimation of paternal master signifiers,[1] identifies with what those symbolic structures leave outside: the bodily drives, nonsense, sound—those phenomena associated with the original object that, with the imposition of the paternal metaphor, had been banished to the non-status of what is not whole and lies outside of the bounds of knowledge, the "crumbs" of meaning, so to speak, the discarded, the idiosyncratic remnant. Such is the subject who has undergone full analysis and whose symbolic landscape—like Oedipus's—has as a result been ravaged. Both Benjamin and Lacan know that these energies lying outside of symbolic structures (Lacan calls them "drive energies") and liberated with the incremental demise of the transcendental authority of Father-law, release a new force—not least in the field of language which now awakens from a deep sleep.

This chapter therefore moves into the realm of "the symptom" both in its literal and metaphorical senses: these are also the non-symbolic realms where the martyr-allegorist immerses himself to begin the process of re-making, re-mastering, and re-intending the fragmented world. He must do so, however, without pretending that meanings are either eternal or total, or that they supersede the world of nature which is transitory, always changing, and marked by creaturely suffering and death, so as not to deny what modernity means. The martyr-allegorist, like Lacan's *sinthomatic* post-oedipal subject—and like the post-oedipal Trauerspiel—lives in the key of incompleteness and mourning, de- and re-constructing meaning in bits and pieces *for himself*, while the energies that had once bound traditional authoritative meanings are now entangled with corporeality and materiality. My argument here will be that Lacan and Benjamin both think of the mourning and writing processes—processes defined by recovery and preservation as well as constant transformation—as ethical positions that are to function as inoculations against totalitarian positions (Gault 2007, 73).[2] For Lacan they are "inoculations," because they stave off the construction of new authoritative signifiers (and their symptoms) in favor of a different sort of knowledge; for Benjamin they are "inoculations" because they use the new energies that are released in the modern state of emergency—and that are in danger of being used for purposes of tyranny, as we saw in Chapter 1—in a "coming" philosophy that no longer attempts to separate subject from object, subject from subject, and body from mind in the traditional manner.

1. *Martyr-Allegorist and* Sinthome

Lacan's notion of the *sinthome* (Lacan 1975–76/1999) describes what is left to the subject after the end of analysis, after the deflation of the Father-image, the Oedipus, the law, and after the existence of the Other of the Other and even the blinding misrecognitions of the ego have evaporated. The question the *sinthome* answers to is, "How does the subject live after analysis and the demise of master signifiers? What supports her to live?"

The *sinthome* understood as phenomenology and experience is the subject's identification with and immersion into the symptom (which rarely makes a total retreat), the corporeal remnant and side-product of the inscriptions of symbolic signifiers. After the superego of the Law has been deflated and the symptom has been "read" in analysis—that is, interpreted, its meaning retrieved, leaving the material shell—the subject must find a way to *be* or, more hauntingly, a way for "deserving to live" (Lacan 1975–76/1999, 185).[3] It is tempting to read Oedipus leaning on his daughter Antigone in *Oedipus at Colonus* as leaning on his *sinthome*. She remains to him after he has seen—so much that he is blinded—through all else.

Like Benjamin's concept of "origin," Lacan's *sinthome* is both a return to and a distortion of a phenomenon, in this case a psychophysical one: it returns to the root of the subject's psychic structure—the interrelations of Real, Symbolic, and Imaginary—and it dislocates these relations, the rings in the Borromean Knot.

Borromean Knot

The fascinating thing about the *sinthome* is that it appears both in the case of the post-analytic subject and in psychic systems threatened with psychotic dissolution. As a fourth ring, it holds together the other three that are threatening to come apart in a sort of psychic state of emergency, a crisis of legitimacy—specifically, the absence, or at least significant waning, of the Father function. Like Benjamin's *Ursprung*, and like his idea of the "ruin," the fourth ring as *sinthome* points to a breached, perhaps even broken, symbolic realm and a potentially catastrophic inundation by the real. It embodies a peculiarly modern post-catastrophic knotting of the subject. "The sinthome," says Lacan, "is situated at the place where the knot slips, where there is a lapsus of the knot" (1975–76/1999, 97). It marks that site in Benjamin where the baroque king's crown—the symbol of law, authority, meaning, identity—slips.[4] Lacan's *sinthome* and Benjamin's martyr-allegorist survive in a mode of being that is no longer held in place by sovereign meaning but by these post-sovereign subjects' relationship to corporeality and the object world. Two main structural features of the *sinthome*, which are functionally related to the allegorist's reconstructive mode, make it possible for a subject shaped by absence of the father function (and thus the oedipal constitution of the subject) not to become psychotic and to construct for him- or herself an alternative mode of being. First, there is the *sinthome*'s unusual relationship between symbolic and real, connected by the fourth ring, the *sinthome*, which translates for the subject into a different mode of relating to the abyss of the real, to corporeality and materiality, and thus to knowledge. Second, this structural deviance leads to a differently structured and differently functioning ego, where the imaginary (the optical illusion of sovereignty) does not dominate: as the *sinthome* establishes itself, the imaginary and its phallic meanings slip away. Both of these features are intimately related to a subject's language use, the nature of his symbolic function: the real is an "energetics," says Lacan, and it finds its way into this symbolic in an unusual manner. Benjamin, too, understands *Trauerspiel* language (the language of the martyr-allegorist) as having opened itself up, anomically, to an energy that upsets the shape human language has taken in its normative historical development:[5] for instance, in its new and strange incorporation of sound. Differently from the humanized and full language of tragedy, language in the *Trauerspiel*, according to Benjamin, when it is not consumed in endless palavering, tends toward lament and sound. It also tends toward music, a "suprasensuous nature"; that is, it becomes more than human-historical, infiltrated as it is by the anxiety-provoking part-objects, the banished remainder of nature: "the interplay between sound and meaning remains a terrifying phantom for the mourning play . . . [The *Trauerspiel*] concentrates in itself the infinite resonance of its sound" (Benjamin 1916*a*, 60–1). It is, in other words, invaded by real elements.

Lacan's *sinthome* is a re-inscription of the symptom (which is itself an inscription), in particular the purely physical shell of the interpreted symptom that is left over after the analysis, into the context of art and writing. It is defined by a structure that is homologous with Benjamin's "origin" insofar as it seems to "return" to the unimaginable source of the subject only to reemerge in a symptomatic dislocation. But while the symptom repetitively seeks to re-symbolize itself, the *sinthome* rests in writing and art. It is characterized by *anomie*—an incursion of the real into the subject's symbolic status—as well as by corporeality (the "creaturely"), passion, and mourning, the affects that characterize Benjamin's martyr-allegorist. Lacan presents Joyce's writing, in particular in *Finnegans Wake*, as *sinthomatic* writing, and it is not by chance that it is a modernist who embodies the *sinthome*, though Lacan does not comment on this fact. Joyce and *Finnegans Wake* are examples, for Lacan, of "baroque" language, which approximates *lalangue*—his word for the non-communicative, chaotic, and polysemic substrata of language. Modernist language experiments are fundamentally "returns" to this "baroque." It is Joyce's particular "haeresis" (Lacan 1975–76/1999, 15), however, that interests Lacan aesthetically and clinically in its own right. Lacan's theory implies, though it does not state, that modernist aesthetics reflect a historical crisis of authority and legitimation whose origins lie in the Baroque. This fact in itself establishes a point of connection between this theory and Benjamin's *Trauerspiel* work.

The Joycean *sinthome* is writing as art, a liberation of the symptom into art. Specifically it is, Lacan says, the art of the "artificer." It is also the embodiment of passion and affect insofar as, in the shape of the physical symptom, it had been partially pure *jouissance*: trauma and ecstasy. The symptom, as opposed to the *sinthome*, is partially a signifier, insofar as it carries a message that can be read, on the inscribed body, analyzed and recovered (Lacan 1966, 455); what is left over from that reading process, however, its other part, is opaque, un-analyzable, and as such a mode of pure enjoyment of the unconscious. This is the *sinthome* (1975–76). Translated into *sinthome*, this *jouissance* finds expression in art where it stands as *savoir*—unconscious and esoteric half-knowledge. The *sinthome* is thus a signifying formulation that moves beyond the workings of the symbolic—that no longer *demands* symbolic containment— and beyond notions of full analysis and meaning. It allows one, Lacan says simply and esoterically, to live. Thus, writing, as Lacan conceives of it here, goes beyond and falls outside of symbolic and imaginary representation and approximates idiosyncratic expression of non-signifying substance.

There is a pronounced structural similarity between this interpretation of the writing of Joyce in particular, structured by the failure of the paternal signifier and by modern meaning-crisis, and the vicissitudes of language in Benjamin's figure of the baroque martyr-allegorist. For Lacan the psychoanalytic and aesthetic truth of Joyce's writing is the dissipation and structural absence of the Name-of-the-Father (his personal father having been mostly absent and alcoholic) and Joyce's own consequent self-construction by way of his *sinthome* through his written art. This art is not captivated by and contained within imaginary and symbolic meaning, but is instead infused by the *jouissance* of the real, as in *Finnegans Wake*, where linguistic distortions and dislocations that foreground the production of sounds abound. Lacan refers to this self-rescue of Joyce from a dissolving and uncontrolled psychosis—a malignant foreclosure of the symbolic—as a "decision," a "*haeresis*" (heresy, meaning an "act of choosing"), and adds that moreover Joyce is a "heretic" like Lacan himself (1975–76/1999, 15). One assumes he means that they both have a "heretical" relationship to language and symbolic containment on the whole.

It is this rescue of self by the self that I wish to foreground here. "One must choose the way by which truth is to be grasped," Lacan says in reference to such "heretical" choices or decisions. That particular truth is a matter of "*savoir-faire*" (1975–76/1999, 15). Writing the symptom, says Philip Dravers in his interpretation of this Lacanian seminar, means unknotting and re-knotting RSI—the trinitarian topology of the Borromean knot, the Real, Symbolic, and Imaginary—heretically: in Joyce's writing the Borromean trinity RSI that underlies the structure of subjectivity is replaced by Joyce's own construction (Dravers 2005, 6). While it is true that this self-rescue is not possible in any definitive and lasting way, as language continues to speak the self rather than the other way around, it is nevertheless the case that the *caesura* between Father-law and self-construction comes to have the same function as Benjamin's repeated explosions of the definitive symbol into fragments that lend transformative energies of the real access to language.

Lacan's theory of the *sinthome* offers, I suggest, a theory of the modernist subject that haunts Benjamin's various more or less heuristic projections of the modern subject—or rather: they haunt each other. At stake here is a topography for a new, modern ego that refuses totalizing solutions as well as oedipal orders and containments. The conjunction of Lacan's *sinthome* and Benjaminian inundations in the *Trauerspiel*'s mortifications of modern subjective sovereignty makes it possible to envision a modern subject that resists assimilation by any totalizing system and comes to rest in its own corporeal and creaturely self.

Let us look more carefully, then, at Lacan's structure of the Borromean knot, which combines the interdependent orders of subjectivity into individual and social identities. R(eal), in Lacanian theory, is the element of unshaped, unfissured, thing-in-itself, existence; S(ymbolic) is figured as hole: it empties out and represses the Thing, and makes existence signifiable and thus bearable in language and law; I(maginary) supplies consistency, visibility, and representation.[6] The three orders interrelate in such a way that the third order always cuts through and delimits the other two. In other words, it is both a balancing act and necessary trinity; of the three orders it is the real that can be catastrophically dissolving for the other two, even while being itself formless, while S and I limit its incursions and dangers (Dravers; Lacan 1975–76, 11). On the other hand, S and I can be catastrophic in their own right.

The real appears in the form of sound in Benjamin's *Trauerspiel* book. Sound, like the *sinthome*, lacks clear outline and is irruptive. Both, and this is the main point here, have a restorative power that veers away from and is subversive of intentional meaning in favor of a different kind of significance altogether. In the formation of a *sinthome*, the ring that sews back together a Borromean knot threatening to come apart (in reaction to a deflation or foreclosure of the Name-of-the-Father), the real and the symbolic orders become directly interlinked and are no longer mediated by an imaginary, which now slips away. Or better: is overcome. This formula makes up the kernel of Lacan's analysis of Joyce's aesthetics. I want to suggest that it also describes what happens when Benjamin's martyr is suddenly invaded by the *sound* of language. The slipping away of the imaginary in the baroque martyr results in subjective fragmentations, traumatic intrusions of the real, and loss of containment and representation. This unraveling threatens subjectivity with psychosis and fantasmatic fragmentations of the body image. Such psychic events have profound effects on a subject's language. The fourth ring, the *sinthome*, forestalls the slip into psychosis by an emergency re-knotting and distorts and transforms real irruptions into constructive florescences. This unfolding and re-knotting occurs, for Benjamin and Lacan both, in particular in writing.

2. *Writing*, objet a, *Ursprung*

By introducing a non-signifying opaqueness into language, the *sinthome* acts as a parasite upon the symbolic; at the same time, however, it provides an uncontainable excess, and it has the function of supplying "even a vital tress of subjectivity which binds together what would otherwise remain a 'paranoid' three [RSI]" (Dravers). In other words, ultimately the symptom, far from being all malady and destructive incursion, prevents totalization within subjectivity with or without art, by constantly reintroducing fragmentation, anti-meaning, and materiality[7]—the same abjections that face the baroque martyr and martyr-allegorist in the catastrophic crises of the Baroque—into the subject's symbolic framing. The *sinthome* is an evolution of the symptom in that it supplies both real *jouissance* and an element of artifice with which the *jouissance* can be allowed to appear—however transitorily. The *savoir-faire* of artifice corresponds to the Benjaminian allegorist's momentary masteries through convention.

Conceptually, Lacan has resonance for Benjamin's martyr-allegorist in two ways: through the notion of the *objet a* on the one hand and that of the master signifier on the other. While *objet a* refers to the incarnated cause-of-desire, evanescent embodiment of the inexorably un-encounterable first object, the master signifier is the central signifier that an individual chooses to stabilize meaning for herself, to totalize the "half knowledge" associated with *objet a*. The master signifier is as deluded as is the illusion of unity achieved by the subject's copulation with knowledge, as Lacan puts it throughout *Encore 1972–73* (Lacan 1998); "copulation" because *jouissance* enters into the pursuit of knowledge which tries to make up for the hole at the center of the Symbolic as well as the non-existence of the sexual relation—in other words, the loss both of the original object and, forever, of the *objet a*.[8] The *objet a*, on the other hand, the cause-of-desire, keeps desire alive by incorporating the little bit of difference which produces desire; the *objet a*'s very incompleteness, its fragmentary nature as well as its evanescence, the always only partial identifications that it enables, constitute both the subject's experience of "being," as Lacan calls it, and its drive toward self-emptying, self-destruction, and death. In this sense it provides a psychoanalytic explanation for what Benjamin calls *Ursprung*. It is possible to see an important connection between the dynamics of the *objet a* and the attitude of Benjamin's martyr: the reality of *objet a* subverts any subjective claim to sovereignty. In the end, *objet a* is defined as the leftover, the remnant of the real after the introduction of the symbolic. More importantly, the theory of the *objet a* helps explain Benjamin's insistence on immersion as the central characteristic of the martyr and the martyr-allegorist. The *objet a*'s function in constituting subjectivity is to subvert, by the very nature of its own logic, any conception of subjectivity as stable, positively identifiable, or sovereign.[9] Ross describes the process of immersion into and identification with *objet a* this way:

> The only way for the subject to escape the perpetual cycle of incomplete identification with its residue of difference (that keeps desire alive) is to

achieve complete identification, emptying itself out in a full transferral of its content into something other than itself. In other words, the subject would have to undertake the utmost realisation of the logic of predication, not only relating "I" to "that," but emptying "I" into "that" so completely that "I" would cease to signify altogether in an instant of pure subjective negation. If "the *objet a* is the lining of subjectivity" (Bowie 176–7), then we may think of this radical negation as an instance of the subject turning itself inside out, bringing together "the alpha of human experience" with "the omega of death" (Bowie 165). (Ross 2002)

Given Ross's (unnecessarily) totalizing representation of the process of identification ("complete identification") with *objet a*, one might at first object to bringing it into too close a relationship with the allegorist; but we also know from Benjamin that it is precisely the constellations of the "extreme" elements of a genre or any phenomenon that approximate its "truth." The extremity of the "complete identification" does correspond in important ways with the martyr's extremity.

Jacques-Alain Miller's depiction of the *objet a* as explosive throws additional light on the Benjamin-Lacan conjunction. In Miller's hands, Lacan's psychoanalytic dictum, "There is no Other of the Other"—no personalized God, no transcendental guarantee of stability behind the oedipal "guarantee" (which is no real guarantee) of the Name-of-the-Father and the symbolic order—and Lacan's final devaluation of the Other, leads to the converse statement, that *a*, on the contrary, does exist. The Lacanian Other, the Other that functions, is not real. That is what allows us to understand that *a* is real, that this *a* as *plus-de-jouir* founds not only the Other's alterity but also what is real in the symbolic Other. It is not a matter of a link that integrates, but of an articulation of extimacy—intimate living conditions with what is utterly unknown (Miller 1994, 81). I understand Miller's statement as describing a central aim of psychoanalysis: the transformation of a metaphysical relation to reality into a material and corporeal one. This is also Benjamin's aim in theorizing a modern subject who in his movement out of a pre-modern metaphysical universe immerses himself in a *sinthomatic* materiality in order to be of no use to the totalitarian elements within modernity.

Keeping the very real existence of *objet a* in mind makes it easier for thinking to shift into the perspective of contingency of Benjamin's martyr. The reality of *objet a* re-concretizes the inevitable abstractions of Benjamin's materialism: for instance, the notion of the subject submerging himself in the object. Miller's description of the reality of *objet a* corresponds to what occurs in Benjamin's martyr's psyche and language. Miller demonstrates the relationship between the field of the Other (the symbolic order) and the *objet a.* In terms of the latter's explosiveness its *real explosiveness* is relevant to understanding not only Benjamin's phenomenology of baroque man but also his philosophy of exploding the "*es war einmal*" of historicism[10]–both on the part of the individual facing his own history (in the manner of the Angelus Novus) and of the historiographer facing the "official" historical record.

The *objet a* can take on the "semblance" (Miller 1994, 85) of the symptom, insofar as the symptom both means something (in its cover, the interpretable symptom) while also functioning as disruptor of the signifier—exploding its coherence, even annulling its meaning. Identification with the *sinthome* on the part of the subject—as a mode of living, as an ethics—means placing the *objet a* in the position of the master signifier:[11] essentially, it means making it the (anti-)signifier that (dis-)orders a subject's symbolic field according to the timbre of the symptom. Benjamin does this in his creation of the martyr position, though he tends sometimes, but not always, to theologize the position. Correlatively, the *sinthome* expresses a faithfulness—to transience and corporeality. This again points to the *objet a* as both underlying language (as the cause-of-desire) and lying outside of it (Metzger 1997, 161).

As the real within the symbolic, the *objet a* signals *anomie*: in this, too, it corresponds to the irredeemably anomic condition of Benjaminian *Ursprung* as well as to the leap between divine and human language. Benjamin's idea of translation—repeated acts of throwing off constructs illusorily pretending to eternity for the sake of unveiling "language as such," even if just for an instant—which is of course an act intimately implicated in identification, lays bare the transformability of language, of desire, and thus also of reality. Further, the leap, breach, and absolute difference that *objet a* embodies is part and parcel of Benjamin's understanding of writing: as human language, writing cuts into the infinity of language through momentary limitation; as "stirring writing"—drawing actual concrete strokes on paper—it brings elements of corporeality, materiality, and contingency into the symbolic field of language.

Lacanian theory identifies the position of the analyst with *objet a;* the analyst must *be objet a* in order to reestablish the gap—the breach between cause-of-desire and expression of loss—necessary for the life of desire. Here we see even more clearly the similarity between *objet a* and Benjamin's *Ursprung.* The *objet a* implies both enjoyment (in its status as embodied representation of the original object), which interrupts clarity of meaning,[12] and, from the perspective of the Symbolic, sacrifice, as *a* always represents what is sacrificed and necessarily relinquished. It is in this sense that the analyst is identified with *a:* he or she contains the kernel of enjoyment, which, usually is sacrificed to the analysis—even as this enjoyment continues, in the person of the analyst, to muddy the waters of the analysis. For these reasons, being *a*, the analyst "shoulders" the *sinthome*. The analytic scene, then, is also a scene of martyrdom—for both analyst and analysand—as the hope is that eventually the analysand will identify with his or her own *sinthome* and not require that someone or something else be it for him.

But what does it mean, concretely, to identify with the *sinthome*? Art and writing produce the identified-with *sinthome*: Lacan links the function of art to the real by way of the blank of the fourth ring, where art reaches the symptom. In doing so he makes passing reference, instigated by a member of the audience (1975–76/1999, 40–41), to the myth of the lamella,[13] thus "substantiating" art. By "lamella" Lacan means the immortal, unstillable life force of drive energy, what I have been referring to as psychophysical "contingency," the leftover corporeal substance after the symptom has been interpreted. In "reaching" the symptom, art in fact reaches into what precedes (this can be understood both psychoanalytically and theologically) the signifier—that "leakage" that I noted in Chapter 1. In other words, entering the mortification and fragmentation processes in one's relation to truth as I have described that process in relation to the martyr-allegorist. In Lacan, this means identifying truth with the "half-said," in the form of a kernel of libidinal, non-sensical excess that rises so strongly to the surface both in the Baroque's obsession with ostentatious, excessive, and resounding language and in Joyce's jokes and language-games. Both are libidinally charged, both arise from the body and its drives.

At the same time, however, the *sinthome* as the fourth ring is also what holds a "self" together: it produces its own container, out of writing. *Sinthome* and writing thus function as a "skin" that offers consistency, even as this "skin," this "outline," has no predetermined form; it is a mobile deflatable, re-shapable container which deploys linguistic explosions and dislocations. As a non-imaginary shaper and because of its charge by the real over the imaginary, the *sinthome* privileges ear and sound over eye and image. Hence the psychoanalytic resonances of Benjamin's references to sound in the *Trauerspiel*. In that sense, too, the *sinthome* rescues a subject from the deadly fixation of and captivation by the gaze associated with totalizing knowledge.

3. *Lacan's Joyce:* Sinthomatic *Subject,* Sinthomatic *Topography*

Accessing "a little piece of the real" as truth or as a Benjaminian "origin"—shaped and provisionally contained by the consistency of a manipulatable

"skin" and by artifice (the art of the self-made man, as it were), all in order
to undo a threatened total disintegration of the signifier—can occur, says
Lacan, "through little bits of writing" (1975–76/1999, 68) whose matrix
topographically is non-imaginary. Joyce's writing is example and proto-
type for all of this in Lacan's Seminar. Joyce's non-relation to his father—
including to his father's nation and everything else that comes with the
"Father" as master signifier—and his partial foreclosure of the symbolic
create his geographical and psychological exile. In order to compensate for
his acute lack of a master signifier—a "baroque" condition—Joyce becomes,
in a way that recalls Benjamin's allegorist, his own "supreme artificer"
(70). The conjunction of influx of the real and *objet a* on the one hand with
"supreme artifice" on the other is what characterizes this strange fourth
ring, the *sinthome*. In addition, there are Joyce's foreclosures of the father
and devaluations—not to say popping of bubbles—of patriarchal authority, followed by constructions of *differing* symbolic authorities. As Patrick
Healy says in his commentary on Lacan's reading of Joyce, in Joyce we find,
instead of belief in an illusory father, someone who is listening to himself
write, almost as a third person.[14] The passage he quotes from *Finnegans
Wake* depicts Joyce's perception of the "imposture of [a de-legitimated]
patriarchy":

> or, an invitation to a larval genealogy, where the kind of hidden philosophi-
> cal mythology in language is exposed, and by a loss of faith in grammar,
> one, as Nietzsche has it, can be rid of belief in God, that the play of larval
> modalities of words and phrases in the hesitant self-doubting of writing can
> overcome the death of God . . . as you sing it its a study. That letter self-
> penned to one's other, that neverperfect, everplanned. . . . (Healy 1997)

Here, writing and reading, and reading one's own writing, replace, without
entirely canceling out, eschatology. Healy adds:

> One cannot assign to Joyce the neat solution of overcoming the death of God
> in the symbolic order of language and culture . . . The construction or fabri-
> cation is not an effort to create some primordial unity to be compared to the
> insatiable desire-as-lack of the patriarchal symbolic order. The thematics of
> the fallen patriarchy is dissolved and liquidated in the *jouissance* of the lapses
> of language. As Lacan would have it, the verbal slip is the radical facet of the
> non-meaning all meaning possesses. (1997)

4. Benjamin and Joyce: Origin and Irony

In a fragment entitled "Secret Signs" in *Short Shadows (II)* (1933a) Benjamin
describes something resembling the phenomenon that characterizes Joyce's

deconstruction of "legal" language and knowledge "in the *jouissance* of the lapses of language":

> A word of Schuler's has been preserved for us. Every piece of knowledge, he said, contains a dash of nonsense, just as in ancient carpet patterns or ornamental friezes it was always possible to find somewhere or other a minute deviation from the regular pattern. In other words, what is decisive is not the progression from one piece of knowledge to the next, but the leap implicit in any one piece of knowledge. This is the inconspicuous mark of authenticity which distinguishes it from every kind of standard product that has been mass produced. (699)

What Benjamin describes here is the true flow of tradition in its dialectical relationship with "origin" and not so much a re-writing of tradition. Nevertheless, aside from being one of the Benjaminian images criticizing the concepts of "progress" and identity, this is also an image of linguistic distortion and dislocation by way of *objet a*—the leap of *Ursprung*. Thus it may also function as an example of Lacanian "extimacy"—the real within the symbolic. In fact, insofar as *Ursprung* is characterized by *Nachträglichkeit*—effects rather than simple actions—and dislocation and distortion, it connects Benjamin's thought to psychoanalysis on the whole.

Joyce's English, too, is injected with alterity, dis-identifying it with traditional "English" and ostentatiously containing its "waste." It is supplemented with something like mania (Lacan 1975–76/1999, 12). As Jacques-Alain Miller puts it, the "Joyce insignia" manipulate "the letter outside the effects of the signifier to the ends of pure *jouissance*." Joyce's writing would even put in question the analyst's discourse because "the subject identified with the symptom closes up in its artifice" as Miller writes (1996). In other words, we see in Lacan's theory of the *sinthome* a subject that becomes quite independent (and thus more of a "self") in its play and *jouissance* with its own symptom. Pure *jouissance* means opening the subject up to the real, to the meaning-free sound beneath the word, to the musical note. Listening to the real (rather than empirically hearing it) means that the subject perceives the drive that is "the echo in the body of the fact that there is speech" (Lacan 1975–76/1999, 17). Willy Apollon puts it even better: "The drive that manifests itself in jouissance comes from farther away than the sphere of individual life" (2002*b*, 125), preceding the subject, as it were. In that it reminds us once more of Benjamin's martyr who falls apart at the sight of the creaturely. What may seem like a contradiction here—How can the "self-made," oppositional *sinthomatic* writer also be so depersonalized?—is not one: it is not a particular identity that is at stake here, but rather the difference between how subject-object and subject-subject relationships are experienced. The *sinthome* offers what Benjamin would consider to be a redeemed experience, the ability to communicate "originally" with all of reality, including material reality. But what does it mean to "communicate originally"?

Joyce's famous epiphanies are defined by Jacques Aubert (who speaks at length in Lacan's seminar) and Lacan as moments of the real foreclosing symbolic-imaginary meaning. While in *The Portrait of an Artist* the epiphany by and large still has the character of an imaginary representation of the religious impulse (Lacan 1975–76/1999, 181), in the later work this foreclosure translates into a refusal of imaginary solutions—that is, hallucinatory satisfaction— in favor of "baroque" linguistic artifice infused with materiality.

This refusal is comparable to Benjamin's allegorist's refusal of the totalizing solution of the symbol. Joycean epiphanies are instances of failure of the Name-of-the-Father's and the Borromean knot and are vacua in signification where the cover provided by the imaginary slips away. These moments are like the still moments of Benjamin's martyr-allegorist's contemplation and immersions, his generalized denigration of meaning and master signifiers, and the momentary liberations from the tyranny of the symbolic that can occur under his watch, when sound is liberated.

The *sinthomatic* in Joyce's writing can also be understood as moments in which the baroque impulse toward allegory re-emerges: stoppage (*Stillstand*), the crumbling of forms, and those efflorescences and ornamentations that are born in between the constant re-writings and reconfigurations of meanings that typify Benjamin's Baroque. By becoming master signifier manipulators, the martyr-allegorist and the *sinthomatic* Joycean writer attempt to master the wounds of symbolic *anomie* by a play with language that also carries with it charges of *jouissance*.

In both cases this results in the publication of personal *jouissance* infusing—and *refusing*—a collective language. The most self-consciously allegorical versions of such re-configurations of meaning take on an aura of ironic artifice. Thus Aubert says about Joyce's writing,

> . . . things move around, artifice is created, when the names of the father are caught up in a game of hide-and-seek; in other words, . . . alongside what looks like a gap, we have the displacement of the gap, the displacement of the name of the father. (Lacan 1975–76/1999, 182)

These displacements follow, as I have said, the movement of the Benjaminian *Ursprung*, described by Weber as a process of "repeat, restore, and at the same time dislocate" (1991, 493). Repetition and restoration imply a return to an origin, the Father, but the returns are always subject to dislocation ("things move around" and there is "the displacement of the name of the father"). The human state of exile, even though overtly it leads to games with convention, can also find instants of "origin" by retrieving, in a sort of imitation of God's original writing, a primordial writing still dripping with—in Lacanian and Benjaminian terms respectively—traces of the Thing and of Paradise, while at the same time ironizing them.

5. *"Supreme Artificers" of a New Ego*

The Lacanian dialectic of supreme artifice and expression in the *sinthome* helps explain the dialectic and ambiguity of Benjaminian allegory, too; it provides a psychoanalytic explanation for Benjamin's projections for a post-catastrophic modern subjectivity that is, I am arguing, covertly psychoanalytic in the first place. One could say that both terms—convention/artifice and expression/*jouissance*—are mortified, by Benjamin and Lacan both, in irony. This mortification, a sort of *rubbing* together, releases for each the other for the sake of its own control. The rubbing is the way in which I have understood and perhaps re-codified "martyrdom." In the "Theological-Political Fragment" Benjamin writes, "nothing that is historical can relate itself, *from its own ground*, to anything messianic" [my emphasis] (1920–21 or 1937–38, 305). And later on: ". . . just as a force, by virtue of the path it is moving along, can augment another force on the opposite path, so the secular order—because of its nature as secular—promotes the coming of the Messianic Kingdom." The longer passage that follows is almost a summary of the *Trauerspiel* book:

> For in happiness [the secular expression of messianic redemption] all that is earthly seeks its downfall, and only in happiness is its downfall destined to find it.—Whereas admittedly the immediate messianic intensity of the heart, of the inner man in isolation, passes through misfortune, as suffering. The spiritual *restitution in integrum*, which introduces immortality, corresponds to a worldly restitution that leads to an eternity of downfall, and the rhythm of this eternally transient worldly existence, transient in its totality, in its spatial but also in its temporal totality, the rhythm of messianic nature, is happiness. For nature is messianic by reason of its eternal and total passing away. (305–6)

"Happiness" and the "messianic," in this passage, correspond to "expression," and "downfall," temporality and transience, to "convention" as well as to "artifice." Through immersion in the "passing away," in convention, and by ironically lacerating and re-writing it in the mode of *jouissance*,

Joyce re-creates the "self," which survives in that way in the *sinthome*, as ironic and enjoying supreme artificer.

Less abstractly, my discussion of the Lacanian *sinthome* and of Joyce adds to Benjamin's theorizing of the modern subject the dimension of the individual modern artist, who, Benjamin intimates and Lacan asserts, is a *sinthomatic* artist, who (successfully) runs the *agon* in the face of the weight of an increasingly meaningless tradition, the latter's catastrophic crumbling, and a resulting threat of reactionary tyranny. The distortions and unfolding of collective master signifiers into contingent and transformative—and often concrete—signifiers that come about through Joyce's (and, through him, Stephen Dedalus's) and the allegorist's writing result from their being "supreme artificers" who re-configure the signifiers they usurp. In Joyce the signifier is, says Lacan, "reduced to what it is—equivocation, a twisting of speech . . . he ends up breaking or dissolving language itself, by decomposing it, going beyond phonetic identity, . . . [thus] break[ing] free from the verbal parasite" (1975–76/1999, 96–7).

This mirrors the vicissitudes of language in Benjamin's Baroque when it becomes excessive and overflowingly ornamental.[15] Both are instances of *lalangue*: "non-communicative aspects of language which, by playing on ambiguity and homophony, give rise to a kind of *jouissance* . . . *Lalangue* is like the primary chaotic substrate of polysemy out of which language is constructed, almost as if language is some ordered superstructure sitting on top of this substrate" (Evans 1996, 97). This same radical ambivalence emerges in the *sinthome* that—as the fourth ring that saves the other three from total disintegration and that takes the shape of Joyce's verbal reconfigurations—neither "heals" nor "paper[s]" over the void. . . . If anything," writes Patrick Healy, "there is only a piling up of catastrophe" (Healy 1997). This is certainly an interesting image in the Benjaminian context. In other words, neither Joyce nor the faithful martyr-allegorist work to overcome absence and fragmentation. Just like the analyst, who shares his position with that of the *objet a* (the cause-of-desire) without believing in its "healing" function, but only in its effects (i.e., in its ability to reconfigure the structures of desire), so too the true allegorist remains faithful to the ruins, the rubble out of which meaning can be constructed.[16] Lacan would agree with Benjamin's general valorization of verbal art as the site where both the impulse toward re-enchantment and the prohibition against it, but also the quest for new forms of experience that can counteract a totalizing and simultaneously dissociative world, play themselves out. *Sinthomatic* writing re-configures, in a new way, an ego that had crumbled in a radical legitimation crisis of the Father, the Symbolic, the Other. The process of rescuing the personality *is* the process of *sinthomatic* writing; the latter provides a support for thinking (Lacan 1975–76/1999, 144)[17] within the gaps of the shards of language many of which are broken and are continu- ing to break.

Unpacking the ramifications of all such convergences constitutes the meat of the second part of this chapter and the following ones—the "*Ponderación Misteriosa*" at the end of the *Trauerspielbuch*, the meaning of Benjaminian "mimesis," and the psychoanalytic case of "Susan": *sinthomatic* writing coincides with the process of configuring a new and very different sort of subject after the mainly imaginary ego with the totalizing inclinations has slipped away upon the failure of the Name-of-the-Father to establish itself. In a strange detachment from itself as broken, in the coming-into-being of a *sinthome*, the function of this "new" ego, Lacan says, "is enigmatic and reparatory" (153). And just as the broken ego, as it were, enfolds itself within its own broken pieces, re-configuring and re-containing itself, and the son, both personally and collectively, shoulders the burden of the absent father (in the same way in which the analyst shoulders the *objet a*), the Joycean art work's truth content stands in a homonymous relation to its frame: its form is also its content. In Benjamin's text, allegory is an allegory that says that everything is allegory; the knowledge that knowledge is untrue knowledge is itself knowledge, which, however, is repeatedly contradicted—for the sake of true knowledge, *savoir*.

6. Writing, Theology, and the "Practice of the Signifier"

With the *sinthome* we can also find ourselves within the dialectic of a negative theology. Lacan says, "We do not believe in the object as such" (1975–76/1999, 36), but rather in the field of tension of the object that is posited as lacking and the subject able to maintain itself as subject only by way of desire for the object. "Our analytic grasp of the knot is the negative of religion" (36), he says, and within this field of tension relations with materiality and with objects encounter the real in non-conceptual ways. In Benjamin this same realm is the one where immersion into the materiality of language takes place, where the subject becomes partially inundated by the object, and is taken hostage by a language that moves it into unexpected dimensions. In both cases we are dealing with a specific kind of materiality. It may be that this language that stands in such a peculiar relationship to the body comes to disarray the traditional subject. The ways in which Joyce disarticulates English gives it another, non-communicative, use. This is Joyce's "savoir-faire" (61). "Savoir-faire" gives "a remarkable value to one's art . . . [perhaps] the jouissance of God" (61), as it seems to lie outside of the sphere of judgment as Benjamin conceived of it in his 1916 language essay, and outside of the law in Lacanian terms. "Savoir-faire" "escapes us, in other words [it] far exceeds the enjoyment [jouis-sance] we can have of it. This absolutely slender jouissance is what we call spirit [l'esprit]" (61). In "The Rat in the Maze," in *Seminar XX. Encore* (1972–73), Lacan defines *savoir-faire* as a particular kind of engagement with the unconscious dimension of language: ". . . the unconscious is knowledge, a knowing how to do things (*savoir-faire*) with llanguage. And what we know how to do with llanguage goes well beyond what we can account for under the heading of language" (1972–73, 139). Lacan's conception of "llanguage" (or *lalangue*) as the unconscious dimension of language, as the speaking unconscious itself, is, in my understanding, a manifestation of Benjamin's "pure language" set off against the language of judgment, as he theorized it in his 1916 essay. For Lacan, "llanguage serves purposes that are altogether different from that of communication," and language "is merely what scientific discourse elaborates to account for what I call llanguage . . . Language is what we try to know concerning the function of llanguage" (1972–73, 138). Like scientific discourse, language "misrecognizes the unconscious" (139). In this sense Lacan's llanguage or *lalangue* is a language suited to Benjamin's "coming philosophy."

Faithfulness to the creaturely, as Benjamin puts it, engagement with waste matter, as Joyce puts it, and a Lacanian identification with the symptom all represent hope for the redemption of both subject and object—redemption from a reified subject-object relationship altogether, as traditional, delu-sionally full "knowledge" comes to be usurped by "half-knowing." It redeems "experience" and, in Lacanian terms, "being" from the limited knowledge of scientific discourse. A more fraught term than "being" hardly exists, and yet it is what identification with the *sinthome* finally provides. To some extent this ability to "be" or "live" is tied to the enjoyment of art, but it is more than that. Aubert asks, whether it is literature that remains, that deserves to survive. The phrase "deserves to live" (1975–76/1999, 184) comes from *Ulysses*, and Aubert applies it here equally to the foundation of art and to the *sinthome* which makes life possible both when the Name-of-the-Father has lost its legitimating power and at the end of analy-sis, when so much deconstruction has taken place and certainty is known not to be had.

I have argued that Benjamin's *Trauerspiel* book struggles with this same legitimation crisis and historicizes it, and I have attempted to show that a Benjamin-Lacan convergence is not only interesting from the viewpoint of intellectual curiosity, but that it grounds Benjamin's intimations regard-ing modern subjectivity in individual experience—and in a praxis for transformed experience. Strengthening the Benjamin-Lacan convergence, Aubert even uses the figure of the king to represent both the failing Father and the failing symbolic word that the king had seemed, imaginarily, to guarantee, but no longer does:

> The problem of the king's word as foundation of legitimacy, the word which even if the mother's belly has lied, allows things to be set right by legitimation. Legitimation, in other words the possibility of bearing the mark of the king, the crown, stephanos; or again, of bearing that other mark which appears in Circe, with Virag, the grandfather who falls down the chimney, labeled Basilicogrammate, with the king's gramme. The problematic of legitimacy which shows itself to be that of legitimation takes a form here, perhaps, in the imaginary dimension, and its recuperation. (187)

Aubert links Joyce's "survival" to the functioning *sinthome* and the alternative use to which it puts the slipping paternal word, namely the use of what he calls "personation," by which he seems to mean the coming-to-life of an incarnated subject, and sound, "and for instance in whatever 'deserves to live,' in melody" (187). What he calls "the voice-effects of the signifier" (187), that is, the signifier embedded in the voice as *objet a*, are dependent on attentive listening on the part of the subject: on the use of the ear, an *objet a* that transcends the realm of the signifier. While Joyce had at first wished to "codify [these effects of the signifier] into rules in an aesthetic science," "fairly quickly he realized that it was not all that linked to science, and that it was, precisely, a savoir-faire linked to a practice of the signifier" (188), a very specific form of writing constructed on the foundation of sound by way of distortion, or, as Lacan puts it, by the treatment of the real by the symbolic.

Given the structural slipping away of the imaginary ring and the implementation of an ego whose function it is to constantly re-configure itself by way of a play with and the (*objet a*) effects of the signifier, Lacan's theory of the *sinthome* implies the (self)-creation of a subject, one that links symbolic to real in a new way and that is fundamentally different from the triple-knot subject which has failed in its "tightrope" task, "with excess on one side, and the Other's absence on the other," as Willy Apollon has described the modern subject (2002*b*, 125). Whereas generally speaking the ethics of Lacanian analysis are about the reduction of *jouissance* in favor of the signifier—that is, the subject's move from symptom to fantasy—the following step, from fantasy to *objet a* is equally important, as it comes to terms with the failing of the signifier and thus with its deflation. What remains is the *objet a*: "The principle of Lacanian analysis is predicated on this failing of jouissance, this lack that pierces a hole in the chain of signifiers and that is signified in the object which Lacan calls object *a*" (Apollon 2002*c*, 140). The "hole in the chain of signifiers," yet another metaphor for Benjamin's martyr, can also take the shape of a hole *in* the signifier, a dissociation of signifier and signified and the breaking out of individual letters from the whole signifier and from whole meaning. The letter brings with it a trace of the real and is linked to the drive, as compared to the signifier which is symbolic and struggles to keep the letters "covered" by meaning. In Apollon's words, "It [the letter] becomes linked to the hole the signifier surrounds, and traces a path, on the edge of the organism in the symptom, for the death drive where jouissance returns to challenge the effects of the Law. The 'letter' acts as an edge outside the signifier toward the exteriority of the jouissance as real" (2002*c*, 109).

Dialectically, the letter both supports the signifier as a dam against the real, yet, loosened from the signifier, it opens up a door to a seeping *jouissance* and comes to support the symptom, which is a writing of *jouissance*. Generally *jouissance* must be reduced by the signifier, but the signifier partially fails in this, and the subject must survive by making its own law. What emerges is a subject that survives both the tyranny and the waning of the Law-of-the-Father, and its survival implies an ethics: first, in the sense of faithfulness to the material object world, and second in that it survives the catastrophic changes wrought by loss of faith in traditional notions of sovereignty, authority, and power:

> In time, after the subject's encounters with whatever is the anguishing knot of the real in the unconscious, the desire to be cured yields to the ethical requirement of a truth that is incommensurable with the knowledge of science or psychology. The false need of belonging within which the stakes of the ego identifications justify themselves, disappears with the return and recognition of a desire bearing its own markers with no regard for the demands of the Other than the symbolic limits of social or citizen coexistence. (Apollon 2002*c*, 140)[18]

I am arguing that this Lacanian ethics is a concrete version of Benjamin's ethics of martyrdom. The case of Susan in Chapter 6 will demonstrate this Benjamin-Lacanian ethics most concretely.

7. Sinthomatic *Ethics and the Baroque*

At work in the subject who constructs his or her own *sinthome*—not only in response to the threat of a psychosis and the dissolution of the Borromean knot, but also post-analytically[19]—is a search for an irreducible substance (what Lacan here calls "being"), which lies also at the basis of Benjamin's theologically inflected materialism. Historically, I argued in Chapter 1, the search originated in the processes of secularization—*Deontologisierung*, as Makropoulos refers to them—and the resulting rise of contingency in the modern individual's experience, together with depersonalization, anaesthesia,[20] and enchantment. Benjamin, I argued, presents—documented in the *Trauerspiel* of the Baroque—two responses to this problem: (1) to search for—and find—imaginarily "authentic" meaning by dominating, taming, and overpowering contingency by imposing meaning upon it (this is the Counter-reformational, Carl Schmitt's, and fascism's solution); and (2) to use contingency in order to build new *jouissant* artifice[21]— the martyr-allegorist and the *sinthome*, as I have demonstrated in this chapter. This means a personalized art or praxis that cathects the body and its drives as well as its relations with the material object world in a language that has widened its parameters to include experiences that may in many cases still be dormant. Makropoulos calls this second modality a "contingent subjectivity" (30). Lacan's *sinthome* and the work of Joyce exemplify it.

By way of Lacan's theory of the *sinthome* I have opened up the ways in which we may read Benjamin's projections for a modern subjectivity by focusing both on the figure of the anti-canonical modernist writer as well as on the psychology and experience of the figure of the martyr-allegorist who, as subject, continues to require experience of non-verbal, non-signifying "substance" in order to overcome the emptying out of experience in modernity. Just as *Ursprung* in its dislocating action performs the task, as Benjamin puts it in his Sixth Thesis on the Philosophy of History, of "wrest[ing] tradition away from a conformism that is about to over-power it" (Benjamin 1940/1969, 255), the *sinthome* too works within an ethics of recuperation and against assimilation. It forms an integral part of Lacan's ethics of psychoanalysis. Now the "individual conscience" (Makropoulos 1989, 29) is forced to become a stabilizing ground itself, to become a demiurge who is not only swayed but also shaped by his or her own constructs. In the *sinthome* such constructs, such artifice, move away from and distort master meaning. To a large degree this was *not* the case for the allegorist; nevertheless, Benjamin's allegorist continues to be overcome by the melancholy and (self-)destructiveness that continue to seep *jouissance* in ways that are unpredictable. In fact, one could say that the *sinthome* would have to be a central support in the establishment of what Makropoulos refers to as a modern and coherent *Lebenswelt*, resting on a new ontological foundation of the real (35).

II The Post Catastrophic Subject

1. *Ponderación Misteriosa*

Chapter 1 and the first part of this chapter frame the somewhat bombastic ending of *Origin of the German Tragic Drama*. They contain ramifications for the psychology, phenomenology, and, in the end, ethics of subjectivity in modernity. To summarize, the problem of the individual that Benjamin confronts in his *Trauerspiel* book is that modern subjectivity is shocked, reified, fragmented, and depersonalized, making it vulnerable to seductive compensations in the form of domination, grandiosity, control, on the one hand, and isolation, rest, and illusion of immortality on the other. Throughout Benjamin's work, from his early statements regarding modernity's siege on meaningful experience, in his descriptions of the modern world of meaning and relationship as empty, to his preoccupations with perception in ordinary and extraordinary conditions, in particular in relation to modern technology, the topography of the subject is central to it all.

Language is always central to his analysis. The structure and experience characteristic of allegorical intention and intuition, as a specific sort of language, is central to the transformations of "baroque" modern subjectivity.[22] Allegory recognizes that modern experience has been emptied out with the evanescence of metaphysical guarantees and that language is fundamentally fallen. Thus the allegorical mode is both tragic and comic, both despairing and ironic, insofar as all it can do is point to what is not. This constitutes its hopeless hope. Nevertheless, the final passages of *The Origin of German Tragic Drama*, climaxing in "*Ponderación Misteriosa*," are a grand finale of esotericism from which emerges, fragmentedly and negatively, an idea of subjectivity that gestures toward the messianic. These pages present difficult reading, and interpretations of them abound. The difficulty has to do with voice: in whose voice is Benjamin speaking? The voice becomes heavily ironic here as Benjamin takes on the point of view and the language (in particular the language of judgment, "good and evil") of the Counter-reformation.

The central issues are the topography and the vicissitudes of allegory. Allegory, Benjamin now says, had been characterized by three illusions: "the illusion of freedom—in the exploration of what is forbidden; the illusion of independence—in the secession from the community of the pious; the illusion of infinity—in the empty abyss of evil" (Benjamin 1928/1998, 230). Allegory is determined by Satanic temptations, and its nature is "evil" because of its secession from God and its immersion in pure materiality. However, Benjamin's voice is not wholly fused (even if only ironically) with the Catholic one; allegory is also "evil" from the point of view of Benjamin's 1916 language essay where fallen language is said to be consumed by the desire for "knowledge." While allegory can, if it remains true to itself, resist the closures of absolutism and totalitarianism, it is also driven by the desire for knowledge, thus remaining irresolvably dialectical. It breaks up totalities (it separates itself from the community) and this provides its liberatory value; but it can also be so mobile as to never make possible a *Stillstand*, necessary for the formation of "philosophical constellations" (Benjamin 1928/1998, 231)—and that problematizes the first value. Baroque allegory does not know itself; it does not know what it is doing. In any case, in its fall into the "bottomless depths," Benjamin now says, allegory encounters a limit in an "about-turn into salvation and redemption" (232). That is, an arc comes into being: what had pointed unceasingly downward toward material reality now swings up. What this means for allegory is that it no longer refers to transitoriness by way of its form, but transitoriness is "displayed as allegory." It is contained within a frame of representation; it becomes myth. The graveyard in which allegory had recognized history is, it turns out, "Golgotha" (a symbol), which, as we know, moves in the direction of resurrection: "Ultimately, in the death-signs of the baroque the direction of allegorical reflection is reversed; on the second part of its arc it returns, to redeem" (232). In its attempt to overcome melancholy and thus the "evils" of subjective knowledge and "overnaming," allegory transforms into God's world—specifically a Christian God's world. But this lurch upward means leaving behind the things of transience and decay, the catastrophes of history, "the most fragmented, the most defunct, the most dispersed" (232):

> All this vanishes with this *one* about-turn, in which the immersion of allegory has to clear away the final phantasmagoria of the objective and, *left entirely to its own devices* re-discovers itself, not playfully in the earthly world of things, but seriously under the eyes of heaven. And this is the essence of melancholy immersion: that its ultimate objects, in which it believes it can most fully secure for itself that which is vile, turn into allegories [note the self-referentiality], and that these allegories fill out and deny the void in which they are represented, just as, ultimately, the intention does not faithfully rest in the contemplation of bones, but faithlessly leaps forward to the idea of resurrection. (232–3)

Allegory, whose "origin" is materiality and transience, natural history embodied in the corpse, is thus betrayed: "Allegory goes away empty-handed" (233). Things get increasingly more complicated here as Benjamin tries to show that the configuration in which allegory leads to its own apotheosis (and thus becomes "faithless") is a totalizing and stabilizing one which in reality has nothing to do with "faithful" allegory, which is dialectical and material. The allegory that is allegedly constituted by "knowledge of evil" is "'nonsense' [*Geschwätz*]" (233) as "There is no evil in the world," given that "'God saw everything that he had made, and, behold it was very good'" (233). The existence of "evil," the judgment of "material communities" as "evil," is thus an illusion proper to the allegory that moves toward its own *Umschlag* in order to redeem itself (and not the world), and thus proper to the inflation of the subjective, which thus, with the arrogance and contempt typical of assumptions of omnipotence, loses touch with the objective world. This inflation of the subjective, though it presents itself as leaving subjectivity behind as "evil," suffers from the same flawed and faithless Christian reversal. A subjectivity that lets go of itself only when it believes to be mirrored by the fullness of God, has been faithless and mythical all along. Such belief is typical of a psychology of omnipotence.

Faithless allegory is a consequence of the Fall and human beings' growing distance from the language of names. While the language of names had made possible the appearance of the martyr-allegorist and his attentiveness to objects, faithless allegory is the culmination of the fall into guilt—that is, "abstraction": "For good and evil are unnameable, they are nameless entities, outside the language of names, in which man, in paradise, named things and which he forsakes in the abyss of that problem. For languages the name is only a base in which the concrete elements have their roots" (234). The concrete, Benjamin implies here, would be the aim of faithful allegory. But the swing upward, allegedly away from the "abstractions" that had led to the appearance of melancholia and mourning, actually means a smug and self-satisfied abandonment of concrete things as "evil."

What does faithless allegory encounter in its upswing? Given that allegory comes to turn away from things (the erstwhile "satanic" immersions into the elemental) and onto itself (as transparent image of God) as a source of salvation, it is not surprising that it should be a mirror. And this takes us into Benjamin's treatment of baroque subjectivity, understood here as a concern with what is actually an assimilation of the self to the authority of "omnipotent" master signifiers, a filling of the self by way of the mirror:

> Here the unconcealed subjectivity triumphs over every deceptive objectivity of justice and is incorporated into divine omnipotence as "a work of supreme wisdom and primial love," as hell. It is not appearance, and, equally, it is not satiated being, but it is the reflection in reality of empty subjectivity in the

good. In evil as such subjectivity grasps what is real in it, and *sees it simply*
as its own reflection in God. In the allegorical image of the world, therefore,
the subjective perspective is entirely absorbed in the economy of the whole.
[my emphasis] (234),

and the objective world is forsaken.[23]

And now follows Benjamin's description of the "baroque balcony." The
balcony is the object of an optical illusion that greatly increases the appearance of grandeur and enormity of whoever stands there from down below.
Benjamin precedes it with his reference to Saint Theresa whose visions
represent the height of an inflated subjectivity as "hallucination." Such
visions have been used historically by leaders and institutions as a foundation for their authority and power: it is "the miracle," precisely the image
and vision of "faithless" allegory, subjectivity mirrored and dissolving in
God, used by the Catholic Church in the Counter-reformation as the mythical guarantee of its authority (234). Benjamin's reference to the "miracle"
takes us right to Schmitt's theory of sovereignty, where he writes, "The
exception in jurisprudence is analogous to the miracle in theology" (Schmitt
2005, 36). Hence Benjamin describes the Baroque's self-characterization as
self-referential, inflated, grandiose, and narcissistic: "What else can be the
purpose of the constant references to the violence of the supporting and
supported forces, the enormous pedestals, the doubly and triply augmented
projecting columns and pilasters, the strengthening and reinforcement
of the interconnecting elements. . .?" (235). The symbols and structures
representing overwhelming power and the manipulation of the viewer
down below culminate in what the mighty soaring pilasters and monumental pedestals actually support: a balcony. An empty space. Subjectively,
one is to imagine—hallucinate—the Sovereign-God standing there. On the
other hand, objectively, there is no one there, and this fact turns the baroque
symbolism of power into ostentatious spectacle,[24] just as it turns that
baroque "upswing" of allegory that loses itself—empties itself, in fact—
into miraculous delusion and phantasmagoria. This alternative to the
"miracle"—seeing the empty balcony as empty—is an allegory for *Trauer-*
spiel allegory that remains "inadequa[te]," "deficient," uncontained, and
not yet "thought through" (Benjamin 1928/1998, 235). In this sense the
German tragic drama is a true "origin," a potentially revolutionary, perhaps anarchic, *Ursprung*: while the Southern Counter-reformation drama
reinstates myth and is thus a reactionary return to foundationalism in the
wake of the loss of the transcendent, the Northern play dislocates that
return and insists on remaining unfinished, a fragment. This is the source
of its messianic and revolutionary energy: ". . . for this reason the German

Trauerspiel merits interpretation. In the spirit of allegory it is conceived from the outset as a ruin, a fragment. Others may shine resplendently as on the first day; this form preserves the image of beauty to the very last" (235). For in this Benjaminian text, all totality and closure are related not only to the tyrant but also to the deceitful power institution that claims to have brought about universal reconciliation.

The balcony's emptiness functions as a clue toward deciphering a Benjaminian ethics, which is always ultimately related to the "expression-less," *das Ausdruckslose*. As Koepnick (1996) puts it, Benjamin's ethics "maintains that the inner truth of morality is neither revealed by gestures and immediate expressions nor communicated through an iconic signifier. The ethical resides outside of language and pictorial representation and therefore also negates a transformation into an aesthetic spectacle. . . . " (271). Interpretative possibilities abound of this, as Weber says, "demonically equivocal" (1991, 500) ending; my focus is psychological, ethical, and political.

2. *Ethics of the Subject:* Encore *Lacan and Benjamin*

The "about-turn" of allegory into its own apotheosis coincides with a state of exception in which only the miracle, according to Schmitt, can lead to decisiveness and wholeness. Allegory's "about-turn" into the closed, self-reflexive faithlessness of the "mirror," which puts a stop to the "downward" drive, corresponds to the Schmittian dictator using the "miracle" to suspend not only the old law and put himself and his decision in its place, but also to suspend contingency as such. "Faithless" allegory puts an end to its own state of *anomie*. According to Benjamin in his Thesis VIII (1940/1969), such a state of emergency leads to a continuous state of emergency where "the things" are abandoned, remain unredeemed, and where history accelerates its course toward continuous catastrophe. "Faithful allegory," on the other hand, would translate into contemplation of the creaturely—the animate and inanimate objects of material history—for the sake of its recollection (Weidmann 1992, 23). Pensky (1996) speaks of faithful allegory as "an affective reaction to the theological condition of fragment, loss, confusion," a "collecting" that takes place in both the individual and the collective historical realms and always requires individual attention. He writes,

> Collecting establishes a particular gaze, in whose healing power one first discerns the origin of that Kantian 'disinterestedness' with which the subject

first encounters things lifted from their consignment to objects for the subject, objects of cognition or of usefulness, and with gratitude sees in nature
the state of things divinely arranged to fulfill the subject's need for signs of
a postponed redemption of subjectivity and things . . . The collector lifts the
things out of the cycle of production and consumption . . . (1996, 186)

We saw in the first part of this chapter how Benjamin's insistence on
the fragmentariness of truth finds an echo in Lacan's formulation for the
truth of the subject: "[truth is] the impossibility of telling the whole truth"
(1972–73/1998, 95). Instead, given the irreparable loss that characterizes
the symbolic order, and in a heightened, *baroque* way, the consciousness
of the subject at the end of analysis, truth will be represented in the ruin,
the fragmentary torso of the half-said, the not-whole. In *Encore* (1972–
73/1998) Lacan refers specifically to the mystic who "sides" not with "the
winner," but with the "not whole," not only because of the truth of fragmentariness, but also because the *jouissance* of the real leftovers gathers
there and because *lalangue* is to make up for the loss of the real around the
formation of the paternal symbolic:

> Mysticism . . . is something serious, about which several people inform us —
> most often women, or bright people like Saint John of the Cross. . . . One can
> also situate oneself on the side of the not-whole . . . despite—I won't say their
> phallus—despite what encumbers them that goes by that name, they get the
> idea or sense that there must be a jouissance that is beyond . . . They experi-
> ence it but know nothing about it . . . (76)

Lacan goes on to say that his *Écrits* are "of the same order." The jouissance
is produced precisely "thanks to the being of signifierness," an involvement
with language and the signifier that goes beyond their phallic function and
that is "a good at one remove" (77), even as it is dependent on living within
the signifier:

> . . . the subject turns out to be—and this is only true for speaking beings—a
> being (*un étant*) whose being is always elsewhere . . . The subject is never
> more fleeting (*ponctuel*) and vanishing, for it is a subject only by a signifier
> and to another signifier. (142)

In the later Lacan, too, then, like in Benjamin's notion of allegory, subjectivity is arbitrary convention *as well as* expression, passion, jouissance.
It grows out of "attentiveness to the creaturely." Such attentiveness implies
a (re-)collection of what has been consigned to the "waste heap," as well
as a re-inscription of this materiality into the material reality that is to
be read.

3. Reading and-Writing

Like Benjamin's "faithful" martyr-allegorist, when he is understood as a reader and writer, Lacan's mystical subject, or the subject fully alive in language, "approach[es] the One in a way other than the intuitive, fusional, amorous way" (Lacan 1972–73/1998, 47). The latter would correspond to the "faithless" turn to the symbol in Benjamin. "The One" here refers, as Lacan puts it, to "[t]he One everyone talks about all the time [who] is, first of all, a kind of mirage of the One you believe yourself to be" (47)— a "mirage." The subject ought to approach truth differently, as Lacan describes it in "Love and the Signifier" (1972–73/1998) where he explains how letters function and what they "are" by reference to set theory. He says, letters "are like," and then, no, they *constitute* or *create*, assemblages of absolutely heterogeneous and different elements, forever irreducible to the One, always sliding and thus always bringing with them a friction of *jouissance*. Saussure's profoundest insight was, according to Lacan, "that no signifier is produced (*se produit*) as eternal . . . [though] it would have been better to qualify the signifier with the category of contingency. The signifier repudiates the category of the eternal . . ." (1972–73/1998, 40). Nevertheless, he goes on, what else can take us back to origins, to *Genesis*, but the signifier?[25]

> Isn't it clear to you that [the signifier] participates, to employ a Platonic approach, in that nothing on the basis of which something entirely original was made *ex nihilo*, as creationism (*l'idée créationiste*) tells us?
> Isn't that something that appears (*apparaisse*)—insofar as your laziness (*laparesse*) can be shaken up by any sort of apparition—in the Book of *Genesis*? *Genesis* recounts nothing other than the creation, from nothing, in effect—of what?—of nothing but signifiers.
> As soon as this creation emerges, it is articulated on the basis of the naming of what is. Isn't that creation in its essence? (1972–73/1998, 40–1)

This is the strange, dialectical nature of the signifier: convention yet also *Ursprung*.

Language in Lacanian thought is unconsciously permeated by what he calls *lalangue* or *llangue*, which is "original" in the Benjaminian sense. *Lalangue* is made up of the unconscious storehouse of language fragments that permeate and thrash around inside the subject, pieces of language variably infused with resonances of meaning, significance, and *jouissance* for the subject. *Lalangue* makes up the unconscious and has effects that go much further than communication, since, as Renata Salecl puts it, it affects "body and soul." It is thus the swimming storehouse of fragments,

variably loaded with *objet a,* the cause of desire. Salecl quotes Jean-Claude
Milner:

> Llanguage is made of a bit of everything, of what wallows in the gin-mills
> and of what we hear in salons . . . it is possible to find meaning in everything
> . . . The llanguage is the storage, a collection of traces which other "subjects"
> have left . . . [it is the way] each subject inscribed its desire into language,
> since the speaking being has to have a signifier to be able to desire . . . again
> in signifiers . . .

and she goes on,

> Through the remainder of what is spoken we find not only something more
> than an individual speaker's intention, but something more than the sum of
> the speech acts of the members of a linguistic community. Llanguage thus
> represents the return within language of the contradictions and struggles that
> make up the social, the persistence within language of past contradictions
> and struggles, and the anticipation of new ones. (Salecl 2001)

Salecl's leap between individual and collective jouissance and language as
a storehouse of the traces and marks of contingency and *objets a* makes it
possible to conceive of a collective *lalangue*—such as the language of the
Baroque that Benjamin examines in his study of the *Trauerspiel.*

Joyce's writing is, in Lacanian terms, permeated by *lalangue.* In *Encore*
Lacan writes:

> What happens in Joyce's work? The signifier stuffs [*vient truffer*] the
> signified. It is because the signifiers fit together, combine, and concertina—
> read *Finnegans Wake*—that something is produced by way of meaning
> (*comme signifié*) that may seem enigmatic, but is clearly closest to what we
> as analysts, thanks to analytic discourse, have to read—slips of the tongue
> (*lapsus*). It is as slips that they signify something, in other words, that they
> can be read in an infinite number of different ways. But it is precisely for
> that reason that they are difficult to read, are read awry, or not read at all.
> But doesn't this dimension of "being read" (*se lire*) suffice to show that we
> are in the register of analytic discourse? (1972–73/1998, 37)

Joyce's esotericism in his engagement with language is shaped out of dislocations and distortions that express both corporeal and psychic processes
while also engaging the materiality of the signifier itself. The distortions
not only of words, but of letters, too, with the result of producing resonances within the body, bring Joyce's writing into close proximity not
only with analytic discourse but with baroque writing as well. Again in
Encore (1972–73), Lacan says, "I am situated essentially on the side of the

baroque" (106), by which he means his analytic discourse. He opposes it to the discourse of the master—knowledge in the Benjaminian sense—which he associates with "speaking as a winner" and with "Sunday," a reference to dogmatic and institutional (Counter-reformational) Catholicism. All of this comes to a head, he says, in Hegel's absolute knowledge and discourse. Being "on the side of the baroque" in this context means essentially doing what Benjamin does in his *Origin of German Tragic Drama*: referring and relating to the body and to the creaturely as what "grounds being" (Lacan 1972–73/1998, 110), but not in any way that allows any taking possession of the body or of achieving satisfaction for it. Baroque art, says Lacan, shows the body in various broken ecstasies of *jouissance*, but never in the act of copulation (consummation):

> In everything that followed from the effects of Christianity, particularly in art . . . everything is exhibition of the body evoking jouissance . . . but without copulation . . . [N]owhere more blatantly than in Christianity does the work of art as such show itself as what it has always been in all places: obscenity. (1972–73/1998, 113)

The word "obscenity" is here to be taken in its most literal sense: *ob-* ("onto") and *caenum*, "filth" or "waste." Being "on the side of the baroque" means being on the side of a disarraying, anxiety-provoking, *jouissance*-liberating fragmentariness that concerns both body and psyche, that emerges again and again by way of its own countless translations, distortions, and dislocations. My shorthand for it in Benjamin's *Trauerspiel* book has been "martyrdom." It means being in a relationship to language that moves away from the language of judgment, of the master, of the Father, taking the position, instead, of the martyr—but also often the sadist (in the form of the allegorist)—in regards to language.

What is it that results from this *jouissance*? To a large extent the answer to this question remains as enigmatic in Lacan as it does in Benjamin, as far as empirical reference goes. This "what" is related to what Benjamin refers to at the end of his book, when he speaks, obscurely, of what has yet to be "thought through" (1928/1998, 235) in relation to the *Trauerspiel*. At the end of "On the Baroque," Lacan points in the direction of the contingent and the future:

> The economy of jouissance is something we can't yet put our fingertips on. It would be of some interest if we managed to do so (*qu'on y arrive*). What we can see on the basis of analytic discourse is that we may have a slight chance of finding out something about it, from time to time, by pathways that are essentially contingent. (1972–73/1998, 116)

Such "contingency" would, then, for both Benjamin and Lacan, seem to play the main role in the structure of a new and ethical subjectivity that would remain true to the objects in its *Umwelt*.

Ethical in what way? First, in the way of keeping one's attentiveness focused on the materiality of history, its contingent elements, rather than on the narcissistic ideas that seek to encapsulate history. Such an ethics also means remaining true to one's own history and *jouissance*-driven engagement with one's own contingencies. Second, subjectivity is ethical insofar as it concerns the subject's relationship to other subjects. Lacan's vision—which I believe to be an only somewhat abashed messianic view— of the post-analytic space (Benjamin's "post-catastrophic" subject) is that it does not structure subject-object relationships, no matter how dialogic they may be, but subject-subject relationships. This is a view that exceeds Christian beatitude:

> The relation of being to being is not the relation of harmony that was prepared for us throughout the ages, though we don't really know why, by a whole tradition in which Aristotle, who saw therein only supreme jouissance, converges with Christianity, for which it is beatitude. That gets us bogged down in a mirage-like apprehension. For it is love [for Lacan, a false harmony and imaginary closure of the gap] that approaches being as such in the encounter. But this encounter is always a missed encounter. (1972–73/ 1998, 145)

When Lacan now goes on to explain why "love" is—and should be—a "missed encounter," he also throws light on Benjamin's "being on the side of the [German] baroque" insofar as this *Trauerspiel* aesthetic and ethics finds no closure—thus eschewing apotheosis in the closed and static space of the "mirror"—because the subject is in fact already filled to the bursting point with *a* (traces of the real). Lacan goes on to say here that "true love gives way to hatred" (146) where "true love" is false fusional oneness, "faithless" enchantment by and with the symbol. In totalization the tendency toward sacrifice will realize itself; the *Trauerspiel* book's "empty balcony" will be filled by a leader and "Golgotha" will repeat itself in a curse of eternal sameness, of the dark night of myth.

PART 2

CULTURES OF MIMESIS

Introduction to Part 2

Lacan's Saussurianism—that is, the view of language as a formal system of elements in which the relation between signifier and signified is arbitrary—could seem to pose a problem in my Benjamin-Lacan conjunction. Benjamin's conception of the mimetic in language, his ideas about "pure"—"Name"—language are decidedly anti-Saussurian. The contradiction is considerably diminished, however, by two crucial elements in Lacan's and Benjamin's thought: these are the roles that contingency and the book of *Genesis* play in their philosophies of language.

Lacan writes concerning Saussure's definition of the signifier that "it would have been better to qualify the signifier with the category of contingency" (Lacan 1972–73, 40) rather than with arbitrariness and "eternity." I will return to this question of "contingency"—by which Lacan means accident, uncertainty, and also materiality—below. The signifier and language in general lie, for Lacan and Benjamin, outside of intentional control. At the same time, for both of them language points "backwards," toward *Ursprung,* virtual site of memory, of truth, and transformation. This is the site of the signifier, of the letter, and of writing. For Benjamin striving toward *Ursprung* through writing is a way toward "profane illumination"; it is also an action. Moreover, it counteracts the enchantments of mythical thought and of phantasmagoric cocoons in a manner that is actually quite Lacanian.

The focus of the following chapters is on the act of writing and reading as acts of "profane illumination"— in Benjamin, in psychoanalysis, and in the thought of some of Benjamin's contemporaries. For Benjamin, reading and writing are aspects of the "mimetic faculty." In later chapters I will show what such acts may contribute to psychoanalysis and to the psychoanalytic relationship. The latter is our best model for what redeemed

Benjaminian subject-object and subject-subject relationships might look like: dialogic structures that survive the deadening and reifying forces of modernity. The psychoanalytic and the Benjaminian relation are both dependent on the psychophysical effects of a catastrophically experienced "martyrdom," an immersion into body-language.

Most of Benjamin's short esoteric pieces of the early 1930s, the years leading up to and including the Nazi seizure of power and Benjamin's exile in 1933, may be read as enactments of the "other" philosophy that Benjamin had announced in his 1918 "On the Program of the Coming Philosophy." There he had written that a philosophy that would "undertake the epistemological foundation of a higher concept of experience" (1918/1996, 102) would include a radically revised concept of the subject-object relationship, an opening up of empiricist knowledge to a different sort of knowledge altogether, as well as a way of thinking about the subject that would allow for its presentation not only in terms of identity but also in terms of its alterities. At issue is Benjamin's critique of Kant: the impoverishment of Kant's concept of experience, the reduction of cognition to the subject's "knowledge" of the object world in empirical terms alone, and the banishment of the absolute, including the category of theology, from experience and cognition both. There has been a Kantian trend in reading Benjamin, especially in its emphasis on his attitude toward modern technology, endorsing the *Entzauberung* (disenchantment) of modern experience at the moment that, with the development of modern technologies (in "The Work of Art in the Age of Its Reproducibility" [1936]), art and experience both register and further the waning of aura. Others counteract this trend somewhat by insisting first on the continuity of the theological dimension in Benjamin's thinking and second on recovering from within his middle and late work the traces of the theological 1916 language essay. I am most interested in allowing Benjamin's early overt theological impulses to transform, at least partially, into concerns with corporeality, physiological forces, the drives. In Part 1, I said that the metaphysical impulse in Benjamin returns, secularized, from below, in a preoccupation with a fragmenting real that has psychological and political ramifications. In any case, in reading Benjamin it is necessary to combine the emphatically secular and materialist *and* the theological impulses—just as Benjamin does.

Benjamin's mimesis essays are also engagements with the "pure language" carried by the cast-offs from the master signifiers. Gerhard Richter's *Walter Benjamin and the Corpus of Autobiography* (2002) has guided readers through this "mimetic Benjamin" in this sense. As in his autobiographical texts on the whole, in the "mimetic" texts Benjamin gives voice to an "other" mode of thought, a messianic and esoteric mode that is, as Richter puts it, unavailable for use by ideologemes assimilable by fascism:

> For Benjamin, "language has a body and the body has a language" (3:138), and both remain suspended in the corporeal subject that is perpetually caught between construction and dispersal in the act of self-portraiture . . . They perform "useless" concepts with every undoing of the self, staging a negation of fascism with every trope—or turn away from—an essential, fully legible self. (Richter 2002, 15)

This would imply exploding the continuity of a cultural tradition by interrupting it for the sake of attentiveness to a previously unthought thought at the point where Benjamin inserted this "coming" thought of his. This, as Adorno had said, was founded on the paradox of the "impossible possibility" (Richter 2002, 15) to include that thought that had historically been excluded. I intend to take this reading of Benjamin into more specific and concrete psychoanalytic directions.

Part 2 concentrates on the relationship between Benjamin's thought and psychoanalytic trends more contemporary to him; simultaneously, we will see how the idea of psychoanalysis as it developed over time was, in itself, a historically determined idea. The central concrete link between Benjaminian thought and psychoanalysis is provided by Benjamin's notion of the "mimetic faculty" and some similarly-minded trends in the thought of Sandor Ferenczi, Melanie Klein, and the post-Kleinian W. R. Bion (Marion Milner will be my focus in Part 3.) Linking these analysts and Benjamin is a mounting preoccupation with the phenomenon of psychic "catastrophe" that coincides with various therapeutic mechanisms of mimetic immersion. As I showed in Part 1, the main question for Benjamin at the exhausting end of the *Trauerspiel* book is how to retrieve and preserve "experience" in the modern era. Experience is salvaged for Benjamin by exploding the catastrophic shells of deadened life within phantasmagorically dissociated existence in which there is neither time nor contact. Mimetic practices have the power to blast open reified experience.

In Chapter 3, I will first contextualize Benjamin's fascination with mimesis. Freud's disciple Sandor Ferenczi, *College de Sociologie* member Roger Caillois, art historian Aby Warburg, and the poet R. M. Rilke are just some of the names associated with the surge of interest in mimesis in the 1910s, 1920s, and 1930s, much of which is (consciously or unconsciously) premised on fundamental psychoanalytic discoveries. I will then unfold the psychological and political import of the mimesis phenomenon in Benjamin's short and often esoteric "mimesis essays" of the early 1930s.

Chapters 4 and 5 develop the ground shared by Benjaminian and post-Freudian and post-Kleinian mental topographies by outlining the dialectic of mimesis as assimilatory mimicry and mimesis as recollection, of phantasmagoria and historical awakening, and of "cocoon" and "catastrophic change." In Chapter 5, I align Benjamin's critiques of intentional meaning and communicative language with the theories of experience and "thinking" of Wilfred R. Bion. I also present the ways in which some of Melanie Klein's most basic concepts—of the fundamental role of destruction, reparation, and identification in the construction of self—resonate both with Benjamin's diagnosis of modernity and his intuition about the fundamental importance of mimetic faculties for the individual. I focus concretely on the mimetic phenomena in all three, leading into a discussion of inscription, writing, and body experience in Bion's clinical theory and in Benjamin's mimesis and graphology essays of the early 1930s.

In general, by referring back to *The Origin of the German Tragic Drama* and the implicit theory of subjectivity it contains, in these chapters I extend and shift in a whole new direction the work that has already been done in interpreting the more esoteric categories of Benjamin's thought: corporeality, language, the messianic, and "the psychophysical problem."[1] I deviate from and extend these and a number of other critics' work by bringing together in a new way the "creaturely" and corporeal, the latently psychoanalytic, and the theological elements, both latent and manifest, in Benjamin "psychophysical" corpus.[2]

Chapter 3

Transformative Mimesis

1. Origins of Benjamin's Mimesis

Ideally, none of Benjamin's texts should be read in isolation from each other; as happens when picking up a single word from within the realm of language, any one Benjaminian text brings the others with it. For the sake of external clarity, however, the main "mimetic texts" I will be concerned with in this chapter are "The Lamp," "Doctrine of the Similar," "Agesilaus Santander" (second version), and "On the Mimetic Faculty," all written in 1933. None of these texts in particular can be read without reference to the groundbreaking 1916 essays, "On Language as Such and on the Language of Man," already touched upon in Chapter 1, and "Task of the Translator" of 1921.

At the root of Benjamin's mimetic texts lies his ever-developing notion of experience. On the one hand, he addresses again and again what has occurred to the human sensorium in the early twentieth century as it is bombarded by the fruits of a technology that is developing in leaps and bounds and that is increasingly allied with war. Benjamin distinguishes between *Erlebnis* and *Erfahrung*, both translated as "experience." While the latter is largely what is on the wane in modernity, the first is defined by impoverishment incurred by the traumatic nature of modern experience: *Erlebnis* means living through a moment by defensively draining it of affect. It is a hypertrophic protective shield—the notion that, in his Baudelaire essay, Benjamin takes from Freud's theory of trauma in *Beyond the Pleasure Principle* (1920)—that shuts experience down. In "Experience and Poverty" (1933c) Benjamin insists on the necessity of circumventing the shock of the new technologies by adapting the human sensorium to them, by adopting "a new kind of barbarism":

> For what does poverty of experience do for the barbarian? It forces him to start from scratch; to make a new start; to make a little go a long way; to begin with a little and build up further, looking neither left nor right. Among the great creative spirits, there have always been the inexorable ones who begin with clearing a tabula rasa. . . . these creatures talk in a completely new language. . . . and what is crucial about this language is its arbitrary, constructed nature, in contrast to organic language. (732–3)

There is a clear connection here between these "creatures" of the "new barbarism" and Benjamin's allegorist. The analytic pair, too, "mak[es] a new start," in the "construction" (or "artifice," as Lacan would say) that follows the razing of a schizoid "reality." Benjamin here also insists on the political significance of accepting "the new barbarism," as only it can inure against the seductions of the false unities projected by fascism—the other response to the shock of modernity, the "shadow of approaching war": "Holding on to things has become the monopoly of a few powerful people, who, God knows, are no more human than the many; for the most part, they are more barbaric, but not in the good way" (1933c, 735).

In addition, Benjamin claims that the value of experience was diminished to devastating degrees when Kant, placing a barrier before the absolute, limited it to the realm of empirical science.[1] Benjamin is primarily interested in recuperating a mental and experiential *space* in which the modern individual can renegotiate and reconfigure his relationship to other persons and objects, to present and past, as well as to the broken pieces of tradition while imagining other ways of being.

In this recuperation of experience in modernity, Benjamin's path is a delicate one, as it had been in *The Origin of the German Tragic Drama* as well: to accept the monumental transformations in personal and collective experience wrought by modern technology and not to deny them the way fascism attempts to do, as Benjamin shows in "The Work of Art in the Age of Its Reproducibility" (1936). It means accepting the fragmentations of modernity without violent framing, unifying, and monumentalizing devices. At the same time it is necessary to attempt to recover substance and significance within modern existence, the "absolute" within "immanence."[2]

Susan Buck-Morss's essay "Aesthetics and Anaesthetics" (1992) on Benjamin's preoccupations with the problems of enchantment and disenchantment breaches the question of the very possibility of *Erfahrung*, though without touching the question of the absolute, the messianic. Buck-Morss shows how Benjamin's aesthetics are connected to perception and to the corporeal:

> *Aisthisis* is the sensory experience of perception. The original field of aesthetics is not art but reality—corporeal, material nature. . . . It is a form of cognition, achieved through taste, touch, hearing, seeing, smell—the whole corporeal sensorium. (6)

The concealed origin not only of art but of the psyche as well is the body, just as Freud's mysterious "navel" in dream interpretation (1965),[3] like the "turbinal" excrescences in the "Dream of Irma's Injection,"[4] disappears into the body. "Experience" is thus linked to the nervous system and its environment. In modernity, experience is characterized by shock; defense against it develops into the creation of a new virtual psychic organ—a "protective shield." Its function is not only to defend against shock, but also to make up for the psyche's retreat from sensorial immediacy and its consequent anesthesia. Drug addiction is of course our most obvious contemporary form of compensation (Buck-Morss 1992, 21). Benjamin, however, diagnosed an even more insidious, because all-encompassing and cognitive, form of compensation, an addiction to what he termed "phantasmagoria": the creation of a dream- and wish-reality:

> Beginning in the nineteenth century, a narcotic was made out of reality itself. The key term for this development is phantasmagoria. The term originated in England in 1802, as the name of an exhibition of optical illusions produced by magic lanterns. It describes an appearance of reality that tricks the senses through technical manipulation. (Buck-Morss 1992, 22)

Buck-Morss further characterizes phantasmagoria as "a total environment, a privatized fantasy world that functioned as a protective shield for the senses and sensibilities of [19th century bourgeoisie]" (1992, 22). Phantasmagorias provide narcissistic control. Buck-Morss's phrase "optical illusion" recalls Benjamin's use of it describing the delusional compensations of the Counter-reformation Baroque's projections of omnipotence and totality. Wagner's operas did this well, too,[5] as did the utopian fantasies propagated by Fascism. The overarching function of the phantasmagoria is to conceal complexity, contradiction, and irony.

Phantasmagoria is clearly also a psychoanalytic concept. Bion defines schizoid and psychotic personalities in terms of the ability or refusal to tolerate the transformation of infantile super-concrete perception and primitive "thought" via actual things into thought that renounces the thing itself. The schizoid or psychotic subject rejects abstract thinking because he rejects the whole concept of representational limitation;[6] in hallucination, the category under which phantasmagoria falls, a thought is transformed into a sense impression that does not have meaning, but instead yields pleasure or pain. "Marx made the term phantasmagoria famous," writes Buck-Morss,

> using it to describe the world of commodities that, in their mere visible presence, conceal every trace of the labor that produced them. They veil the production process, and—like mood pictures—encourage their beholders to identify them with subjective fantasies and dreams. Adorno argues that the deceptive illusion of Wagner's art is analogous. (1992, 25)

Phantasmagoria is the fantasy of a total—and totally controlled—mental and physical environment. Hallucinations and phantasmagoria both reflect the return of myth and fate to modernity, its re-enchantment. Both Bion's understanding of hallucination and Benjamin's phantasmagoric anesthesia are defenses against the traumatic assaults of modernity on the sensorium; both emphasize the malignancy of phantasmagoria, its hallucinatory and violent elements, and its link to war.[7]

Benjamin made it his task to document as well as explode the cocoon-like slumber of the nineteenth century by way of reading and re-inscription processes and to recover the intricacies of linking that constitute the experience of truly waking life. He saw such faculties as individual defenses against fascist manipulation and fascistic narcissism. Benjaminian reading and re-inscription processes were to emerge from an experience of "martyrdom," that is, a new sort of corporeal experience and corporeal thought.

Miriam B. Hansen names such Benjaminian body-thought with Benjamin's own term: "innervation." "Innervation" counteracts the neurological and psychiatric effects of perceptive, emotional, and cognitive anesthesia. With this concept Benjamin modifies and relieves, partially at least, the "new barbarian" ascetic response to modern overstimulation; he knew, Hansen suggests, that such asceticism could not possibly suffice to build an authentic political alternative to fascism. "New barbarism" negates. It means walking away empty-handed, an important gesture for Benjamin at the end of the *Trauerspiel* book and again in his autobiographical "Agesilaus Santander" piece discussed below. Alone, however, such asceticism could never stand its ground against fascism, no matter how high the moral ground, just as renunciation of *jouissance* is not enough for the subject to live at the end of analysis, once the fantasy has been traversed. Additionally, as Adorno pointed out to Benjamin, such a renunciation "came close to identifying with the aggressor" (Hansen 1999, 313).

The difficult, if not impossible, position in which Benjamin found himself—a dialectic between a world from which the absolute had disappeared and the rushing in of compensations that were to carry the weight of an uncanny leftover energy—is exemplified by the reference in his "Theological Criticism" (1931*b*) essay to Kafka and Hofmannsthal as emblems of modernity and modern *anomie*. Benjamin reads Kafka's work as pervaded by forms, gestures, language, meaning, and law that no longer "know" their own content: tradition and transmission have failed (Benjamin 1934*a*).[8] The forms return as "threatening, enigmatic gesture," more uncanny than the depth of Hofmannsthal's "posthistorical" (and elegiac) commitment to form:

Both [Kafka and Hofmannsthal], the reader will find, were encountered at the very heart of danger. Kafka, in Prague, in the camp of the degenerate Jewish intelligentsia, where in the name of Judaism he renounced Judaism, turning his back on it with a threatening, enigmatic gesture. Hofmannsthal, at the heart of the collapsing Hapsburg monarchy, where, in a kind of post-historical maturity, he entirely transformed the energy on which it had thrived into formal structures. (Benjamin 1931*b*/1999, 428)

Similarly, in his mimesis texts Benjamin's attention becomes focused on the site of the "disappeared" absolute, its traces (Benjamin 1994, 565). Kafka alluded to a disappeared Scripture in such a manner that the distinction between "content" and "form" itself fell away, and it was the empty shells, the physicality of the "gestures" themselves, that—allegorically, not symbolically— were to become the sources of *Erfahrung*.[9] Benjamin thought that the mimetic faculty could open up the empty shells of the unredeemed things; traces of the absolute could be found in their folds, their "waste." This recovery activity links the mimetic collector who performs it to the martyr-allegorist.

Forms of "innervation" undermine the purely renunciatory "new barbarism." The Lacanian *sinthome* is a form of innervation. Menke (1991) and Richter (2002), like Hansen (1999), show that Benjamin makes the realms of the mimetic—in ancient times associated with divination, magic, and enchantment—usable in emotionally significant acts of reading and writing. In secularized modernity, a fundamental displacement has taken place. Benjamin writes, "in the course of centuries, the mimetic power, and with it the gift of mimetic perception, have disappeared from certain fields—perhaps in order to flow into others" (Benjamin 1933*b* 695): for instance, into a mimetic reading of script. This scene of reading as "profane illumination" is neither poorer nor "worse" than what the mimetic had offered in the past, says Benjamin. For Menke (1991, 111), such reading takes place in a dialectical space that involves corporeal elements: the body is both inscribed and read, both the recipient of inscription and its reader. It emits and receives the gaze. In addition to this conspicuous, maybe even mentally disarticulating, presence of corporeality, Benjamin places emphasis on the visual and aural materiality of the letter. This new emphasis on materiality emerges primarily through the displacement of the spoken to the written word as it does, for example, in the allegorical traditions of the Baroque, the realm of emblems and hiero-glyphs, as for Benjamin writing is, even if largely unconsciously, a physical gesture.

The element of corporeality in Menke's understanding of Benjamin's thought is similar to Miriam Hansen's understanding of the role of "innervation" in the period that followed Benjamin's overtly theological one. Benjamin's examples of "innervation" are, says Hansen, the best alternative to the "new barbarism," to emotional stuntedness, and to compensatory fascistic fusional experiences. As "a neurophysiological process that mediates between internal and external, psychic and motoric, human and mechanical registers" (Hansen 1999, 313), innervation is a new mode both of perception and affect that emerges with the new sensorium that characterizes Benjamin's "profane illumination." It even makes possible a new "fascination."

"Innervation" makes reading and inscription corporeal. It is intensive (rather than referential), active, and bound up with the mimetic faculty, "the capacity to relate to the external world through patterns of similitude, affinity, reciprocity, and interplay" (Hansen 1999, 329). It is also at play, I want to point out, in the experience of the analyst when she participates in the analysand's mental space, as we will see, "transcending the traditional subject-object dichotomy . . . [It is] a mode of cognition involving sensuous, somatic, and tactile forms of perception; a non-coercive engagement with the other that opens the self to experience . . ." (Hansen 1999, 329). It is "affectively charged, excentric perception" (Hansen 1999, 332).

Innervation implies a mode of being open to contingency and to what Benjamin calls "the creaturely." Like Benjamin's mimetic experiences, it refers to an affective vulnerability that lies also at the center of the abjection in Benjaminian martyrdom, the ostentatious parading of the *objet a*, for the modern subject. Surrealism, which for Benjamin aimed to achieve "profane illumination" (Benjamin 1929a/1999, 209),[10] also aimed to "locate," however negatively, the *objet a* in language, bypassing communicative reference and "to the point of explosion" (210). In all these cases the object unleashes the abject, the unspeakable "cause of desire," and thus the subject's disarray. These are the conditions necessary for reconceived subject-object/subject-subject relationships.

Surrealism approached such intensities in its play with the materiality of words and letters: ". . . it is as magical experiments with words, not as artistic dabbling, that we must understand the passionate phonetic and graphic transformational games . . ." (Benjamin 1929a/1999, 212). Words and bodies intermingle in Surrealism, and Benjamin claims that this intermingling has consequences not only for communicative language—denuding speech and language to allow for a glimpse of "pure language"—but also for the seemingly coherent "self":

> . . . language seemed itself only where sound and image, image and sound,
> inter-penetrated with automatic precision and such felicity that no chink was

left for the penny-in-the-slot called "meaning." Image and language take precedence. . . . Language takes precedence.

Not only before meaning. Also before the self. In the world's structure, dream loosens individuality like a bad tooth. This loosening of the self by intoxication is, at the same time, precisely the fruitful, living experience that allowed these people to step outside the charmed space of intoxication. (1929a/1999, 208)

Caygill links Benjamin's theory of experience immediately to the dissolution of "self" and defines it finally as that which folds "time, space and the absolute in configuration" (1998, 79). Benjamin had expressed his desire for this in his "Program of the Coming Philosophy." He extended and transformed Kant's concept of experience by including the absolute within it, but, against Hegel, he refused "any attempt to grasp or comprehend the absolute through finite categories" (Caygill 1998, 2). Benjamin did so also in his figure of the martyr who expresses, in Caygill's words, Benjamin's "recognition of the absolute in the decaying ruins of modern experience" (1998, 151).

Let us superimpose on this image that of corporeality in which the "absolute" consists of the breath that animates a body subject to decay and finitude. Breath belongs to the body, which dies, but it also represents the absolute for Benjamin because it animates language and speech. This breath embodies an oscillation and discontinuity between immanence and the absolute that characterizes Benjamin's "innervated" experience. It also points to an experience of the "self" that has shifted from an alienated and pacified subjectivity into a subjectivity that is on the one hand always already animated by the Other and on the other defined linguistically and corporeally, and thereby opened up.[11]

Caygill's reading of Benjamin's short pieces on "Naples" (1925/1996) and "Moscow" (1927/1999) exemplify the open and discontinuous model of subjectivity and the rigid, closed, and totalizing subject respectively. "Naples," with its arcades and passageways that are "discontinuous, offering possibilities for sudden passages through undisclosed routes" (Caygill 1998, 122), stands opposed to "Moscow," with its architectural acts of monumentality, stability, and eternity displaying the reactionary stance and reminiscent of the Baroque Counter-reformation monumentality that Benjamin describes at the end of the *Trauerspiel* book.

While my readings of Benjamin's mimetic texts do agree very much with Caygill's presupposition that the "motivation" of Benjamin's work "[shifts] from problems of signification and expression to those of inscription and the mark" (1998, xiii), I am less comfortable with his contention that for Benjamin "experience is not primarily linguistic, that it does not take place within the field of linguistic signification" (xiii), simply because I regard such inscriptions and marks as a form of language, and because Benjamin tells us in "The Mimetic Faculty" that the experience that we have lost may still be recoverable, but only because it has concealed itself within language. Moreover, even when Benjamin moves out of the explicitly linguistic sphere and into bodily phenomena, this "out of" and "into" terminology is misleading, as the body is itself permeated by language, the perceptual world is structured by it, and the body is "constructed and disarticulated"(Richter 2002, 54) by it. I will explore this issue in relation to another claim made by Caygill: that each time the messianic appears in Benjamin's work Benjamin risks "laps[ing] into dogmatism" (1998, 149). I will examine instead the ways in which the messianic relates to a specifically liberating relationship to language.

In modernity, then, experience, hollowed out and desensitized by the traumatic nature of modern life (technology, mechanization, urban life, and war), demands to be recovered. Shattered and fragmented, it must be retrieved from scattered objects and imagery containing in some way corporeal experience and physical memory, as well as remnants and traces of what has been banished from modern life's parameters that, like Ariadne's thread, could lead out of the narcissistic cocoon of phantasmagoria. Benjamin's theory of mimesis is crucial in this process. The "mimetic faculty" enables the re-collection of objects, thrown out and often seemingly dead, that re-articulates, by way of a disarticulating mimetic experience, their origins, lives, and afterlives. In his short 1932 piece, "Experience," Benjamin writes, "Experiences are lived similarities"; "[e]xperience and observation are identical," and "[o]bservation is based on self-immersion" (Benjamin 1931 or 1932/1999, 553). These statements also characterize the analytic relationship. Through "self-immersion" into the analysand's mental space the analyst can aid the analysand in articulating it, in an infinite variety of constellations. This is a process of embodied reading and writing. The constellations express, in similarity and difference, relationship as such—language "as such," the explicit Benjaminian aim for a revolution of experience. The analytic immersion in tandem into mental space is an example of what Benjamin names "non-sensuous similarity" (1933*d*, 722).

2. Mimetic Fascinations in Cultural Context: Mimesis as "Origin" and Survival

Benjamin wrote his mimesis essays in a context in which the phenomena of mimesis and mimicry were receiving attention from a number of different directions. In the context of psychoanalysis, they were being investigated by Sandor Ferenczi, who had always been, within Freud's immediate circle, the analyst most in tune with the relationship between psyche and body, the body's abjections, its "creatureliness": the gestural body, the body in the grip of death-driven repetitions, and the body as its own sign. Ferenczi's work on "tic" (1921/1926), which I will look at below, can be correlated with a work like Rilke's novel *Malte Laurids Brigge* (1910/1990), one of whose most memorable passages not only describes an anonymous by-passer in the grip of a convulsive tic, but also the trau-matic encroachment on personal space typifying modernity. Malte's expe-rience of Paris is traumatizing:

> Electric trolleys speed clattering through my room. Cars drive over me. A door slams. Somewhere a window pane shatters on the pavement; I can hear its large fragments laugh and its small one giggle. Then suddenly a dull, muffled noise from the other direction, inside the house. Someone is walking up the stairs: is approaching, ceaselessly approaching: is there, is there for a long time, then passes on. And again the street. A girl screams . . . (Rilke 1910/1990, 4)

As for Freud, for whom mimesis and mimicry were surely involved in iden-tificatory phenomena and ultimately originated in narcissism—which, in the most basic of ways, is defined by assimilation and absorption and the grandiose style—the mimetic for Ferenczi was closely allied with the death drive.

Ferenczi differed from Freud, however, in that the mimetic could also provide a necessary step away from the deadly enchantments of assimila-tion and grandiosity. In this sense Ferenczi would have been of interest to Benjamin, though there is, as far as I know, no indication of mutual awareness. Ferenczi analyzed Melanie Klein, and I am interested in the line of descent and the transmission, conscious and unconscious, of thoughts (conscious and unconscious) regarding mimesis, because it seems at least partially to hold the key to the problem of experience. Mimesis in this wider cultural context functions as a Benjaminian "origin." It returns in Klein's theory as "identification" and "projective identification." In the hands of Bion, who in turn was analyzed by Klein, "projective identifica-tion" was transformed into the phenomenon of "reverie," a productive idea when it comes to fleshing out Benjamin's theory of mimesis, as we will see.

Being produced tangentially to the Ferenczi-Klein-Bion trend—and to the psychoanalytic movement on the whole—was the uncategorizable work of Roger Caillois on mimesis and mimicry. Caillois was active in the College de Sociologie in Paris in the 1930s, and his famous text on insects and mimicry is to be read as a work of fascist symptomatology—as is, in a different way, the art historical and anthropological work of Aby Warburg. The connection of Benjamin's work to both opens up an expansive horizon of cross-fertilizations between discourses and disciplines, linked by the mimesis trope and taking place in those frenetic months before Hitler's ascent to power. Wider cultural concerns with the mimetic, which I can no more than briefly touch upon in what follows, are reflected also in the poetic literature that had permeated these cultural realms. I can make only brief mentions of texts by Trakl and Rilke, the most mimesis-driven of poets of that particular historical and geographical context, while I will spend more time on Mallarmé's "Igitur," in particular in the hands of Yves Bonnefoy.

Attempting to provide a cultural context in this manner is no doubt extraordinarily insufficient; nevertheless, pointing even in this cursory manner to what I believe to be some of the key cultural events moving in parallel fashion with and framing Benjamin's work, goes some way toward moving his "mimetic faculty" away from his own surprisingly vapid references to astrology and placing it in a context from where it becomes possible to think of his "tasks" and "faculties" as concrete ideas for psychological and ultimately political praxes.

A. Mimesis and mimicry

In the context of his work on mimesis in Adorno, Josef Früchtl (1986) takes what he calls the maddening and opaque concept of mimesis back, beyond Plato and Aristotle, to its darker origins, where, however, it turns out to be no more univocal: it is afflicted with over-determination and semantic emptiness simultaneously (4). Its etymology includes the meaning "dark" with all of the following as well: "revelation," "allowing to emerge from darkness," and "switching," "deceiving," "tricking," "exchanging," and "transforming"; it is also defined as the act of showing something that presents itself—deceptively—as the original. Secondly, "*mimos*" refers to the actor in Bacchic cults performing a dance in which, through word, music, and movements, a story is told (8). "Mimesis" is then profoundly and archaically related to physical gesture, sound, and body, all relevant to Benjamin's theory of the mimetic faculty. As in Benjamin's description of children's play in which the body performs similitude to all sorts of objects, these acts bring out the "non-sensuous similarity" between things. Also relevant to Benjaminian mimesis are the simultaneous obfuscation of single origins and concurrent destabilizations of identity that are implied in the more archaic meaning of "mimesis."

This historical ambiguity of the idea of mimesis is as important to Benjamin as it is to its other explorations taking place in Benjamin's immediate cultural context in the 1920s and 1930s, where we see a small, possibly esoteric, but certainly intense, explosion of interest in the psychological and anthropological significance of the phenomenon. This explosiveness may have had something to do with mimesis being inhabited by the death drive and linked to trauma; Freud had published *Beyond the Pleasure Principle* in 1920, in which the death drive was presented, among other things, as the drive to disappear, to fold and dissolve into the primal mass, which is how writers and intellectuals were characterizing the phenomenon of mimicry. "The end is the origin," Freud had suggested, a phrase that, as if by mimetic magic, also appeared in works by, among others, Karl Kraus and Walter Benjamin. The death drive is at work in mimesis in the undoing of articulation and difference performed by mimicry. Mimicry emerges as the dominant modern perversion of mimesis, and, as its subcategory, must be differentiated from it. Mimicry, object of fascination in these years for anthropologists, psychologists, and biologists and onto which they latched as if they were grasping for a disappearing mimetic faculty within the epidemic of its very perversion—can be seen as the death drive in action: in its various manifestations, the same phenomenon emerges—fear, shock, and petrification allow an organism to blend and disappear into its environment and to undo its own difference.

B. *Roger Caillois*

Caillois, together with Georges Bataille, Pierre Klossowski, and Michel Leiris, was a member of the heterodox College de Sociologie, the anti-fascist institution of the 1930s where Benjamin is known to have attended lectures and seminars.

Caillois's relevant text, on the surface entomological, is poetic and allegorical. In this 1938 piece, "Mimicry and Legendary Psychasthenia," Caillois relates mimicry between the organism (particularly insects) and its surroundings directly to the phenomenon of fascination, crucial in both mimicry and mimesis: he describes "butterflies" that "achiev[e] the effect of a snake's head capable of deceiving lizards and small birds, which are frightened by this sudden apparition" (18), for example, the objective always seeming to be ensnarement by fascination. Caillois goes on to describe how mantises' "legs simulate petals or are curved into corollas and resemble flowers, imitating by a slight swaying the action of the wind on these latter" (20). He describes instances of identification of some of the elements of one species with another; often these are rather extreme, for instance, when some butterflies'

> imitation is pushed to the smallest details: indeed, the wings bear grey-green spots simulating the mold of lichens and glistening surfaces that give them the look of torn and perforated leaves: . . . everything, including the transparent scars produced by phytophagic insects when devouring the parenchyma of the leaves in places . . . (22)

Note here too the way mimicry is associated with imagery of laceration and being devoured as well as the extremity that continues to characterize all of Caillois's examples from the world of insects. He goes on to say that these phenomena have never really been satisfactorily explained: self-protection by way of camouflage and by causing fright fails to account for the extremity of some of the examples of mimicry that can end up rather gruesomely for the imitator. Additionally, it seems that mimicry is after all not a tool of utility, but is bizarrely self-destructive:

> Generally speaking, one finds many remains of mimetic insects in the stomachs of predators . . . Conversely, some species that are inedible, and would thus have nothing to fear, are also mimetic. It therefore seems that one ought to conclude with Cuenot that this is an "epiphenomenon" whose "defensive utility appears to be nul." . . . The case of the Phyllia is even sadder: they browse among themselves, taking each other for real leaves, in such a way that one might accept the idea of a sort of collective masochism leading to mutual homophagy, the simulation of the leaf being a provocation to cannibalism in this kind of totem feast. (24–5)

Caillois then finds anthropological corroboration ("Tylor, Hubert and Mauss, and Frazer" [25]) for his intuition regarding the archaic and regressive nature of mimesis as mimicry, which is not only "primitive," not just tragically counterproductive, but also a horrifying reality of entrapment, a spell: "*an incantation fixed at its culminating point* and having caught the sorcerer in his own trap" (27). Its "end would appear to be assimilation to the surroundings" (27): a "psychasthenia" (psychic weakness), in fact, as the unconscious's spell-binding capacities wreak enough havoc on the being's body for it to "assimilate[]" (27) to the point of its own disappearance. Mimicry seems to obliterate space itself and is originally traumatizing.

Schizophrenics, Caillois goes on to say, share a disappearing mimesis with mimetic insects: invariably schizophrenics suffer from a prohibition of space for their bodies: "dispossessed souls," Caillois calls them, to whom space seems to be "a devouring force" (30) as it assimilates them to it, entrapping them in a "cocoon" of disappearance:

> Space pursues them, encircles them, digests them in a gigantic phagocytosis. It ends by replacing them. Then the body separates itself from thought, the individual breaks the boundary of his skin and occupies the other side of his senses. He tries to look at himself from any point whatever in space. He feels himself becoming space, dark space where things cannot be put. He is similar, not similar to something, but just similar. And he invents spaces of which he is the "convulsive possession." All these expressions shed light on a single process: depersonalization by assimilation to space, i.e. what mimicry achieves morphologically in certain animal species. (30)

Much of this imagery addresses Benjamin's in both the *Trauerspiel* book and the mimesis essays: on the one hand, we have come across this experience of spatialization in the *Trauerspiel*, as well as the sense of having become the "convulsive possession" of space. Depersonalization was also a part of the baroque man's experience, this falling apart of symbolic and real. But Caillois emphasizes the opposite outcome of depersonalization: the self's disappearance rather than its transformation. Caillois's mimetic and depersonalized self disappears into a black hole, while Benjamin's self is disarrayed, but not disappeared by, the history of ruins. On the contrary, depersonalization like mimesis in Benjamin has in its aim a new "attentiveness to the creaturely."

For Caillois, on the other hand, one need not look only to schizophrenics to understand this self-destructive assimilation to space, "necessarily accompanied by a decline in the feeling of personality and life," where "life takes a step backwards" (30). Certain physical (mimetic) contractions of caterpillars that stand bolt upright suggest "hysterical contraction," and, Caillois asks, "is not the automatic swaying of mantises comparable to a tic?" (31) What Caillois is tracing in the world of insects and plants (later he would reach even farther back to stones, minerals, stalactites [1964]) is the "beyond the pleasure principle," "a sort of instinct of renunciation that orients [the creature] toward a mode of reduced existence, which in the end would no longer know either consciousness or feeling—the inertia of the élan vital, so to speak" (32). One may read Caillois allegorically: he sounds an alarm bell informing all who listen that modernity enables the return of the repressed in the form of archaic mimicry—"archaic" in the sense in which Benjamin and Adorno use it --that is neither innocent nor playful, but a defused death drive. Distance is obliterated, and everywhere living beings stand petrified, mimicking an encroaching threat, mimetically warding off pervasive obliteration by a defensive assimilation to the hostile surroundings. Petrification, tic, and the archaic lead us to psychoanalysis—specifically the work of Ferenczi.

C. Sándor Ferenczi

Ferenczi's analysis of tic in his 1921 essay is based on his experience with shell-shocked World War I soldiers. He describes tic as "an unconscious reminiscence of [a] real sensation" (151) that had irrupted traumatically. As reminiscence, however, it is characterized by having taken the shape of a "physiological reflex [rather] than . . . repression," an "[a]breaction [which] is a more archaic method of relieving accrued stimulation" (153). Its archaic nature relates it to the world of animals and children. Ferenczi correlates tic with "echolalia" (146)[12] "echopraxia" (163)[13] "imitation mania" (157)—symptoms that are also seen in "deep hypnosis" (163)—and mimicry in general: the tic repeats the attitude the body was in at the moment of shock (156). It is also closely related to catatonia and its negativism and rigidity (147): on the one hand, the *tiqueur*, like Caillois's butterflies, becomes petrified in the face of the outside world and attempts to blend in with the flora, perhaps even with minerals, and thus regresses not only ontogenetically but phylogenetically as well; on the other, he negates the outside world, and this act drives him into a severe narcissistic regression. As the function of the *tiqueur*'s "imitation mania" is both to blend catatonically into a threatening external world (and thus supposedly undo the threat) and, ironically thus to cover up this regression into the farthest reaches of a disappearing ego, the *tiqueur* vacillates between catatonia (rigidity) and cataclonia (convulsive movement) and between mutism and excessive, echolalic talk. And thus we see Benjamin's martyr embodied in the shell-shocked modern *tiqueur*. For Benjamin both mutism and echolalia (in the incessant palaver of the *Trauerspiele*, their *Geschwätz*), are pathological scenarios. In Ferenczi, too, we see traumatic attacks on meaning and authority, the symptoms of which appear in the field of language. Here too language is broken up and ruined. Ferenczi, post-Freudian in his thinking about language and in a manner that echoes with the world of Kafka, seems fully aware of the psychic and affective value of the fragmentations and the fragments themselves. This Ferenczi-Benjamin convergence highlights an important aspect of Benjamin's mimetic "strategy": mutism and *Geschwätz* for him are both potential pathological scenarios that need to be combated. The first typifies the culture of fascism—where language is replaced by mass identification and is drowned out by the sound of endless marching boots—a culture in which the death drive is beginning to defuse from the bounds of civilization; the second typifies that touted history of progress in which an exaggerated symbolic activity begins to point to its own emptiness—and thus toward its own collapse into mutism once again.

Like every other "adaptation-reaction," Ferenczi goes on, with time tic develops into an instinct, meaning that it—like the mimetic reaction described by Caillois—has in fact transcribed the psyche. Mimicry becomes a way of not experiencing, a way of defending against shock by defending against perception of and stimulation by the external world altogether. Buck-Morss lists a number of emerging nineteenth-century techniques of such "defenses"—administered by others with the self's cooperation or self-inflicted against an external world threatening to become too stimulating. All of these are self-destructive forms of mimetic self-petrification and immobilization: "To the already-existing Enlightenment narcotic forms of coffee, tobacco, tea, and spirits, there was added a vast arsenal of drugs and therapeutic practices, from opium, ether, and cocaine to hypnosis, hydrotherapy, and electric shock" (1992, 17).

The more dialectical approach to mimesis, which Benjamin shares, and which straddles the realms of aesthetics and psychoanalysis, does not end with the stasis of petrification. This particular kind of mimetic process, which is psychological as well as contemplative, may be imagined as a diver entering an underwater wreck, spellbound and fascinated by what opens itself up to him there. He does not remain—and drown—there, however; he emerges from the encounter transformed in some way, with a different sort of knowledge. In such a catastrophic experience, motivated by extreme anxiety, or emptiness, or being closed out from experience, an individual chooses immersion. Through interruption and absolute stoppage, through a caesura in consciousness and intentional communication, such an abjected subject may allow himself to tumble through space, as it were, from object to object, slashing through the barriers that had separated "self" from "other," subject from object.[14] In the more dialectically mimetic scenario, however, the subject does not disappear in shock, obliterated, leaving the reified objects in the end untouched; instead he moves among the things, the "material community," any sense of "sovereignty," untouchable and omnipotent, broken. Subject and objects have fallen out of the spellbinding myth of History, the history of "progress."

Dialectical mimesis, avoidance of obliteration by mimicry, involves a corporalization of language, or, in Benjaminian terms, the translation of the "material community" into names. Corporalization of language, the recognition that such non-intentional, non-communicative language inhabits and gives life to body and mind both, lies at the center of Mallarmé's poetics. In his quest to un-assimilate pure visuality from intentional and instrumental vision and make it uncanny, Mallarmé links physical perception as such to language. Poetic language is thus married to a non-human and intensely material form of perception. Mallarmé's prose piece "Igitur" stages this marriage and helps us understand what Benjamin means by immersion into the "material community," that act he had first mentioned in his 1916 language essay and so important to understanding his notion of mimesis as survival.

D. Yves Bonnefoy and Mallarmé's "Igitur"

In his beautiful essay on Mallarmé's "Igitur" and its relation to photography, "Igitur and the Photographer" (1999) Yves Bonnefoy reveals the influence on modern and avant-garde poetry of an entirely new phenomenon emerging with the advent of photography: shadows, evanescent presences, evidence of "something else" captured, unconsciously, by the camera, troubling details popping up in the viewer's field of vision, what Bonnefoy calls "indexes, the aspects of the outsides of things whose inventory and relation remain the sole conceivable matter for investigation, in the light of a truth also available only from the outside" (334). In other words, what Mallarme's piece signals is the riddle of subject and object, subjective and objective knowledge. It announces the emergence of that traumatic onslaught of materiality that Benjamin describes in *The Origin of German Tragic Drama*, when history spreads out, time becomes space, and when Kant's "solution" to the problem of the thing itself, the reduction of experience to the internal categories of understanding, is rejected as well. For Mallarmé this seemingly other exteriority of experience translates into an experience of "Nothingness," a disappearance of meaning by the "fearsomeness and enigma" of the opacity of things: ". . . in the room are those drapes that we can so easily imagine stirred by the bottomless absence feared beyond. As essential in Mallarmé as in Poe is this presence of drapes, of closed furniture, heavy objects contracted in their opacity . . ." (334), Bonnefoy continues. In Mallarmé, the disappearance of meaning exacts not thought (on the disappearance of meaning), but rather the recognition that something far more primal is called for: a sort of corporeal confrontation. With the disappearance of meaning, subjective knowledge and the power to represent too fall away, their blind, illusory truths forcing their disappearance, and what is left is "pure perception" (335). Communicative and intentional language fails as well. On this eve of the absence

of language (which remains nothing *but* an "eve"), the senses are victori
ous, what Lacan called the "lamella," the undead object, the life that
cannot be given support in the symbolic order (Žižek 1993, 176–82).
Mallarmé's choice is to "look as photography looks," says Bonnefoy, like a
"new barbarian," but also enacting a sensory immersion into the phenomena. Mallarmé privileges some sort of pure vision, claims Bonnefoy: ". . .
Mallarmé wants to accomplish consciously—wants to accomplish as an
ultimate act of consciousness, at the threshold of a new age—what the
photographic machine does outside any consciousness . . ." (335). Even
the word is to become visual, and Mallarmé "reduce[s] himself, through
the depth of himself, to a photographic image; from depth to surface—and
back to depth, since the photograph now carries evidence of meaning
(without speaking it, to be sure!), not language." Though it is not entirely
clear what Bonnefoy means by "language" here, it seems that what
Mallarmé is attempting to do is to find the "pure" (not mechanical, but
unintentional, unknowing) word through photographic (unintentional,
unconscious) visuality. The metaphor of photography enables Mallarmé to
conceive of pure language, his real concern, and its relationship to the
"material community."

"Pure visuality"—in "photography" or as a metaphor for pure language—demands immersion into phenomena:

> . . . pure visuality in the center of which consciousness would be plunged,
> before its rebirth as a finally liberated word. This door, for example: pure
> visuality. Behind it we know in our lived existence that there is a corridor and
> other places for action, but now it is to be seen as simply a being-there with-
> out function or name, without anything except in the unthinkable. (336)

Passing over the threshold into this "pure visuality" involves, says Bonnefoy,
"descend[ing] with him into the twilight of meaning, identifying himself
with his character through the interior of this look of transgression and
silence" (336). Mallarmé's attempted identification is an immersion into
things which effects the transformation not of space into time (the establishment of symbolic thought categories), but of time (the medium of the
symbolic) into space (the real), as Igitur says: "To be sure, I have done everything so that the hour [the clock] sounded would remain present in the room,
becoming for me nourishment and life—I thickened the curtains . . ." (337).
The result of this operation is that

> Mallarmé succeeded in these pages—in deep moments of the text where his
> labyrinthine expression discourages understanding and so approaches
> silence—in giving almost the sensation of the thing seen in its being-there

infinitely foreign to all thought, all presence to the world. He has almost rejoined it in its essential "chance," that proof of our nothingness, at the very instant when this chance vanishes along with the thought that gave us an inkling of it. So that from the absolute an absolute of absence flowers before his eyes and ours. (336)

The "flowering" of absolute absence: it is the Lacanian Thing that performs itself in absolute singularity; it is also the Benjaminian pure word and "origin."[15]

Immersions of this sort privilege the partial drives. Not just the scopic drive, but those other orifices and their objects as well. The ear:

> [Igitur] listens to the tick-tock of the pendulum. He descends so far in his listening to each sound that the expectation of the next sound is effaced with the memory of its meaning, and this beat—this "hesitant oscillation"—seems to stop, an instant of the outside of time after which time will not start again, at once interminable and, if I dare say it, atemporal, but only as the same invisible and omnipresent reverse side of the human thing that the eye also foresees. (337)

Here one can see concretely, as it were, an example of a positive transformation of the baroque malaise described by Benjamin into a leaking out of substance from which emerges not only the annunciation (and not the realization!) of the pure word and thus the origin of the poetic, but also the promise of naming, and thus redeeming, things mortified by reification and "overnaming."

Imaginary captation (vision anchored in control and totality—control of totality) fizzles out into thin air, and what is left is the heavy thing, the obstacle of the unknown and uncontrolled, non-imaginary body:

> The mirror is obviously the very place where the Mallarméan experience can complete itself. There, among the furniture and drapes reflected in the depths of the mirror's water—in the freezing of this "water," where the hour also vanishes—the watcher of Midnight can perceive far off his own image, suddenly the supreme object of reabsorption of meaning, "a vague figure" disappearing in the horror of having to remain itself without, for all that, ever knowing anything about itself or even thinking that any knowledge might be possible: the head in the reflection being another than he—or, rather, being that of the other, the unknown one, the visible thing empty of meaning, this chance at once null and impassable for which no words can be found to lead it back into the land of human meaning. (337)

Mallarmé's quest for "pure vision" outside of knowledge and intention leads him to attempt to build a constellation of "pure things" (in language, of course, but a "full" one)—what he calls "Beauty." This is a performance in which things are not represented but present themselves, threatening the viewer (Igitur, Mallarmé) with annihilation. Here things are simultaneously "full" (producing anxiety and jouissance) and forever fleeing, present in the moment of their, and the viewer's, evanescence. This moment, atemporal, evanescent from the start, already fled at its own emergence, spells instantaneous liberation from the concept and the image, like the sinthome. Igitur's "moment" occurs when he sees the usually banished shadow of his own image in the mirror; it enables him to disregard the narcissistic vision and to immerse himself into the shadow, no longer concealed from him by imaginary fixations. The immersion is productive—for Bonnefoy, in terms of photography, but for my purposes simply as an example of where and how looking awry, and playing with points and lines, it is possible to emerge out from under the concept:

> Is it not true, in fact, that this image in the mirror where all Igitur's presages, all his fears, are concentrated but also where he attains supreme lucidity is something very like photography as I described it just now: a figure in the depths of paper that permits the paralysis of all meanings through an epiphany in the image of chance details, of an infinite with no reason, that are obviously the denial of the dream of personal being? (338)

Mallarmé's enigma of the subject-object relation, and of their mutual embeddedness, central to modern art, also forms the center of Aby Warburg's idiosyncratic theory of the art of the Renaissance. Warburg's *Pathosformeln*, pockets of affect, spots of "nonsense" finding expression usually in inchoate textures of folds and hair, and deployed within the otherwise rationalistic representations of individual sovereignty in the paintings of the High Renaissance, have effects that are strikingly similar to Igitur's experience of his mirror-shadow as described by Bonnefoy. Warburg's *Pathosformel* is precisely "a figure in the depths of paper that permits the paralysis of all meanings through an epiphany in the image of chance details, of an infinite with no reason, that are obviously the denial of the dream of personal being." At the same time, Warburg's manner of thinking about mimesis acts as a bridge into Benjamin's dialectics of mimesis.

E. Aby Warburg

Aby Warburg was a German Jewish art historian and cultural theorist; his cultural theorist orientation enabled him to establish iconology—the study of the work of art as a product of its cultural environment. Like Benjamin,

Warburg achieved fame mainly posthumously (mostly in the 1970s). Also like Benjamin, for Warburg, "God dwel[t] in the details" (Rosand 1999). Born in 1866 into a wealthy and prominent Jewish banking family in Hamburg, Warburg exchanged his birthright as the first born son to take over the banking business for his younger brother's promise that he would provide Aby with all of the books he would ever want throughout his lifetime. Warburg's work—beginning with his dissertation on Botticelli in 1893 and up until 1929, when he died—is collected in a volume entitled *The Renewal of Pagan Antiquity: Contributions to the Cultural History of the European Renaissance* (1999). Impatient with the sterility of formalism, Warburg's ultimate goal as an art historian was to write the history of the psychology of human expression. He thought that throughout time art works acted as aesthetic containers for the specific psychological stances of individual cultures. Art thus fulfilled a crucial function and could be read symptomatically. In his methodologically unorthodox—anti-systematic and open-ended—work he attempted to reveal the psychological development of social and cultural life through the interpretation of its art. His particular acuity in doing so, by focusing on paintings' detail—human gestures, facial expressions, physiognomy and garment, ornament and handwriting—makes him one of the most fascinating cross-disciplinary and cross-cultural critics of the early twentieth century. Like Benjamin, Warburg was drawn to the irrational, to magic and religion, and his emphasis is non-logocentric; unlike Benjamin, he purported to be the guardian of Enlightenment even as he insisted on the fundamental importance of irrational immersion into or empathy with cultural artifacts to the life of a civilization.

One notion emerges from Warburg's work as fundamental to both his philosophy and methodology and as the phenomenon that he claimed was fundamental to a life-affirming and tolerant culture: this is the notion of *Denkraum*, literally "thinking space," critical distance (Brosius 1997; Gombrich 1986, 224; Steinberg in Warburg 1995, 69). A work must contain its own *Denkraum* and in turn it must provide it to its viewer. Similarly, as a historical collection of symbolic forms, art has always provided the spaces in which humans symbolize their emergence from the inchoate. "Primitive" peoples and children generate(d) "memory images" to defend against a cryptic and terrifying nature: such images Warburg called "phobic reflexes" (Gombrich 1986, 218). They are very much like tic in this sense, with the important difference that "within" the phobic reflex space is provided for expression, no matter how unconscious that expression may remain. Viewing and experiencing art means "reading" it— again, no matter how unconsciously—through an immersion into psychic expression, and doing so in an especially delimited space. Art works contain both the phobic reflex and its progressive symbolic evolution. Every work, aside from its manifest content, will always also contain within itself pockets of almost pure affect: these Warburg called, in his *Mnemosyne-Atlas*, "*Pathosformeln*" ("pathos formulas"), those residues of the real, the inchoate. Warburg remained fascinated with their intrusions and the kinetic elements all his life and insisted on their curative function: they provide a door, he claimed, to an archaic dispossessedness (the primal moment of threat and a point of origin where human creation first takes place) and open the door to the *Denkraum* in which symbolic identification "originally" occurs. Frozen mimicry is overcome within the space of the *Denkraum*. Warburg presents both *Pathosformeln* and this *Denkraum* as necessary to the individual's survival. In the scenarios described by Caillois and Ferenczi the real enters traumatically, abolishing space and distance in modernity and reducing the individual's body to a body that twitches mimetically. *Denkraum*, all of these writers within the same decade seem to fear, is being threatened with obliteration in modernity. Modernity means being frozen in position, mimetically catatonic, and "schizophrenic."

Warburg's professional life was framed by a visit he paid to the Pueblo Indians in Arizona in 1895: he spent a few months observing their religious rituals and returned to Europe with a large collection of photographs which he displayed during at least two lectures. In 1918 Warburg suffered a nervous breakdown and was hospitalized in the sanatorium "Belle Vue" in Kreuzlingen, Switzerland, and placed under the care of Dr. Ludwig Binswanger. In April of 1923, after an almost six-year stay at Belle Vue, Warburg requested to be allowed to prove that he had regained his sanity by way of a lecture for the doctors and patients of the hospital.[16] His topic was the "*Schlangentanzritual der Pueblo-Indianer*"—"The Serpent Ritual of the Pueblo Indians" (Warburg 1995)—based on notes taken twenty-seven years earlier in Arizona. Presenting the gist of this legendary lecture provides me with a way of visualizing more concretely the way in which Benjamin's "mimetic faculty" is to have a curative function within traumatically encroached upon psyches.

There were three parts to the lecture. In Part 1 Warburg discussed the function of the serpent image for the Pueblos: the serpent is a mimetic representation of lightning. The function of the hieroglyphic "naming" of lightning by way of serpent designs on *Kachina* dolls, pottery, and in dances is to conjure rain. Part 2 described the Indians' masked dance, and Part 3 considered the relevance of image-language to European culture. Two elements concerning the ritual were crucial to Warburg's lecture. First, he claimed that the Indians' serpent ritual had been replaced within modern

America by electricity: lightning had been "captured," put to instantaneous use, its writing obliterated, and brought about an instantaneous "usage" of the forces of nature, a capture that emblematizes an instrumental reason that Benjamin had associated with the emptying out of experience in his "Program for a Coming Philosophy." (We will see a return of the lightning image in Chapter 6: electric shock.) Second, the Indians, who in the ritual danced with live rattlesnakes, threw the live snakes back into nature after the ritual, while "[t]he present-day American [of European stock] feels no awe of the rattlesnake. It is killed, or at all events not accorded divine honors. The response to it is extermination" (Gombrich 1986, 225).

Symbols, for Warburg, have the function of writing down, as it were, in a space opened up for just that purpose, a relationship between symbolic and real that is not immediately captured by the imaginary and instrumental reason. The written symbol, the handwriting of the ornaments and folds in painting, are not residue-free. Residues of the chaotic and irrational remain everywhere and uncannily in cultural symbols. *Denkraum*, where affect is thought through, contains what Warburg thought of as the split nature of the subject: at work in the space (*Denkraum*) of the serpent ritual are a primary mimesis (the image of the snake that frames for the first time a threatening force of nature), irrational immersion into the image (its sacralization, that is, re-contacting the real through it), mimicry (the Indians mimicking the snake which mimics lightning), and the symbolization (lightning is the *sign* for water) that takes the Indians beyond their petrified helplessness before nature and their "assimilation" into it; in other words, that liberates them from a paralyzing magic. The written symbolization of *Denkraum* liberates from paralyzing mimicry and does so through acts of mimetic immersion.

Warburg used his lecture and his active thought to prove his "sanity"; however, his lecture itself participated in a mimetic operation insofar as it mimed his own struggle to free himself from the paralyzing enchantment of his mental illness, including the cocoon of Binswanger's hospital. Warburg's idea of *Denkraum* provides a clear model for the action that is involved in Benjamin's understanding of mimesis—the mimetic faculty. The latter takes the shape of "reading" and "writing" and of finding access to a new mode of perceiving and experiencing oneself through the Other and through *Denkraum*. This Other includes not only what Benjamin calls the "material community," but also one's own corporeality; both are necessary, for Benjamin, for a redeemed experience.

CHAPTER 4

WALTER BENJAMIN'S "MIMESIS"

Mimesis and mimetic practices are always productive, not mere reflection, in Benjamin. Counter-intuitively, Benjaminian mimesis uncovers difference; it perceives similarities that lie concealed, and in doing so lends voice to what had historically been silenced.[1] Largely a capacity that has been lost, Benjamin says, mimesis and the mimetic faculty have withdrawn into the realm of language, and there we must recollect them, keep them alive and translate them into other spheres of life. The "once powerful compulsion to become similar and to behave mimetically" (Benjamin 1933d/1999, 720) had, when we "had" it in the past, meant the capacity to experience an original relatedness "grounded" uncannily in the abyss of the other.

While Weigel (1996), too, like Weber, insists that it is in distortion, the folds of "origin," that Benjamin seeks "truth," immersion into them uncovers, in single flashes, a new immediacy. The material of these folds, the origin of revelation, is, for Benjamin, language, the work of art, or perception. The material is momentarily stripped of its communicable element, as it is in Mallarmé's "Igitur." In "Problems in the Sociology of Language" (1934/2002) Benjamin discusses such non-communicative elements of language: "the resonance [of] the purely phonetic side of language" (69) which, as we saw, rose to the surface in the seventeenth century, "linguistic expression[s]" that are "oral drawings" (71), the "language of children," that "exists as a socialized language on the one hand, and as egocentric language on the other, [t]he latter . . . ha[ving] no communicative function" (82). Like Mallarmé's language, they all point to the mimetic nature of language, which as it were uncovers and invites the subject producing and also reading it into an immersion into its opacities in the hope that in this way the subject may be moved to recognize the relationality that language itself communicates. Benjamin ends this essay by quoting neuropsychiatrist Kurt Goldstein on the problem of aphasia:

> One could not find a better example to demonstrate how wrong it is to regard language as an instrument. What we have seen is the form in which language emerges in cases where it can be no more than an instrument. Even in the case of normal people, it can happen that language is really something quite different . . . As soon as human beings use language to establish a living relationship to themselves and to others, language is no longer an instrument, no longer a means, but a manifestation, a revelation of our innermost being and of the psychic bond linking us to ourselves and to our fellow human beings. (85–6)

Benjamin goes on to explain even more denotatively the ethical and political significance of reaching for "language as such," the mimetic immersion-inviting elements of language. He does so in a letter to Martin Buber. It deserves to be re-quoted here at length:

> The opinion is widespread, and prevails almost everywhere as axiomatic, that writing can influence the moral world and human behavior, in that it places the motives behind actions at our disposal. In this sense, therefore, language is only one means of more or less suggestively *laying the groundwork* for the motives that determine the person's actions in his heart of hearts. What is characteristic about this view is that it completely fails to consider a relationship between language and action in which the former would not be the instrument of the latter. This relationship would hold equally for an impotent language, degraded to pure instrument, and for writing that is a pitiful, weak action and whose origin does not reside within itself, but in some kind of sayable and expressible motives. . . . Every action that derives from the expansive tendency to string words together seems terrible to me, and even more catastrophic where the entire relationship between word and deed is, to an ever-increasing degree, gaining ground as a mechanism for the realization of the true absolute, as is the case among us now.
> . . .
> Every salutary effect, indeed every effect not inherently devastating, that any writing may have resides in its (the word's, language's) mystery. . . .
> My concept of objective and, at the same time, highly political style and writing is this: to awaken interest in what was denied to the word; only where this sphere of speechlessness reveals itself in unutterably pure power can the magic spark leap between the word and the motivating deed . . . Only the intensive aiming of words into the core of intrinsic silence is truly effective. (Benjamin 1994, 81–2)

I wish to bring the assignment of the deed's power (in the form of effects) to the "speechlessness" of language into relationship with the notion of the "act" that the end of analysis incorporates, the *sinthome*. Understanding how that works in a true convergence of Benjaminian and psychoanalytic thought is the topic of Chapter 5. Here I will unfold the main elements of Benjaminian mimesis.

1. Mimesis, Imitatio, Language

The "cause" (i.e., the cause-of-desire, the *objet a*) of mimesis and mimetic acts is the subject-object relationship: phylogenetically, the identificatory relationship with the mother, embodied in the mother's face; ontogenetically, the relationship with an "origin" that, in the containing Judeo-Christian narrative, is told in the story of God's creation of human being and in the *imago dei* idea. Given Benjamin's theological framing of his philosophy of language, it makes sense to start here. I will return to phylogenesis in Chapters 5 and 6.

The Christian theologian Leo Scheffczyk's analysis of this idea and the verse of *Genesis* 1, 26, "And God said, Let us make man in our image, after our likeness," is striking in this context. He begins, in his book, *Der Mensch als Bild Gottes*, by saying that every theological doctrine has to begin with *imago dei* (xiii), with a being-similar-to, and that this verse has been and continues to be the object of enormous "fascination" (xiii) among exegetes and speculative theologians, insofar as the features of the god-human relationship are inexhaustible. Most interesting is the element that he calls, in German, the "*Imago-Rest*," the trace or remnant of a pre-verbal identification with the divine in the human being that cannot be lost (xxviii): it refers also, in my mind, to the "little piece of the real" that opens up an equally "inexhaustible" abyss within the subject, having to do both with the body not fully covered by language—and, as we have already seen, to the "origin" of language, the lost Thing, that "unforgettable first object," the mother, the "Sovereign Good."[2] Scheffczyk goes on to say that the translations of the Hebrew words in *Bereshit* 1, 26 adumbrate Benjamin's mimesis: the Hebrew for "imago"—*demut*—and "likeness"—*salam*—allows the otherness in the creation process to emerge: *demut* translates into "that looks like" or "they looked like [but weren't]." The difference between this and "in our image" is that in the former distance and difference are clearly retained; there is similarity, but not identity. The second word, *salam*, translates best as "silhouette" ("*Schattenbild*," in German), and also *gestalt*, statue, shadow, adumbration. In this context God is not only the source of the possibility of reflection and reflective existence (*Denkraum*), an existence in self-presence, but of alterity. There is an abyss, an irreducible difference, in the face of God, an insight that Susan, if I may reach ahead to Chapter 6 again, comes to gain by way of her re-inscription of her own "origins" in her painting of the holey face entitled "My Mother" (Chapter 6, Figure 31).

The idea of the abyss in the face (of God, mother, humans, or angels) in Jewish tradition is interesting in this context: in the complicated structure of laws and prohibitions regarding the representation of human beings, one convention that finds acceptance is to give three-dimensional representations of human beings a broken nose (Schwarzschild 1975, 32). Since a material representation of what is antithetical to matter—the soul—is impossible (and forbidden), breaking a part of it makes reference both to its "other," the "soul" perhaps, and to the fraught relationship between contingent matter and the absolute.

The figure of the abyss in the face, and the concrete example, the broken nose, are in complicated ways part of Benjamin's notion of mimesis. They are also reminiscent of the Lacanian *sinthome* and its ethics insofar as they allude to the act of identifying with the symptom that undermines the imagistic, imago-obsessed ego. Perhaps, in this sense, one could speculate that in part the Judaeo-Christian injunction to imitate God is also a command to identify with the real, with alterity. As the mimetic always refers to what is primordial, it stands in close relation to Benjamin's notion of origin. The "eddy" of the origin that fragments and distorts (Introduction) may also be thought of as language in the form of broken shells standing before the origin. Words as "broken shells," as shattered nose, and as abyss, echoes the kabbalistic image Benjamin inserts into "Agesilaus Santander" of the "perishing angels": "The Kaballah relates that, at every moment, God creates a whole host of angels, whose only task before they return to the void is to appear before His throne for a moment and sing His praises" (1933g/1999, 714).

Because there is no representational or conceivable original to be had—there is no such thing as a whole word that does not carry its own non-identity within itself—the human mimetic faculty is necessarily always a failure when it is regarded from the point of view of recovery as full restoration. Benjamin and psychoanalysis are agreed on this. From the perspective of "origin," however, mimesis is about processes of reading and writing, which include physical gesture, the actual physical act of inscription, as well as the pictorial character of written language: ". . . the written word," Benjamin writes,

> —in some cases perhaps more vividly than the spoken word—illuminates, by the relation of its written form [*Schriftbild*] to the signified, the nature of nonsensuous similarity. . . .
>
> Graphology has taught us to recognize in handwriting images that the unconscious of the writer conceals in it. It may be supposed that the mimetic process which expresses itself in this way in the activity of the writer was, in the very distant times in which script originated, of utmost importance for writing. Script has thus become, like language, an archive of nonsensuous similarities, of nonsensuous correspondences. (1933d/1999, 721–2)

The necessary brokenness that for Benjamin lies at the origin of mimesis, that central reality of destruction, would then seem to be related to the Jewish *Bilderverbot*, the prohibition of images. The *Bilderverbot* underlies at least partially what are figured in Benjamin's mimesis and translation work as defensive "detours" through language (language defending, i.e., against encountering the Thing as the Highest Good, the absolute against which Kant had erected a barrier), but not only language: thinking, too, for Benjamin, is structured in this way. Detour as deviation, "phobic reflex," in order not to be inundated, in its extreme form is common both to psychological dissociation (defense against trauma) and, counter-intuitively, to the Benjaminian experience of mimesis. It is true of dissociation in the sense that its extreme splitting lends definition to, or releases, the absolute; it is the sort of splitting that the *Trauerspiel* performs as well. Benjamin's mimesis thus moves in paradox fashion: on the one hand, it seeks the Highest Good by way of immersion, as we saw in Part 1; on the other, it deviates away from being inundated by it. Fed by its origin, this detour blossoms into linguistic infinity and ornamentation. The *Bilderverbot* functions as the "detour" sign, pointing away from the origin, which both beckons as the source of redemption and points away from itself. This paradox explains Benjamin's image for messianic intensity:

> If one arrow points to the goal toward which the profane dynamic acts, and another marks the direction of Messianic intensity, then certainly the quest to free humanity for happiness runs counter to the Messianic direction; but just as a force can, through acting, increase another that is acting in the opposite direction, so the order of the profane assists, through being profane, the coming of the Messianic Kingdom. (1920–21/1937–38/2002, 305)

Altered states of consciousness are also common to both dissociation and mimesis. The mimetic experience suspends, for an instant, conceptual thought and the subject-object division that characterize western post-Kantian thought and experience. From the point of view of Kantian cognition, to be "known" and gazed at by the object may be experienced as engulfing, even traumatically so. Language is a dissociative and thus defensive conduit. Benjamin implies that, in order for a transformation in thinking to come into being, neither the subject nor its language must become petrified by a traumatizing experience of alterity, of the uncanny, nor must it negate this "failed" encounter entirely. But then, in Benjaminian mimesis, language actually comes to the rescue. Language is the most "faithful" *imitatio dei*, as it is both original and insufficient over against the image.

It is here, then, in this context of the peculiarly Benjaminian inflection of *imitatio dei*, that we can begin to understand what Benjamin means by "non-sensuous similarity." In an explanation for why Judaism makes no use of symbols, Abraham Heschel writes that the only symbol of God is man: "What is necessary is not to have a symbol but to be a symbol" (1998, 126) he writes, and this surely reminds us of the Lacanian *sinthome*.

2. *Reading*

The figure of "detour" plays an important role in "Agesilaus Santander," one of Benjamin's most esoteric texts of 1933. In this scene in which Benjamin describes, however obscurely, the process of his "task" of "reading" in the face of the historical catastrophe of a triumphant Nazism, it is the "detours" on the way back to the "origin" by way of the other— detours that read like Freud's "detour" of Eros in the face of Thanatos, as he describes it both in *Civilization and Its Discontents* (1930) and *Beyond the Pleasure Principle* (1920)—that seem to contain a space of survival. Here Benjamin describes his relationship to the painting of the Angelus Novus by Klee (which also became the model for the Angel of History in his 9th Thesis in the 1940 *Theses on the Philosophy of History*) that hung in his room:

> ... he [the angel] has made me pay for having disturbed him at his work. By turning to his advantage the fact that I was born under the sign of Saturn— the planet of slow revolution, the star of hesitation and delay—he sent his feminine aspect after the masculine one reproduced in the picture, and did so by the most circuitous, most fatal detour, even though the two had been such close neighbors. He may have been unaware that in doing this he brought out the strength of the man against whom he was proceeding. For nothing can overcome my patience. Its pinions resemble those of the angel: they need but a few movements to hold it stationary in the face of the woman whom it is determined to await. (713)

Interruption of the usual at the moment of catastrophe and a turn in a different direction in order precisely to circle around the "origin" without being assimilated by it characterizes the movement of this passage. This is also how Benjamin saw his critical and historical task on the whole. In the mimetic experience, a psychological, perceptual, and linguistic experience, following an immediate perceptual stimulation, the dissociative reaction to the encounter with alterity expands the perceptual jolt, before spreading out into linguistic commentary. This is one reason some critics' emphasis on images in Benjamin's work may be problematic; it would be a mistake to claim that image is central in Benjamin's thinking about mimesis.

Similarity, or mimetic returns to origin, can at most appear in "flashes," momentarily and virtually, and thus are always linked to perishing. In fact, it appears that the mimetic cannot even appear without being enveloped in a semiotic—that is, functional and communicative—language: ". . . the mimetic element in language can, like a flame, manifest itself only through a kind of bearer. This bearer is the semiotic element. Thus, the nexus of meaning of words or sentences is the bearer through which, like a flash, similarity appears" (1933d/1999, 722). In order for the flash of the mimetic to be realized and to be effective, it has to be received—or read. Reading becomes the human task *par excellence*[3] in these pieces as it transforms into the task of recognizing what is "original." In "Doctrine of the Similar," Benjamin writes:

> . . . at this deep level access opens to a peculiar ambiguity of the word "read-ing," in both its profane and magical senses. The schoolboy reads his ABC book, and the astrologer reads the future in the stars. In the first clause, read-ing is not separated out into its two components. Quite the opposite in the second, though, which clarifies the process at both its levels: the astrologer reads the constellation from the stars in the sky; simultaneously he reads the future or fate from it. (1933b/1999, 697)

The "two components" are, in German, (1) *lesen* as reading, and (2) *lesen* in the sense of *auslesen*, that is, "sorting out," "picking out." Thus "read-ing" becomes not simply a process of combining the elements provided in order to make them signify, but also a process of picking out what otherwise would remain invisible, and moreover, to do so with an eye toward the future.

Benjamin's notion of mimesis, seen through the scriptural and scripto-rial prism of the "perishing angels," is also a thought image (*Denkbild*) for the creation of the new. Out of the perishing emerges hope—hope for the new, for the other, and also "hope for the dead" (50), to use a phrase of Caygill's, the hopeless hope. The new emerges by way of recovery of origin and its transformation. Writing brings forth the new, but so does reading, as one ". . . read[s] what was never written" (1933g/1999, 722). It is also an image for the process of psychoanalysis. A beautiful sentence from Benjamin's "Epistemo-Critical Prologue" to his *Trauerspiel* book encour-ages this particular correlation: it describes the philosophy of both the many returns to "origins" for the retrieval of novelty (in the sphere of thought and of aesthetics) and the subject-subject relationship: "Tirelessly the process of thinking makes new beginnings, returning in a roundabout way to its original object. This continual pausing for breath is the mode most proper to the process of contemplation" (1928/1998, 29). In mimesis, too, the Benjaminian mimetic engagement with an other does what it does in relation to things and works: immersion and retrieval of alterity.[4] In the context of the critic's "digging" into the work, she sets in motion, by way of translations that emanate from the origin, the work's afterlives.

In psychoanalysis this scene translates into a similar sort of unfolding process of the alterities that, in the state of repression, had relegated the subject to a state of mimicry, rigidity, and slumber.

3. *Das Gedichtete (The Poetized)*

Whether or not Benjamin was aware of other work on mimesis—some of which I have so briefly referred to by way of Caillois, Ferenczi, Warburg, Mallarmé—being done (most likely, he was), his approach to mimesis responds dialectically to the problem of mimicry. He attempts to rescue "mimesis" from petrifying and inundating mimicry through language. Benjamin's mimesis is not about disappearing; on the contrary, it is to be a tool for retrieving what has been "disappeared." For even though mimesis contains mimicry (disappearance, transience, assimilation) within itself, this moment is always dialectically opened up by mimesis's retrieval of divergence and distortion. In sum, for Benjamin, mimesis retrieves alterity. From beginning to end (both phylo- and ontogenetic), the mimetic faculty "misses" the mark of a unifying identification.

Mimesis's most "original" (in the Benjaminian sense) material is the body, as it is also for Caillois, Ferenczi, Warburg and, as we will see, Klein: the "[d]octrine of the similar," as Bettine Menke rightly observes, is to some degree a doctrine of gestures, of those corporeal processes that "generate similarity" (Benjamin 1933*b*, 694), gestures that, as she says, achieve "inscription" and thus participate in what, in and on the body, can be read (Menke 1991, 114). Much of Benjamin's *Berlin Childhood Around 1900* (1932–34/2006),[5] together with "Doctrine of the Similar" and "On the Mimetic Faculty," refers to children's bodily imitative play:

> Children's play is everywhere permeated by mimetic modes of behavior, and its realm is by no means limited to what one person can imitate in another. The child plays at being not only a shopkeeper or teacher, but also a windmill and a train. (1933*g*/1999, 720)

Play is the school of the mimetic faculty, and correspondences in nature as well as the environment stimulate and awaken it. Dance produces similarity, and "the newborn" (Benjamin 1933*g*/1999, 721) is in full possession of it, in part because the newborn is all body at first, a body dependent on other bodies at that.

In "The Lamp," another piece within the "mimetic series" and one in which Benjamin says once again that mimesis "continues to function nowadays only in children" (1933*e*/1999, 691), the mimetic faculty is described

as a fundamental structure of the human sensorium and psyche and as a particular way of relating to the external world:

> At first, at the moment of birth, [childhood] makes itself similar to the most distant things in the deepest, most unconscious stratum of its own existence, so as subsequently to enable the objects of the world around to accrete, layer by layer. (691)

So it seems that children's inborn mimetic faculty has to do with traces of a non-judgmental and a more than functional perception of the "material community." It is a particular form of perception, a faculty that "reached far beyond the narrow world of perception in which we are still able to perceive similarity" (691). Benjamin then goes on to describe himself as working to retrieve that form of perception: the "formative powers" of similarity have "formed in [him] the image of chairs, stairwells, cupboards, net curtains, and even a lamp—objects that surrounded [him] in [his] child-hood" (692). Is it possible for such a retrieval to occur when we have lost so much? In "Doctrine of the Similar" Benjamin says that "language now represents the medium in which objects encounter and come into relation with one another" (1933b/1999, 697). This is where the mimetic faculty's transformation through time has found refuge:

> True, our existence no longer includes what once made it possible to speak of this kind of similarity: above all, the ability to produce it. Nevertheless, we, too, possess a canon according to which the meaning of nonsensuous similarity can be at least partly clarified. And this canon is language. (1933g/1999, 721)

A particular kind of reception and production of language may make it possible to (re-)induce a mimetic network of relationships among objects within the consciousness of a listening and reading subject: "[S]imilarities flash up fleetingly out of the stream of things only in order to sink down once more" (1933b/1999, 698). I have shown this to be psychologically at work in Benjamin's baroque man, who attempts to survive by creating a "material community" for himself. Later we will see how Marion Milner engages in readings of this sort in her analysis of Susan's drawings. In much of psychoanalytic theory that forms the background to Milner's work, the newborn comes to form its entire, albeit primitive, world of per-ception in the "field" of the mother's "face," which it encounters mimeti-cally. The face forms another link between the ontogenetic and phylogenetic worlds of experience. For Benjamin this link between inner and outer, that for him like for psychoanalysis is a wider object world, is the fact that the newborn appears to have emerged into the world with a full potential for the unfolding of language. Even if that potential will increasingly be obfuscated by "chatter," this unfolding focuses the field of mimesis.

It is only language that can return us—via all sorts of detours—to true "origins," that is, to the collaborative creative process that Benjamin had described in his 1916 language essay. It does so by showing repeatedly that its very possibility is dependent on encountering, and somehow only partially containing, alterity. In language a mimesis that both turns to the origin and allows alterity to realize itself is called "translation," and it emerges from constellations:

> . . . the concept of nonsensuous similarity is of some relevance. For if words meaning the same thing in different languages are arranged about that signified as their center, we have to inquire how they all—while often possessing not the slightest similarity to one another—are similar to the signified at the center. (Benjamin 1933g/1999, 721)

While the original Word is not (anymore) available to us, the act of translation, which posits the idea of an original (as opposed to its empirical instantiation), points to a mode of residence within human languages which, under the best circumstances, circle around the "pure" but lost, absent, Word. This virtual original Word is creative, precisely because of its own virtuality and the various translations it implies in reality.

But "origin" as "*Ursprung*" is also very much a reversal, an "*Umkehr*," an idea that Benjamin took from Hölderlin. In "The Task of the Translator" (1921/1996) Benjamin says about Hölderlin's Sophocles translations that they return virtually to the "revelation" of Holy Writ:

> Hölderlin's translations from Sophocles were his last work; in them meaning plunges from abyss to abyss until it threatens to become lost in the bottomless depths of language. There is, however, a stop. It is vouchsafed in Holy Writ alone, in which meaning has ceased to be the watershed for the flow of language and the flow of revelation. Where the literal quality of the text takes part directly, without any mediating sense, in true language, in the Truth, or in doctrine, this text is unconditionally translatable. To be sure, such translation no longer serves the cause of the text, but rather works in the interest of languages. (262)

Weigel notes that for Hölderlin *Umkehr* was to recover the "Oriental element" that had disappeared in Greek tragedies (Weigel 1996, 140). In his essay on Goethe's *Elective Affinities*, Benjamin notes that in "the poetized" (*das Gedichtete*), "something beyond the poet interrupts the language of poetry" (1919–22/1996, 341), something that traverses and "ruptures writing," as Richter (2002, 89) writes, something "that cannot be reduced to authorial control" (Benjamin 1914–15*c*/1996, 20). Perhaps, as Benjamin writes, "the unities of art and life, whose unities themselves are wholly ungraspable" (1914–15*c*/1996, 20), an "indeterminacy of the shaping principle" (23), something before meaning.

Benjamin's 1914–1915 work on Hölderlin reflects a fascination in his cultural environment with Hölderlin's enigmatic and uncanny work. The rediscovery of Hölderlin was very much in vogue with Rilke and his followers, with Stefan George and his circle, and many other *literati*; the George Circle especially attempted to imitate such Hölderlinian language. Rilke's work represented certainly some of the most successful Hölderlin-inspired poetry; but Trakl's poetry deserves mention, too, as perhaps a more striking example of poetic language tending toward "pure language." An example of *das Gedichtete*, the "poetized," tending toward "origin" in Trakl's poetry is the word "Laβ" in "An den Knaben Elis." Here are the first two stanzas:

> Elis, wenn die Amsel im schwarzen Wald ruft,
> dieses ist dein Untergang.
> Deine Lippen trinken die Kühle des blauen Felsenquells.
>
> Laß, wenn deine Stirne leise blutet
> uralte Legenden
> und dunkle Deutung des Vogelflugs. (Trakl 1917, 20)

There is really no equivalent in English for "*laß*": "*laß es*" could mean "leave it!" as the imperative form of "to leave"; "*laß es gehen!*" on the other hand, would be "let it go!" "*Laß es gut sein*," "leave it be." But "*laß*" alone is more difficult, as "let," in English, cannot stand alone. It can hardly do so in German. The closest translation would be a gesture: a fist opening up. "*Laß*" conjures up Meister Eckhart's "*Gelassenheit*": "*gelassen*" is the past participle of "*lassen*" and its imperative form, "*laß*." Yet the imperative here is a peculiar combination of imperative form and semantically, absolute passivity. "*Laß*" is an example of meaning "plung[ing] from abyss to abyss" "until it threatens to become lost." It functions in the poem as an "indeterminate shaping principle," the abyss from which the rest of the poem emanates, the abyss of language, deep reversals, "origin," and transformation. The rest of the poem unfolds the abyssal origin of "*laß*" as well as its ultimate corporeality.

In Hölderlin and Trakl's poetry, as well as in Benjamin's descriptions of mimetic language digging toward original language, communicative language retreats, a process that Richter refers to as "poetic excess encoded in [the Benjaminian conception of] *das Ausdruckslose*" (2002, 31). This is

precisely what "*laβ*" is: an instance of *das Ausdruckslose*, expressionlessness—intentionless, semantically indeterminate language that tends toward
the physically gestural. Instead of precise and exhaustive legibility there are
intensities of the body, "something expressionless" that "refuses to be represented" and thus also refuses any sort of stabilizing inscription as fiction.
Richter rightly claims that this "unreadable physiognomy" is the site of the
ethico-political, as it eschews imposed stabilizing decisions:

> . . . the ethical is precisely the undoing of a readable physiognomy. It is what
> departs from the body as a legible text. On the far side of expression and leg-
> ibility, the body's retreat signals its politics: its uselessness for an ideology of
> stable bodies and stable hermeneutic meanings. (2002, 72)

Das Ausdruckslose is what Harold Bloom has called a "frontier concept"
(1991), neither language-as-meaning nor pure corporeality, but something
in between that deconstructs both. This is language, says Richter, at its
most political, when "the linguistic moment breaks out of the syntax of the
body. Language encounters the ethical when it transgresses its own laws"
(2002, 72). It is a pulsating real within the symbolic, uncontainable, a
remnant of the other in both spheres, *objet a*: bodily gesture that escapes
meaning and language that "no longer serves." It is the "retreat" from
expression (as "expressionlessness") that, as Richter also notes, separates
Benjaminian physiognomy and graphology from the fascistic uses made of
reading bodies (physiognomy), stars (astrology), or any other perversion of
mimetic practices. Ascetic withdrawal and retreat from self-presence[6]—the
emptiness required for the creation and recognition of the other—deter-
mines Benjamin's notion of mimesis. Peter Fenves (2001) has framed such
retreat and withdrawal in the tradition of *epochē*, a suspension of judgment, a withdrawal of belief, in a moment in which the object world is lost,
in catastrophe, and destroyed, only in order to be regained.[7] In Chapter 5
we will translate such body-language and *caesuric epochē* into the psychoanalytic register again—this time in the work of W. R. Bion—in order to
concretize Benjaminian mimetic praxis.

Mimetic practices, then, tend away from representation, in favor of
non-communicative, opaque revelation. Benjamin's understanding of revelation is paradoxical Lacanian-style: revelation in psychoanalysis consists
in the vitiation of the recognition-misrecognition opposition. Benjamin's
understanding of language as divided between instrumental, intentional,
and communicative on the one hand and "original" language on the other
finds a powerful echo in Lacan's distinction between the imaginary speech
between two egos, where one wants only to make itself understood by the

other, and the revelatory speech that takes place between two subjects, where the speaker is surprised by what s/he says and the listener responds—silently or otherwise.[8] In the latter case, subjects acknowledge the sovereignty of language instead of the sovereignty of the intending subject. Compare this to the final sentences of Benjamin's 1916 language essay:

> The language of nature is comparable to a secret password that each sentry passes to the next in his own language, but the meaning of the password is the sentry's language itself. All higher language is a translation of lower ones, until in ultimate clarity the word of God unfolds, which is the unity of this movement made up of language. (1916/1996, 74)

BENJAMIN, KLEIN AND KLEINIANS, AND THE NEW THINKING

1. Melanie Klein: Drawing Mental Space

The sort of thinking I will describe in this chapter is what I believe Benjamin aimed at in his "Program for a Coming Philosophy" (1918). Innovatively, I want to suggest that a Benjaminian reading of Kleinian and post-Kleinian theories of the subject may illuminate Benjaminian theories of reading and writing. I turn to Klein and read her in the key of the *Trauerspiel* book.

Klein represents the birth of the human subject in the infant as a harrowing process. Striking about her presentation[1] is that the archaic, not-yet-symbolic state of the psyche is represented in dynamic, often violent, geometric terms: points, lines, circles, and broken lines and circles when objects are projected or introjected. We are here in a realm that precedes any sense of whole self and whole other. From the very beginning, however, there is object-relating. It is violent and frantic because the original subject is haunted by the failure of its own survival. The violence of the movements of fragments (see, for instance, Klein 1946/1987) of what will eventually be a "self," but is at this moment not even a real object, but an "abject,"[2] in its relation to the fragments of the Other is exacerbated when the connection between points is broken, when lines are violently split, or when a heavily drawn defensive container around self-fragments bombards everything around it with part objects used as missiles. Klein's hellish scenarios are characterized by sadistic cutting and hatred-filled splitting. All this happens in fear of annihilation. Klein reads in them overwhelming anxiety, fretting despair, and hatred that fills a pathetic fledgling subject who is really just configuring a livable place for itself, to survive. Before the subject proper comes into being, before it is possible to speak of "self" and "other," lines in the early subject's experience are almost always lines of defense; circles are fortresses keeping something overvalued and omnipotent in and the other—as lack and death—out. Cutting and splitting lines is catastrophic; but so is the omnipotent fortress-circle. All of this activity constitutes mental space.

From the very beginning the infant interacts with the mother who is its first object, though she is at first not seen as "whole," but is reified into good and bad part objects.[3] The infant's phase of acute anxiety regarding this object's role and fears for its own survival, fuelled by defensive aggression and hatred, is the "paranoid-schizoid" position (PS): "its violence is such," writes Kristeva,

> that it does not tolerate . . . lack but attaches instead onto an object-target, a pseudo-object, or an *abject*. There is nothing missing, then, to be desired, but everything wounds, gets wounded, and allows itself to be attacked according to the principles of retributive justice. (2001, 83)

Here both the fear of death and the death drive proliferate and do so in an unending process of fragmentation; splitting and sadism dominate. The overall state is catastrophic in both senses: rigid lines and circles come into being which attempt defensively to counteract thanatic fragmentations: this leads to the infant's, as well as the later subject's, manic and tyrannical delusions of omnipotence and sadism. Such "successful," though delusional, acts of containment are derisive in tone and desperate in aim. The hard, thick, closed outline that rigidly and judgmentally splits phenomena into "good" and "bad" and can transform into missile at any moment as well as founder into fragmentation and abjection characterizes PS. Its momentary rallies are the result of panic and they immobilize rather than calm, spell-bind rather than think. Remaining stuck in PS is the great danger and essentially defines psychotic and schizoid disorders.[4] When this occurs, the rigid PS containers themselves need to undergo catastrophic change.

When the infant becomes able to recognize the mother as whole object who has been in the line of fire of its violently enacted fear of dissolution, it begins to be able to configure the self-other relation along the lines of the "depressive position" (D). The depressive position, analogous, as we will see, to *Denkraum* (Chapter 3) and *Denkbild* (Chapter 6), provides at first a just barely livable, but eventually also a creative, alternative to the violence and catastrophe of PS. D is inaugurated by "mania," experienced as self-preservative grandiosity that, as Klein puts it, "play[s] a positive role in development protecting the ego from unbridled despair" (Kristeva 2001, 78). This interesting phenomenon of mania is marked both by PS and D. "In mania the ego seeks refuge not only from melancholia but also from a paranoiac condition which it is unable to master. Its torturing and perilous dependence on its loved objects drives the ego to seek freedom" (Klein 1935/1987, 132). In other words, mania is imperative in the constitution of an ego. Geometrically, this is a moment—delusional, no doubt—in which the self sees itself contained within itself without needing to resort to violent, or at least rupturing, projections. It is comparable to the illusion of subjectivity that Benjamin describes at the end of the *Trauerspiel* book, the pure subjectivity that mirrors itself as it becomes one with God. Mania makes heavy use of denial: "that which is *first of all denied is psychic reality* and the ego then may go on to deny a great deal of external reality" (Klein 1935, 132). It is also fundamentally ambiguous: in Benjamin's narrative of the martyr/tyrant/allegorist/intriguer positions the "freedom" achieved through a sort of Kleinian mania appears the moment the "allegorist" rescues the martyr from drowning in melancholic brokenness. It is also present in the "new ego" of the *sinthome*—the moment that it heaves its father on its back and evades its own sacrifice to the Law-of-the-Father. Mania initiates a preservative mechanism[5] that will come to define the depressive position and that the young psyche had not known before. It is made manifest in a manic circle. Nevertheless, it scorns the depressive position that it, triumphant in its new selfhood, after all helps bring into existence: those aspects of the subject that acknowledges the other-within-the-self and that, to use Benjamin's terminology, make it "faithful" to the world, the reality of abjection, absence, and lack.

Following the manic moment a more realistic new sense of two subjects—the self and the other—develops and, with it, the reality of loss and incompleteness for self and other both. This is accompanied by melancholia, characterized by self-lacerations and mortification for the earlier attacks, attempts at reparation vis-à-vis the previously attacked and hated object, and finally mourning, in the shape of a piece-by-piece retrieval and acknowledgement of the world that had been all but consumed in the violence of PS.

D allows the subject to transcend the unbroken and solipsistic circle and to enter the real world of objects. It is defined by its reparative and mournful re-collection of objects that are now recognized as having been touched by both self and other and as connecting them. This re-collection is a specific sort of "reading" of world and self: world can be read only following the fragmentation and mortification of a fortified sovereign ego, and the subject-to-be can be read only upon the re-collection of objects in the world which she takes into herself or into which she immerses herself in order to become a true subject. Klein's depressive position corresponds in striking ways to the position of Benjamin's melancholiac and martyr-allegorist: on the one hand, both pick up the fragments of the real in order to piece together "meanings"; on the other, they do so only following a crucial moment of self-dissolution and immersion into these things which have always already been a part of the subject herself. Both the Kleinian and the Benjaminian melancholy subject perform these inherently mimetic acts against a background of anxiety, violence, and destruction. In fact, it is clear that it is precisely the moment of destruction that makes the re-collection and the abject and remorseful re-presentation of objects possible. Re-collection and re-presentation in the depressive position are painful, passionate, and self-lacerating acts. This is where Klein's scenario sounds the most Benjaminian:

> The pain experienced in the slow process of testing reality in the work of mourning thus seems to be partly due to the necessity, not only to renew the links to the external world, and thus continuously to re-experience loss, but at the same time and by means of this to rebuild with anguish the inner world, which is felt to be in danger of deteriorating and collapsing. (Klein 1940/1987, 156)

In directly Benjaminian terminology, the negative moment of PS together with the positive development for "true thinking," brought about by the depressive position corresponds to the position of the Angel of History wishing to repair things and raising the hope that the contemplator and reader of history will attempt to do so, instead of perpetuating the catastrophic course—contemptuous, denigratory, exclusive, omnipotence-deluded—history has in fact taken. Bion replaces Klein's terms PS and D with "dispersion" and "integration." Bion's "dispersion" corresponds to Benjamin's "explosions" out of the continuum of history: "Remaining only or too long in 'D' leads one to a stereotyped form of mind and at the end, to stagnation of thought," writes Neri (2003, 144). Thus the depressive position moves toward the truth that is more characteristic of O, "the realm of insight, of contact with 'all sins remembered' or a free movement towards the depressive position as observed by Melanie Klein" (Sandler 2003, 62). At the same time, too much PS means psychic and mental atrophy and annihilation of both the other and external reality.[6] Similarly, for Bion, in the analytic setting analysand and analyst must both bear the anxiety of hovering somewhere between "patience" (persecution) and "security" (integration) (Bion 1978, 124).

Geometrically, the depressive position is drawn as circles of broken outlines across which a constant exchange between inside and outside takes place. The objects themselves—the early "self" and the other(s)—are experienced as both part objects and whole objects and they include inscribed body parts and embodied thoughts; in time the latter will become increasingly abstract. At this origin, however, thought is still material and objectal.

This basic Kleinian narrative, like its counterpart in Benjamin's *Trauerspiel*, offers a model for returning, in the analytic setting, to the origins of both language and dialogic object relating by way of a re-materialization of both. The realm in which self and other are built up, piece by piece, through a constant exchange of part objects across lines is the realm of affect, corporeality, *jouissance*, and *lalangue*. It can be re-accessed in analysis when analysand and analyst together reactivate this origin within the analytic space. Such reactivation is an archaically mimetic act. A further mimetic act is the projective identification by way of which the analysand invites, so to speak, the analyst into her embodied mental space. In projective identification the analysand (or analyst, for that matter) projects feelings so as to produce them mimetically in the analyst. It is an act of preservation. While projective identification is defined as an action performed by the projector, it is also a receptive, passive act: mimetically, the analyst experiences the analysand's archaic experiences corporeally and emotionally; thus they are retrieved for the analytic space and for the work of mourning. Related modes of access to this space, not necessarily in analysis, result from identifications with the remnants of infancy—symptoms, for example, and other body-experiences—or immersion in an anxiety, the symptom of a barely survived self-dissolution. Yet another path into originary mental space is the experience of art as embodied thought—the *sinthome*.

"Truth" and true thinking for Kleinian analysis, resides in these original processes as well as in their remnants that lie scattered, and most of the time unseen, in a subject's psychic and real *Umwelt* and appear also as "truth content" in works of art. If there is a fault in Klein's thinking, it is that she under-emphasizes—if she emphasizes it at all—the fact that an element of dissolution is still present in the synthesizing action of the depressive position (melancholia), and that objects taken into mental space to be repaired also have a dissolving effect on the subject-in-the-making. Generally marginalized from experience, these remnants from an original "catastrophic" life-and-death experience, are a Kleinian version of Benjamin's "creaturely" phenomena. Lying outside of the synthesizing symbolic realm—part matter, part thought, part body, and part *waste* from the perspective of later mature thought and experience— they are crucially at stake in the subject's negotiation of her mental space with the world. They are what Benjamin imagines the "mimetic faculty" digs for and retrieves. Even within Kleinian thought, though implicitly, such remnants are located in the materiality of the human, animal, vegetative, and object world surrounding the subject. We saw them previously in the clutter of the material and natural world of the German *Trauerspiel*, in what drives the king mad, makes him "creature." The creaturely things make true thought possible. They constitute a field of phenomena that embody the "messianic" in Bion's later elaborations, as we will see—"messianic" because they lie outside of containers and because they emerge from a field of Other-affection—and that break open systems of signification. They are *abject* in their status of lying outside of the symbolic order, of having been *cast out*. The way to reach them—and through them, pathways to untried subjective struc-tures—is mimetic and immersive, physical, affective, and cognitive at the same time. This phenomenology lies at the basis of what Benjamin wanted to imagine as the new thought of "coming philosophy" and as a revolution in experience. It is the phenomenology of the "catastrophized subject." It is catastrophe that makes possible the retrieval of true thought.

2. Catastrophe: Beckett, Bion, Benjamin

Beckett's play *Catastrophe*[7] is emblematic of that modernist literature that has come to be known as a "literature of disaster." It depicts the dissolution of the tragic hero and testifies to the twentieth century's "passion for the real" (Badiou 2007). Like most of Beckett's plays, *Catastrophe* begins and ends with a leftover—of humanity, perhaps, and certainly a leftover of the P(rotagonist). This leftover indicates the historical catastrophes that lie in the background of all of Beckett's work. The sting of this particular play is that at the end, P "catastrophizes"—silences and mortifies—the audience in turn.

On the surfaces of Beckett's plays, only the stark functions and initials of characters remain. Here, this wretched living corpse P that remains occupies a place between symbolic and real: he has no language, no will (until the end, that is), no social identity, only body, a body that signifies. Its real threatens to overshadow P's status as a symbolic subject. The autonomy and identity that seem to define the other two characters, D(irector) and (A)ssistant, are, in P, mortified by death and horror in the marks of historical catastrophe: the signs of the death camp *Muselmann* and of Abu Ghraib. (Throughout P stands—emaciated, ashen-colored, with "claw-like" hands with "fibrous degeneration," and faceless—on a black block, covered form neck to ankles in a black dressing-gown, bare feet visible, face covered, and head bowed.) But the play also unveils com-mercial art that commodifies suffering as obscene. With this self-reflection, the play uses catastrophic force in its attack on itself as representation. With P's obliterating final gaze at the audience, representation is blasted and dissolved. In a devastating mimetic moment, like P, the audience too goes silent.

"Catastrophe" is the central trope in a constellation of Benjamin's, Beckett's, and Bion's work, and Adorno's work on Beckett. All are haunted and ultimately determined by the historical and collective catastrophes occurring around them. Adorno reads Beckett's work as perennially taking place in a "post-catastrophic landscape," both an effect of and a form of protest against the lie of progress that continues to define the presentation of self of the western world. "Catastrophe" is both how we live in a commodified culture and its total management of life and what we need in order to break out of the stultified and compliant ways in which we live these often blank lives. For all four authors the legacies of the Enlightenment and instrumental reason are irretrievably linked to the terrors of the twentieth century.

Adorno's reading of Beckett (1961) in terms of this double meaning of "catastrophe" helps establish a link between Benjamin's critiques of instrumental reason and the barbarisms underlying the history of "progress." Adorno's critique centers on what he calls the "culture industry" of the post-World War II West and the stultifying cognitive and psychological effects of an order in which everything has become a commodity and reduced to its lowest common denominator—its exchange value. Identity and exchange have devoured all other difference. Links between human beings and between things and human beings have become perverse or have dissolved entirely. The state of affairs that Adorno describes—the target of his and Benjamin's critiques of experience—resonates with Bion's description of the fate of links in a schizoid and psychotic mental universe: links (relations) become perverse, cruel, and sterile (Bion 1959), and curiosity—and with it cognitive and mental growth—is thwarted. In Bion psychoanalysis acquires one of its most powerful, if subdued, voices of social critique insofar as groups and societies too become schizoid or psychotic and have largely become so in modernity. From 1934 to 1935 Beckett was Bion's patient.

Benjamin, Beckett, and Bion all seem to agree on one fundamental imperative in regards to psychological domination of this sort: "catastrophize" the subject, undo the Self, dissolve it in the face of catastrophic immobilization. For Adorno's Beckett it is the task of autonomous art, of a culture that resists psychic numbing, to do so. Poetic language and gestural theater have ways of attacking those repetitive links that have been imposed on culture and experience and that have impoverished language, making it instrumental, functional, and inhumane. Bionian psychoanalysis shares an important aim with Benjamin: in order for a human life to relate significantly with its environment language must be materialized, made into a body language. Bion's practice, restricted to a two-person analytic space, shoulders the task of breaking language open, making it strange, difficult, physical, even frightening. Functional language is quite literally attacked and wounded. The practice entails suffering.[8] Out of exposure to, even persecution by, a language that has the power to awaken areas in a subject's mental space that had been immobilized and rendered inaccessible arises a new capacity for experience of oneself in relation to objects.

Historical catastrophe and the "catastrophizing" resistance to it that Beckett's *Catastrophe* displays characterizes the work of Benjamin and Bion both and has deep-reaching and often destabilizing effects on their language and their ideas.

A. W. R. Bion

Bion is the most idiosyncratic of the British psychoanalysts associated with the London-based Tavistock Clinic.[9] The Clinic was founded in 1920 by a group of analysts to treat the traumatic effects of "shell-shock." Bion himself is said to have declared that he had "died on the battlefields of Flanders" during World War I. Freud and his immediate circle had initiated the study of "war neuroses" in 1919. Freud was called upon to offer his expert testimony on shell shock before the Austrian War Ministry in 1920. Partially, Freud's theory of trauma had its origins here: the nature of the events that he thought led to the symptomatology of the war neuroses correspond to the phenomenon that we now call trauma. The ego is overwhelmed. Instead of organic injury, Freud commented, traumatic cases were better described in terms of catastrophic "mental change" (Freud 1920/1961). Freud advocated psychoanalytic psychotherapy—the talking cure—rather than the further traumatizing electric shock treatment that the German military utilized during World War I. While Freud wrote little about the war neuroses, they were central to his subsequent psychoanalytic theory. In 1920 his theory of trauma led to his speculations about the death drive in *Beyond the Pleasure Principle*, where he explored psychic trauma and its cycles of destruction, overwhelming anxiety, and repeated, equally catastrophic binding. One of the most significant outcomes of these speculations was a new sense of the individual's sense of the precariousness of his own psychophysical space and consistency in a modern *Lebenswelt* with such potential to traumatize. Freud's work on the whole had blasted open any notion of the human being as self-sufficient and sovereign. The figure of Beckett's P as a representation of the "catastrophized" self alludes to Freud in a general way—the human psyche is defined by loss, absence, and the repetitive *fort-da* games initiated by the fundamental and traumatic intrusions of absence and death into every individual's life. This he had already established with his discovery of the Unconscious. The historical context of the birth of the death drive, however, points to the specifically modern trauma of technologized global war. Now, in light of these devastations, the modern individual seemed even further catastrophized and fragmented. It was Ferenczi who had emphasized this historical specificity and the historical relevance of psychoanalysis. Bion's war and early work experiences strengthened that Ferenczian trend.

In Bion's work the effects of absence and the consciousness of death become ever more pronounced, until it is fair to say that "catastrophe" becomes the central concept in his view of the psyche. Primal absence and awareness of death are to begin with devastating for every human, says Bion, as his haunting image of the infant torn and consumed by fear of death, needing to be "saved" by his mother's responsive "reverie," shows. Bion himself does not historicize his theory—he seems ambivalent about whether the conditions he describes are general or historically specific, or both. In any case, individual responses to this fundamental condition— reaction to loss—will determine varying degrees of "psychic catastrophe," depending on how catastrophically the initial loss is received as well as on whether the suffered loss is allowed to develop into an "open" psychic system or closes up defensively, unable to accept it. Thus there are two opposing meanings of catastrophe in Bion: catastrophe as a rigidly closed system and catastrophe as the irruption that tears systems open—perniciously or redemptively. Bion, like Benjamin, is interested in "catastrophic" transformations that are significant not only on the level of the individual, but on the level of the collective and culture as well.

Between the two world wars, as Bion's work became increasingly more psychoanalytic, he met Samuel Beckett in London. Beckett began an analysis with him, resulting in what was probably a mutually influential relationship. Something like a Bionian concept of "catastrophe" pervades Beckett's work, as does also Bion's theory of thinking—in particular in Beckett's first novel *Murphy*, which he wrote while in analysis with Bion. Following World War II, Bion underwent a training analysis, first with John Rickman, then with Melanie Klein.

In the British Object Relations world, Bion's theoretical "home," attention has shifted away from Bion's theory of group psychology (primarily in *Learning from Experience* [1962]), which gave him name recognition, to his concepts of "catastrophic change," "transformation," and "thinking," as he gradually moved into less traditional psychoanalytic territory, deviating from the parameters set by Freud and Klein. His heavy emphases on the redemptive possibilities of catastrophe and transformation place him into a productive constellation with Benjamin's intimations of subjective transformation. An individual's "mimetic faculty," Benjamin's central term of the 1930s, is in turn critical to understanding Bion. Like Benjamin, Bion implicates language as body and the body as language in the experience of intrapsychic catastrophe. Ultimately, it is their abiding interest in the effects of catastrophe on subject-object and subject-subject relationships that links them most powerfully. Naturally, for Bion it is the analytic relationship that may throw subjects out of their static psychic cocoons; for Benjamin it is a complex dialectics of reading and writing that has the power to redeem the subject from pernicious enchantment. Both believe that a fundamental transformation in experience can mobilize verbal and non-verbal languages and that engaging with the latter, together with other mimetic, identificatory experiences, can affect thinking itself.[10] This occurs when knowledge appears in an unprocessed and unconceptualized, in some sort of tangible, corporeal, shape. Both believe that recollecting the sources of our knowledge in this way can have significant effects on psychic, physical, and also social well-being. Transformation in thought and exposure to entirely different forms of knowledge are central to Benjamin's and Bion's theories of experience by which they criticize the flatness of a modern existence dominated by instrumental reason.

B. *Catastrophe and "Origin"*

While Bion made catastrophe, catastrophic change, and transformation the cornerstones of his theory, Adorno writes in his description of his friend Benjamin that "he grasped the essential precisely when walls of sheer facticity sealed off illusive essences. . . . [H]e break[s] the bonds of a logic which covers over the particular with the universal" (Adorno 1983, 230). This "breaking" of bonds, this overcoming of "illusive essences," necessitates blasting open the containment of the "universal" in order to liberate the unacknowledged, unspoken, unknown particular, swallowed up by an incessant drive for domination, control, and synthesis. Benjamin practices constant mortification and dissection of conceptual and cognitive containers by "redeeming"—as he describes it throughout his work—things, minds, and language from the commodified life of bourgeois enchantment. The history of "progress" has been catastrophic, not only because "progress" has always moved hand in hand with "barbarism," but also because it has robbed us of our ability to experience.

In his "Angelus Novus" (Thesis IX) from the "Theses on the Philosophy of History," Benjamin writes:

> There is a painting by Klee called *Angelus Novus*. It shows an angel who
> seems about to move away from something he stares at. His eyes are wide,

his mouth is open, his wings are spread. This is how the angel of history must look. His face is turned toward the past. Where a chain of events appears before us, he sees one single catastrophe, which keeps piling wreckage upon wreckage and hurls it at his feet. The angel would like to stay, awaken the dead, and make whole what has been smashed. But a storm is blowing from Paradise and has got caught in his wings; it is so strong that the angel can no longer close them. This storm drives him irresistibly into the future to which his back is turned, while the pile of debris before him grows toward the sky. What we call progress is *this* storm. (Benjamin 1940/1969, 257–8)

In his essay "Commitment" (1962) Adorno comments on Klee's image: "The machine angel's enigmatic eyes force the onlooker to try to decide whether he is announcing the culmination of disaster or the salvation hidden within it" (Rothberg 1997, 66). This fundamental paradox links Benjamin and Bion. It is also the fundamental insight of psychoanalysis: what can emerge from the "single catastrophe" and "wreckage upon wreckage" of fragmentary and fragmented moments in history and the shocked stasis outside of time that they produce, may be, afterwards, a re-reading of these moments in the light of the present so that the present too becomes legible. Only in this way is it possible to awaken from the "nightmare" that is History, for this History of "progress" has limited and deadened the transformability of past and present both. The Benjaminian historiographer explodes moments out of that continuum in order to "redeem" them. Such explosions are not necessarily always joyful or exhilarating in a Nietzschean way (though they are also Nietzschean), as one can see from Benjamin's angel's petrified face and body.

Benjamin and Bion are also linked by the extremes that order their thought and their tropes. While Benjamin talks about the heavy enchantments and drugged sleep of phantasmagoric existence in the nineteenth century, he refers to its messianic interruptions as "explosion," "blasting," "cessation." Bion refers to interruptions of analogously pacifying hallucinations in similarly catastrophic terms:

> . . . this explosion is so violent and is accompanied by such immense fear . . . that the patient may express it by sudden and complete silence (as if to go to an extreme as far from a devastating explosion as possible).
>
> The ensuing state can be most easily expressed by using surgical shock as a model: in this the dilatation of the capillaries throughout the body so increases the space in which blood can circulate that the patient may bleed to death in his own tissues. Mental space is so vast compared with any realization of three-dimensional space that the patient's capacity for emotion is felt to be lost because emotion itself is felt to drain away and be lost in the immensity. (Bion 1978, 12)

The silence Bion describes, and the stoppage a patient may enact in order to forestall catastrophic explosion, take place whenever there is a dramatic change in how a personal or collective history is to be represented, recorded, and inscribed—a change of paradigm. Benjamin expresses something like that in his essay "Problems in the Sociology of Language" (1934/2002), as we saw, regarding expression and "the resonance [of] the purely phonetic side of language" (69) in the body. He had broached this subject already in his *Trauerspiel* book. Such instances of either linguistic catastrophes (Bion) or linguistic transformations (Benjamin) are already familiar to us from Benjamin's *Trauerspiel* as well as from his descriptions of Hölderlin's Sophocles translations (1921/1996). Such changes in language are for Benjamin "original," mimetic, and non-communicative. Benjamin's quotation of Goldstein, which appears in my Chapter 4, reinforces the bridge between Benjamin and psychoanalysis. What Goldstein describes takes place in analysis, where such experiences and moments occur in the relationship between two subjects experiencing forms of mimetic interaction with each other in "language as such," as Benjamin and Lacan would say, and in blankness, silence, and physical shock, as Bion says. For single moments, immersions into "origin" occur. Benjamin seems to speak to Bion's notion of the blankness at the center of O, to which I will turn shortly, when he applies such "blankness" as "speechlessness" to the innermost core of language itself, as we saw in his letter to Buber (Chapter 4). The quoted passage also introduces Benjamin's difficult notion of "writing." Moreover, the idea of assigning the power of the deed (in the form of effects) to the "speechlessness" of language recalls the act that the "end of analysis" that I described in Chapter 2 incorporates.

C. Blasting the sovereign subject

Benjamin's messianism and "Redemption" are dependent not only on blasting open concepts and discourses, but also on dissolving the "sovereign" autonomous subject— the omnipotent, blinded, and violent fantasy of the Self—through self-dissolving suffering. We saw this in the baroque tyrant-martyr. Adorno writes, "In all his phases, Benjamin conceived the downfall of the subject and the salvation of man as inseparable" (Adorno 1983, 231). This statement alone would make Benjamin interesting to psychoanalysis. Catastrophe is an essential element of thought there, too. First, it refers to the spell on things and human beings in alienated and commodified traumatogenic cultures and families. Second, catastrophic blasts open up reified and alienated existences and transform experience.

Dissolving the sovereign Self, blasting its arrogant phantasmagorias, is catastrophic and necessary for Benjamin and Bion both. Bion's thought resonates with such ideas of rescuing the petrified objects within western civilization and its reified institutions and human relations. While Benjamin thought, in his messianic form of historical materialism, of "awaken[ing] the congealed life in petrified objects" (Adorno 1983, 233) within a sleeping bourgeois society entirely assimilated and driven by commodity fetishism, psychoanalysis gives itself the task of awakening the congealed lives of individual psyches. In both cases there is a transformation of historical catastrophe into living expression.

In line with Benjamin's Angelus Novus image, a single pile of loss and destruction may come into view in analysis demanding to be reconfigured in such a way that, with "patience," catastrophes are gradually confronted and allowed to find transformation instead of being swept away by the myth of "overcoming" the past.[11] By "patience" Bion means not so much the ability to defer satisfaction, but something much richer: deriving from *pati*, "to suffer, endure," "patience" carries the truer meaning of "a minor form of despair, disguised as virtue" (Bierce 1911).

D. *Container and contained*

Bion's catastrophe is linked to the relationship between "container" and "contained." The most extreme instance of psychic catastrophe within this relationship is psychosis: the primitive ego overwhelmed by raw, unprocessed sense-impressions and emotional data. Bion calls such data "beta elements," as opposed to the "alpha function" which transforms sense-impressions into thoughts. Beta elements are utterly concrete and are experienced as "things in themselves" that attack from the outside and that the attacked ego needs to repel to survive. This mechanism characterizes the earliest and most basic psychic life, where invading beta-elements are experienced in a struggle to the death. Bion defines psychosis as absence of thought and as consumption by these hyper-concrete attacking beta elements. In the psychotic, beta elements are not contained and without containment there is psychic chaos. This is an extreme form of catastrophe in the container-contained relationship. An entirely smooth fit of contained into container, on the other hand, at the other extreme, amounts to another form of catastrophe: with the final seamless "fit," mental space becomes empty. In between the two extremes lie more or less catastrophic events.

In the realm of language an explosive container-contained relation may take the shape of disturbances between linear, functional verbal language ("container") and a substance of complex emotional meaning ("contained"). In this scenario a speaker may be made into a stammerer (Bion 1978, 106) when his powerfully alive and complex substance explodes the words that cannot contain it, so that the body speaks through the cracks. On the other hand, verbal facility (words as containers) may be so parasitic on the meaning substance that nothing of substance is left; all is swallowed up, and language is reduced to empty prattle. Bion's attitude to such language resonates with Benjamin's attack on the degradation of language into "language as communication," a language that is one-dimensional, closed off from growth, and instrumental (Benjamin 1916/1996).

The potential for "catastrophic change" that a different use of language and a different way of thinking can have is for Bion embodied in the figure of the "mystic," "genius," or "messiah" within a society or group, as destructive force. The "mystic" provokes a backlash of conformity and re-containment by what Bion terms the "Establishment": "stabilization," "hierarchization," "delineation of borders," and some exclusionary way of dealing with "the problem of membership" (1978, 113) reassert themselves. Containment as assimilation and identification translates into closed systems. It refers to uniform, linear, and static narratives of group identity, such as are promoted by historical narratives, the official story, the family. In Beckett's play *Catastrophe* it is P who is contained by D and A (until P breaks out of that containment). Containment rules in the often parasitical Establishment. Benjamin takes that line of thought further when he says that it is the sheer force of iteration that transforms everything into conformity with the status quo: this becomes itself the catastrophe. This is the history of containment of the "messianic idea" (which is destruction in the sense of the Benjaminian "divine violence") when its life is suppressed (1978, 111). In this context especially, Bion's notion of psychoanalysis is of a destabilizing, deterritorializing force that is also a potential mode of social action insofar as it counters the assimilating force of group, culture, and Establishment and activates instead the potential for transformation. Bion's own language seems to seek un-assimilation. In terse, cutting, and often esoteric sentences he makes manifest the inherent necessity for psychoanalysis's own de-containments. Of the analytic session he says that it must elide memory as time (Benjamin's historicism) and concentrate on space. Like history becoming spatial in Benjamin's *Trauerspiel,* the analytic situation too makes mental space concrete: "Time has often been regarded as being of the essence of psycho-analysis; in the growth process it has no part. Mental evolution or growth is catastrophic and timeless" (1978, 107–8). The analytic situation consists of making the patient's mental space available to the analytic couple which immerses itself in it. Analysis is essentially an act of mimetic immersion into the container-contained relationality which defines the human personality: "Descriptions [of the history of messianic thought] . . . formulated with greater precision and sophistication, represent a pattern to which the human personality would be found to approximate" (1978, 114–15). The aim of analysis is the rediscovery of the "messianic idea"—explosiveness and transformability—by way of the "word" or "statement" that expresses mental space (which, as we will see, is neither all body nor all mind, but both) in order to transform the personality into a configuration that is capable of growth. Growth depends on "catastrophic change"—a term as Bionian as the *objet a* is Lacanian. Psychoanalysis itself must rediscover its own messianic idea:

> [P]sycho-analysis, the thing-in-itself, existed. It remained for Freud to reveal the formulation embedded in it. Conversely, once formulated by Freud it remains for others (including Freud himself) to discover the meaning of the conjunction bound by his formulation. (1978, 117)

In other words, to keep re-reading it catastrophically. Much of Benjamin's work and the idea of psychoanalysis both form a constellation around the "thing-in-itself" ("beta elements"): the messianic container-contained configuration, the centrality of "catastrophe." The human personality and the practice of analysis are "a voice reporting that the messianic idea is abroad" (1978, 119).

Ideas about processes of containment and catastrophe make up the heart of Bion's theory and its relationship to a person's capacity for experience and thought. An analysis demonstrates its vitality by concerning itself with these realities, wherefore it must always, directly and indirectly, deal with issues of claustrophobia and agoraphobia, because they are indicators of a patient's relation to containment and rupture (1978, 110). This is a mimetic-immersive reading process of the mental space the patient "draws" in the analysis by way of physical sensations, gesture, and emotional intensities. The value of the analysis lies not simply in its "containment" of such symptoms by translating them into language and preventing "acting out," which in itself can produce symptoms of claustrophobia (being too contained) in the patient; rather, spaces of containment and de-containment are concretely visited by the pair, anxiety and catastrophe are actually lived through. This is one of the central ways in which psychoanalysis is mimetic.

To the extent that an analysis is "about" therapeutic re-containment it betrays the true idea of psychoanalysis. Institutionalized psychoanalysis is good at that, says Bion: quoting Kurt Eissler, he says the more an establishment loads one of its "genius" members down with honors, the more successful it is at containing—and most likely silencing—him (1978, 78). Bion refers to one manner in which the early Christian community perfected its desire to contain and dogmatize its own messianic potential. It combined effective membership regulation with therapeutic know-how:

> In the instance quoted [Mark 9:38] the criterion provided by Jesus seems to be the successful cure and its attribution by the therapist to Jesus. The issues involved are: membership of the group as itself being a symbol of status; status, expressed by the locution "in Thy name" as a therapeutic agent; therapeutic result as a criterion of membership of the group. The solution was empirical but it accepted the criterion of therapeutic efficiency. (1978, 113–14)

Bion shares with Lacan the critique of psychoanalysis as "efficient therapy."

But Bion's affinities with Benjaminian thought—destructive and catastrophic de-assimilation of the materialities and singularities of history from History—are even more pronounced. In his presentation of the fate of the "messianic idea" throughout history, he refers to another history of assimilation of "one Christian Establishment": Catholicism, which thrived parasitically on pagan ideas and festivals that were vanquished and were made to disappear in a "bigger and brighter paganism" (1978, 112).

E. Attacks on linking

Bion's "messianic idea" makes attacks on links within the status quo of convention, the Establishment, the "official story." Conventional and mythical links in historiography and autobiography are undone, catastrophically liberating "new" material (that could also suddenly overwhelm the narrator), breaking down order, hierarchy, and communicative language itself. While the negative meaning of "catastrophe" refers to the Establishment relying to increasing degrees on the closed system as containment, cutting off the messianic idea's demand for transformation and growth, a positive catastrophe can take the shape of "attacks on linking." Bion defines such attacks on verbal thought, emotion, and reason negatively (Bion 1959, 307–8),[12] but I am arguing that they can also take on a messianic force: for instance in what takes place within the analyst herself when she is to renounce memory in favor of listening to the patient in *this* instant, torn out of the continuum of historical memory. Memory and desire project narratives that hijack the patient's words away from the present of mental space because they place them back into the mythical framework of the patient as well as the analyst's own "official" biography, thus dismissing the subject's truth in the now. Such a dismissal is an instance of the container greedily devouring the contained. Instead, the patient must be allowed to tear him- or herself out of the mythical continuum of both the family's and the analyst's memory, and the analyst must be willing to follow into new territory, the unknown (1978, 124). For the analyst this may indeed be a state of suffering as he must "de-contain" even himself.

Perhaps analyst and analysand communicate also non-verbally in such instances, by way of projective identification, and thus by the production within the analyst of "reverie," by way of which she accepts and "suffers" the analysand's projected beta elements, preparing for a working through together with the analysand. These beta-elements must be transformed into dream and thought. The analyst can achieve the first part of this process mimetically:

> Hallucinosis [beta-elements], which can be *observed* by divesting oneself of memory and desire, must have had some corresponding mechanism in the events that led to its inception. If the analyst can take certain steps that enable him to "see" what the patient sees, it is reasonable to suppose that the patient has likewise "taken steps," though not necessarily the same ones, to enable him to "see" what he sees. (1978, 40)

The analyst attempts to "be with" the patient regressed to the level of beta elements, and Bion writes in a footnote that it is this leaving behind of sense-based memory and desire that makes the analytic encounter frightening and potentially dangerous for the analyst (1978, 47, n. 1). In such a relationship slick verbal links are interrupted by something that is not easily named: a form of "suffering."

The analytic task, then, as far as container and contained are concerned, is to subject a catastrophic state of deadly repetition, domination, and inertia to catastrophic attack. Practically this occurs by way of the emergence of a new language forged by analysand and analyst together, a language that remains open to disruption and explosion—from within and without.

Beckett's treatment of language dramatizes both Bion's theory and Benjamin's description of catastrophe in the *Trauerspiel*. In all three the spotlight is on a language that is fragmented, broken, dragged through the mud and wasted, held up as a holey shroud signifying nothing except its own brokenness and inadequacy. Nevertheless, this wasted language is precisely what enables survival, Beckett's Unnameable's, "I can't go on, I'll go on" (Beckett 1953). I mentioned this view of language in the context of Lacan and Apollon. The same ambiguities and ambivalences are very much at work again in Bion: he denigrates language and simultaneously singles it out in his definition of psychoanalysis as the search for the "word" that reveals catastrophic structure as truth, while also, forever insufficient, slipping and falling—like the crown from Benjamin's marionette king's head.

F. O and Origin *(das Ausdruckslose)*

The messianic idea is a catastrophe, what Bion calls "O." Neither the messianic idea nor O are positive concepts in themselves, and they precede the thinking subject. O is, says Bion, the true thought without a thinker. It is the awareness of death that terrifies the infant who projects it into the mother so that he may receive it back in more bearable shape. It is her "reverie," her co-experiencing of the emotion, that makes it bearable. Relating across radical absence and the possibility of shared, mimetic reverie lie at the root of the most fundamental act of all: the formation of relationship. It is a mimetic relationship in that self and other form a constellation, thus a mutual identification, around O. O, like the self-other relationship, is constituted by loss itself and by incompleteness, what for Bion is the only true thought. Without that "true thought" subjects are stuck in the other catastrophe of denial, omnipotence, domination, and repetition.

Bion's theory really does not confine itself to the individual analytic setting. It encompasses theories of knowledge-construction; it also thinks of itself as a preserver of experience. It implies a theory of thinking that is linked to phenomena of destruction and change on a grand scale.

O is "Being," says Bion, an unrepresentable "ultimate reality" (1978, 26) and fundamental background; it is what all representation covers. It is close to Lacan's real as "darkness and formlessness" (26). In Benjamin's terms, one could say that O is the background to God's creative Word (Pizer 1987) or origin as breach (Weber 1991). Since it lies on the other side of form, structure, and representation, it explodes the ordinary word. As "origin" it underlies "the messianic hope, the Oedipus myth, the Babel myth, and the Eden myth . . . [These] are evolved states of O and represent the evolution of O" (Bion 1978, 85). It participates in the adumbrations of meanings of the archaic "mimesis" listed by Früchtl (Chapter 3). True "thinking" emerges from O; with affinities with both Lacan's and Benjamin's notions of pure language, this "true thought" does not emerge from any one thinker but is a "thought without a thinker": "Nobody need think the true thought: it awaits the advent of the thinker who achieves significance through the true thought. The lie and the thinker are inseparable" (1978, 102–3). True thoughts are there to be had. "O," says Bion, "persecutes" the thinker who believes that the thought originated in him alone, which makes him a "liar" (1978, 103).[13] O can create "martyrdom" as a way of suffering a persecution that a subject invites herself, just as it also creates "passion," "passivity," and "patience" in both analyst and "patient." Insofar as the "liar" thinks away from O and creates myth one should associate him with the "ego" as understood by Freud, Lacan, and Bion: as façade and clown. It is this ego that is exploded or just falls away with the appearance of the *sinthome*. Always lurking behind form, O is the explosion of containment. O is ungraspable, and yet, like Benjamin's origin, it is nevertheless traceable in immanent experience, in what Bion calls its "evolutions." In a field of exploded fragments, such as the psychotic's fragmented language, O underlies the entire field, just as the figure of baroque drama, the "corpse" (Pensky 2001), underlies Benjamin's culture of the Baroque. It is linked to destructiveness and death as radical absence, and it negates links, even though links emerge from it. In the analytic setting the analyst embodies O, and thus, in a strange way, also the corpse: "The analyst must focus his attention on O, the unknown and unknowable. . . . [T]he psychoanalytic vertex is O. With this the analyst cannot be identified: He must *be* it" (1978, 27). Analysis, interpretation, and psychological growth are "evolutions in O," similar to the allegorical evolutions in language of the Benjaminian martyr-allegorist. These evolutions, I have argued, undermine the eternal truths of the symbol (Chapter 2) with half-truths, something "half-told" (*mi-dire*) (Lacan 1998, 92).

Why is it important to point out these convergences in Benjamin and psychoanalysis? Bionian psychoanalysis is a concrete form of work that consists of re-thinking and re-configuring the nature of the subject-subject relationship in order to make the analysand capable of experience in O. This intersubjective analysis constructs "relevant constellation[s]" (Bion 1978, 33) made up of self- and memory-fragments that point in the direction of O, toward "at-one-ment," without ever *being* it. O explodes myths. Bion's religious language here ("atonement") is typical and can itself be placed into a constellation with the intrusions into Lacan's writing of "sin" and "St. Thome" in his seminar on the *sinthome*. "Sin" and "atonement" have something to do with Klein's "guilt" and "reparation," and the religious background of all of these terms is a constant in thinking about the subject's relationship with others. The terms are also linked by their embeddedness in and ambivalence toward processes of destructiveness and containment.

Non-totalization for Bion and Benjamin has significance ethically, politically, and aesthetically; but what does it mean to say that the analyst must "be O," the hole at the center, for the analysand (Bion 1978, 27)? Concretely, in the analytic setting it means, for example, that analyst and analysand regard one another as fluid, changing, and kaleidoscopic constellations from day to day in an effort to evade the myths of the past:

> Such belief [that analyst and analysand are the "same" person of the previous day] is suspect as the sign of a collusive relationship intended to prevent emergence of an unknown, incoherent, formless void and an associated sense of persecution by the elements of an evolving O. (52)

Specifically, the sense of the "hole at the center" is brought to bear by the presence of two *bodies* in the room. With Benjamin, Bion views the body as deconstructive of subjective sovereignty:

> The suspension of memory and desire [in approaching O] promotes exercise of aspects of the psyche that have no background of sensuous experiences. Paradoxically, the release of these aspects of the psyche enables them to reveal elements such as the non-verbal muscular movements of the tongue, as in stammer. (1978, 87)

O is destructive in its retreat from linking for the sake of the emergence of something different, something else, which lies at the core of Bion's notion of experience. Much of it is corporeal, and this fact belies Bion's avowed Platonism.[14]

Destructiveness in the realm of O replays Benjamin's emphases on interruptions and *caesurae* at work in his mimetic enterprises: for instance, in the redemptive breaking open of the historical context in order to "blast" out the concrete detail threatening to disappear forever in that great historical amnesia that Benjamin described in his 1940 *Theses on the Philosophy of History:* "In every era the attempt must be made anew to wrest tradition away from a conformism that is about to overpower it. . . . Only that historian will have the gift of fanning the spark of hope in the past who is firmly convinced that *even the dead* will not be safe from the enemy if he wins" (1940/1969, 255). In both cases we have a separating-out, a re-noticing, attentiveness: first regarding the body as the silent patient erased from experience, then, significantly, in the image of endangered corpses, which signify the origin—and the truth—of history.

Bion's concept of O shares in Benjamin's notion of revelation as "origin": the non-communicable abyss, encounterable only in its effects, the transformations that have emerged out of its "eddies." O and *Ursprung* are negative, anti-representational and sudden apparitions of truth as catastrophe and as cut. If O and *Ursprung* are of the order of revelation—and both authors use this sort of language—it is revelation of the subject's experience, through the *sinthome,* of the cut between language and *lalangue,* as

Lacan says; of human subjectivity experienced as "torn apart" and in passion after the Fall, as Benjamin says; and of the knowledge of non-knowledge, as Bion says. In all three cases "revelation" is a paradox in that it is conceivable and traceable only by a mimetic immersion into the effects of its distortions of communicative language (functional verbal language invaded by body-language) and into the body in pain for the salvation that lies at the heart of catastrophe.[15] In abrupt flashes these distorted effects uncover something else when language—or, alternatively, the work of art, "normal" perception, or the functional experience of the body—is suddenly stripped of its functionality and its communicative element is cut open: Benjamin's "language as such" and Bion's stammerer become the material of revelation. Lacan speaks of "revelation" of the subject's desire, Bion about the revelation of the particular "word" that has the ability to stimulate O (the tongue, for example), and Benjamin about the revelations of counter-history.

G. *"Corporeal substance," "the creaturely," Bion's body*

When communicative language is cut open, the "creaturely" appears. Benjamin's deconstructive understanding of the relationship between mind and body makes even more explicit the affinities of his thought with psychoanalysis. For Benjamin, "body" is an umbrella concept giving form to a chaotic amalgam of biological processes; together with the phenomenon of "mind" it makes up what he refers to as "corporeal substance." Like the Lacanian real and Bion's O, corporeal substance can only be thought of as non-conceptual matter. Like "mind," body is a language. Mind and body "are identical, and distinct simply as ways of seeing, not as objects," he writes provocatively in "Outline of the Psychophysical Problem" in 1922–23. "This combined mind and body is the category of its 'now' [*Nu*], its momentary manifestation as an ephemeral yet immortal being" (393). Corporeal substance is an instance of natural history: it exists in history and is simultaneously a singular event; as such it carries the mark of the absolute. Six or seven years later, in his essay on Surrealism, this same energetic "combination" of body and mind would become, as "revolutionary discharge" (1929*a*/1999, 192), energy usable for revolutionary purposes. "Corporeal substance," combining with *das Ausdruckslose*, breaks *through* form. It manifests itself as pleasure and pain, as *jouissance*, and as uncontrollable affect that "culminate[s] in intoxication [*Rausch*]" (Benjamin 1922–23/1996, 394). Within it "no form of any sort, and hence no limitation, is perceived." It is not the "ultimate substratum of our existence, but it is at least a substance in contrast to our body, which is only a function." "Body," as opposed to "corporeal substance," is the empty term with which we misname the latter, which is linked to pure language: "With his body, man belongs to mankind; with his corporeal substance, to God" (1922–23/1996, 395). The distinction Benjamin makes between "body" and "corporeal substance" is crucial: it is here that the *positive* and uncontainable aspects of the "creaturely"—which Santner (2006), for example, does not mention—are located. This "creaturely" opens up a space of silence—for the language-body and the body-language that have been banished from communicative language and from official history. Benjamin's elaboration of this train of thought reminds us that he had already been thinking about his work on the baroque and its laceration by martyrdom:

> The content of a life depends on the extent to which the living person is able to define its nature corporeally. In the utter decay of corporeality, such as we are witnessing in the West at the present time, the last instrument of its renewal is the anguish of nature which can no longer be contained in life and flows out in wild torrents over the body. (1922–23/1996, 396)

I will spend the rest of this chapter following the trajectory of this "last instrument of renewal": where and how does Benjamin rediscover it at the moment of western "decay," and what shape does it take? What part does it play in Benjaminian mimesis, and how do corporeal substance and mimesis relate to psychoanalysis, that other discourse about language, shock, and the materialization of language in the body?

Benjamin goes on to trace the "total vitality" of the life of the corporeal substance in its inevitable dissolution, in "fate" as well as its appearance as "truth content" in works of art. He rejects the "vitalist" temptation in philosophy, which, he says, can end only "in madness": "[T]otal vitality has its conciliatory effect only in art, every other form of expression must lead to destruction. The representation of total vitality in life causes fate to end in madness . . ." (396).

Inundation by the Real in life is "madness" and psychotic catastrophe, the corporeal substance overwhelming symbolic structure. The world of this corporeal substance, the world of the sea and of dream, is the ultimate background world of Bion's O. Benjamin, too, writes, "[F]or in the world of truth, the world of perception has lost its reality. Indeed, the world of truth may well not be the world of any consciousness" (399). Body-world threatens with psychic disintegration unless it is somehow channeled without suffocating it. Sign and physicality as corporeal substance are incommensurable; the latter will always be excessive. This leads Weigel (1996) to categorize physical symptoms as translations without an original, the body the impossible origin. Bion's sense that the body's part objects and drives must come to the rescue of O echoes this Benjaminian combination of body and mind in corporeal substance:

> Jewish mystics in particular find the voice a telling representation of the experience [of O] . . . Psycho-analytical observation certainly cannot afford to be confined to perception of what is verbalized only: what of more primitive uses of the tongue? (1978, 81–2)

Here again is the mimetic moment in Bion and Benjamin: both insist that for the revitalization of experience moments of immersion into this "corporeal" world of dissolution are indispensable.[16] While in 1922–23 Benjamin singles out art as the arena for corporeal substance, his views are modified with the evolution of his materialism. Additionally, Lacan teaches us the intimate relationship between analysis and art. Increasingly, for Benjamin, utopian social aspirations must be fed by the possibilities inherent within the body (Hansen 322). "Aesthetics," writes Buck-Morss, "is born as a discourse of the body." The pre-linguistic, pre-logical, pre-conceptual "senses maintain an uncivilized and uncivilizable trace, a core of resistance to cultural domestication" (Buck-Morss 1992, 6). They endanger the autonomy of Kant's transcendental subject, writes Buck-Morss,

> [n]ot only because they unavoidably entangle him in the world, but, specifically, because they make him passive ("languid" [*schmelzend*] is Kant's word) instead of active ("vigorous" [*wacker*]), susceptible, like "Oriental voluptuaries," to sympathy and tears. (9)

The word "Oriental" here recalls Hölderlin, just as the passivity and the "sympathy and tears" recall the martyr monarch of the *Trauerspiel*. Passively the subject falls hostage to his corporeal substance: to mortality, pleasure and pain, and affect. Miriam Hansen's term "innervation" is again appropriate here:

> the process by which "nerve-force" is supplied to organs and muscles, or the "stimulation of some organ by its nerves." [OED] In [Freud's] (and Breuer's) work on hysteria, however, Freud uses *innervation* more specifically to describe the phenomenon of "conversion," the transformation of an unbearable, incompatible psychic excitation into *"something somatic."* (1999, 316)

Symptoms are innervations. Thus, for example, one of the symptoms of Susan, the case documented in my last chapter, was to blush unpredictably when looked at, which Milner interprets as an unconscious need to let others see "the denied flow of feeling, so that it can be saved from total extinction," to have it "be real through being preserved by those who see it" (Milner 1969, 325n). This is a Benjaminian moment insofar as the suffering body recollects traces of an original affect, demanding to be named. Benjamin historicizes such bodily expression and memory: it is in modernity in particular that the body is subject to shock, inscribed on the body in "painful grimaces and erratic convulsions" (Richter 2002, 69), and it is also in modernity that awareness of the body is "decaying." For Benjamin, the body flickers up as a historical image.

Aby Warburg's *Pathosformeln*, those intensive spots representing bodily expressive gestures, swirls of hair or clothing, are in this sense also mnemic traces, forms of historical memory, carriers, like corporeal substance, of memory.[17] Pieces of the body return to haunt the imaginary wholeness, knowledge, and intention of body and mind both (Weigel 1996, 153). Thus we see a convergence of Benjamin's identification of the origin of modern experience and the birth of psychoanalysis.

Benjamin's aim in awakening "corporeal substance" and "innervation," Warburg's aim in experiencing the petrified agitation contained within the *Pathosformeln*, and the psychoanalytic aim in digging into body-words or word-bodies in patients, is to overcome the silencing enchantments of individual and collective "selves," petrified into defensive cocoons, and to reawaken the senses. Such corporeal recollections are transmitted mimetically from work to viewer, from analysand to analyst, from object to subject, and from subject to subject. In art, for example, Hansen describes as Benjamin having been influenced in this by Sergei Eisenstein's notion of

> physiologically "contagious" or "infectious" movement that would trigger emotional effects in the viewer, a form of mimetic identification based in the phenomenon known as Carpenter Effect (Hansen 1999, 321)

that would re-empower the individual body, which, in turn, has the power to restructure a mental space that has become rigidified.

All of this work shares a theory of writing: recollecting and re-examining the images produced in handwriting are acts performed by body, mind, and language together. This is what Benjamin had meant by "stirring writing" in his *Trauerspiel* book.

Benjamin links corporeal substance and language in ways that undermine Western thinking about the mind-body relation and associate him with the psychoanalytic versions of such frontier concepts. This "body-space" (Weigel 1996), this intensity that Benjamin opens up, is explosive with "uncontainable excess" (Richter 2002, 58). Like Bion's O it explodes the containing functions of knowledge and reality. The body of language and the language of body are both pervaded by the uncanny and explosive presence of real drives that can catastrophically fragment, and, when allowed, transform experience.

Language and corporeal substance come together most perfectly, perhaps, given Benjamin's premises, in the act of naming. Together they constitute paradisal language: as sound is the purest principle of language (Benjamin 1916/1996), and the name "has as its sole purpose and its incomparably high meaning that it is the innermost nature of language itself" (1916/1996, 65), and the name as sound is voiced immediately by a speaker, Adam's physical presence in God's creative act (whether we read this figure literally or figuratively) is a *sine qua non*. Corporeal substance, as being in, reading, and naming the body, is a vantage point that is as crucial to the recuperation of history itself to which Benjamin was dedicated, as it is to Susan's recovery: during the most eventful moments of her recovery, Susan and Milner found that a particular set of recurring curves in her drawings suggested the body-memories of having first sat up as an infant (Milner 1969, 188–9).

3. Leakage and Post-Catastrophic Thinking

What is it that anxiety, symptoms, and the lacerations that original remnants unleash explode out of their contexts? My answers have been "origin," "martyrdom," Lacan's *lalangue*, and "waste." To them we must turn, then. Psychoanalytically speaking, I have said, this remnant is materiality that emerges with minimal defensiveness at "the end of analysis"—recognition of the subject's disarray and identification with the symptom (Lacan). Further, it is the capacity to suffer and to withstand the terrors and "catastrophe" of O (Bion). Third, it is the body—and thus death (Freud, Klein). Benjamin's "corporeal substance," which Caygill refers to as the "absolute," and I have referred to as "origin," is short-hand for all of the above. It judges merely communicative language as lie: truth begins and ends with the "catastrophe" of corporeal substance. Benjaminian immanent criticism, which uncovers this sort of "truth content" in works, traces the distorted and inconspicuous ways in which the absolute manifests itself and thus, as Caygill puts it, aids in inventing the future (1998, 34). Why "inventing the future"? Because it breaks open myth and digs for alternative narratives. Benjamin's historical materialism reveals the absolute folded into the finite—or, in psychoanalytic terms, the real folded into symbolic structures. For Benjamin and psychoanalysis both, the embodied mind is folded into the language of everyday living—in distortions, interruptions, silences: *das Ausdruckslose*.[18]

Kleinian and Bionian theory of psychoanalytic practice provides examples of how pre-verbal and pre-conceptual phenomena, central to Benjamin's understanding of the mimetic, can be re-experienced. Kleinian and post-Kleinian analysis and Benjaminian explorations of such areas in his writings on color, drawing, and handwriting are interested in the question of how to *think* these affective, corporeal, and other-invaded constellations of the subject and how to imagine their enactment.

Bionian "reverie" (Bion 1965/1977) is one such enactment: it involves "knowing," in some way, that one's own self is dependent on being "returned," in bits and pieces, to oneself by the object (whether that be a work of art, an interlocutor, or an other). The not-yet-thinking infant projects beta elements—raw stimuli and fear of death— into the mother who "digests" them and returns them as something more like thought into the infant. This process of reverie is similar to the contemplation of art, and once more I refer to Warburg's *Pathosformeln:* in pockets of almost pure affect, of residues of the real, the viewer of works of art finds real remnants of herself and is enabled to use this projected space as *Denkraum*, the distance and breathing room necessary for experiencing her own corporeal substance. Similarly, through the mother's immersive "reverie," the infant is enabled gradually to build its own mental space as a space that thinks, enabling its corporeal substance to grow. The image-concept of reverie claims that the self necessarily makes a detour through the Other. The relationship between analyst and analysand offers the same opportunity: a meeting of two O's—a mimetic, immersive relationship in which two mental spaces enable the retrieval of corporeal substance for each other. Projective identification results from anxiety and unfolds suffering, "patience," and passion, but revitalizes experience. Holes generate thought.

Pockets of leaked substance in the relationship between a pair of O's or a pair of mental spaces appear in art in a number of other ways, too. Beckett's theatrical work is permeated with paired characters. While those relationships usually take the shape of an endless ping-pong of stereotypical phrases, they are also punctuated by moments (sometimes verbal, more often gestural) that interrupt that sterile catastrophe. In these moments corporeal substance expresses itself and a mimetic encounter between the gesture and its viewer occurs. Examples are Hamm covering his face with a blood-soaked handkerchief (his "old stancher") in *Endgame*, the Auditor's helpless arm-movements punctuating the Mouth's stream of words in *Not I*, and, devastatingly, P's final gesture of lifting his head to meet the gaze of an audience unthinkingly applauding his misery and mortification in *Catastrophe*. It is the task of the analytic pair to release corporeal substance and thereby the future from the analysand's defensively rigidified and empty history.

In "Berlin Chronicle" (1933*f*/1978) Benjamin refers to the sites of mental or bodily memory where such (re-) constructions out of the contemplation of the past occur as "theater":

> Language shows clearly that memory is not an instrument for exploring the past but its theater. It is the medium of past experience, as the ground is the medium in which dead cities lie interred. He who seeks to approach his own buried past must conduct himself like a man digging. This confers the tone and bearing of genuine reminiscences. He must not be afraid to return again and again to the same matter; to scatter it as one scatters earth, to turn it over as one turns over soil. For the matter itself is only a deposit, a stratum, which yields only to the most meticulous examination what constitutes the real treasures hidden within the earth: the images, severed from all earlier associations, that stand—like precious fragments or torsos in a collector's gallery—in the prosaic rooms of our later understanding. True, for successful excavations a plan is needed. Yet no less indispensable is the cautious probing of the spade in the dark loam, and it is to cheat oneself of the richest prize to preserve as a record merely the inventory of one's discoveries, and not this dark joy of the place of the finding itself. Fruitless searching is as much a part of this as succeeding, and consequently remembrance must not proceed in the manner of a narrative or still less that of a report, but must, in the strictest epic and rhapsodic manner, assay its spade in ever-new places, and in the old ones delve to ever-deeper levels. (25–6)

The "scene" describes beautifully the psychoanalytic process as well. Bion refers to what Benjamin calls "the images, severed from all earlier associations" as "mental space." At its core is something akin to "dream-like memory": "The emotional tone of this experience is not peculiar to the dream: thoughts also come unbidden, sharply, distinctly, with what appears to be unforgettable clarity, and then disappear . . ." (1978, 70). Bion wishes for some way of "representing mental phenomena without words" (1978, 42) as words necessarily narrativize.

Such sites of recovery constitute Benjamin's unrepresentable "folds," which I will attempt to unfold in the following section.[19] I understand Benjaminian folds as the pockets of *anomie* that make up the principle as well as the energy of Benjaminian redemption. The "fold" as trope—though it is for sure not merely trope, but a literal realization of *das Ausdruckslose*—is closely related to the *Bilderverbot* that pervades Benjamin's thinking about art, language, the body, and the imagination (Menninghaus 1992, 33). While his early piece entitled "Conversation" (1913–14/1996) is a stunning example of *das Ausdruckslose* and origin as it also unfolds in psychoanalysis, I concentrate here on the later, more corporeal, work. The fold interrupts, "returns" upon itself and its inscription is concealed. While "digging" releases "images" for Benjamin, their function is to point to something else and then to evaporate. Bion's O, too, as the liminal area between body and language, makes the *Bilderverbot* central to his theory of recovery. Benjamin's, Bion's, Klein's and Lacan's thought are brought into a constellation by way of the unspeakable they surround: the hole of extimacy that interrupts representation.[20] The "real within the symbolic," Jacques-Alain Miller's definition of extimacy (1994), is always a matter of an excitatory excess in a provisional and temporary containment. Such martyred, holey language contains the sayable *and* the unsayable—both its own excess *and* its own limitations, and the same sort of explosive tension characterizes the language-body relationship.

Neither Benjamin nor Bion—nor Milner or Susan, as we will see in the last chapter—stop at the abyss, however: out of the hole of extimacy, O, martyrdom, and the fold emerges a life of transformation.

4. Analytic and Benjaminian Relation

Even though in the passage I quoted from his "Berlin Chronicle," Benjamin speaks of "images" that can "stand"—thus sounding like empirical "finds"—it is clear that what this "theater" yields are images whose medium is language. They are subject to distortion and historical transformation, to lives and afterlives. Benjamin's theater of memory and Bion's "mental space" that consists of the materials, in the form of alpha and beta elements, of a person's history, are the originating fount of what Benjamin calls "faithful" allegory. Both are filled with material remnants and ruined "torsos." The psychoanalytic conjunction throws special light on this in the "*erregte Unruhe*" ("excited unrest") that, according to Benjamin, permeates baroque allegory. It now appears that Benjamin's goal of redeemed relationship with objects and other subjects, of "conversation," emerges from it, and that the analytic relationship may concretize it. The destructiveness associated with the encounter of two O's in Bion is defined by the same potentially unbearable anxiety that marks the baroque martyr-allegorist. Bionian analysis must move first from O to K ("knowledge," the always limiting representation via the depressive position), and then from K to O (1978, 36), which, in its most creative transformation into an infinite conversation, becomes F ("faith") (1978, 71). This process is accompanied by a high degree of anxiety, however.

The anxiety in both cases is a product of *anomie*. For Bion, *anomie* comes into being as soon as psychoanalysis recognizes that its field is "nonsensuous" (1978, 57). By "nonsensuous," I believe Bion means an object that remains outside of the everyday reality established and collectively named by a human community. Beta-elements are excessively real and unspeakably proximate objects that lie outside of the Symbolic. Through "evolutions in O" such elements emerge in the analytic space as non-symbolic words, body language, and acting out; they fragment, scatter, and disseminate. Through anxiety-ridden "seeing," "reading," "hearing," and "immersing" processes, in which the willing analyst is ready to encounter such elements—which are "inscribed," as it were, in the analyst's mental space—the analytic pair "receive" them together and begin, through an intermittently appearing depressive position, to forge new unities and constellations among them. In most analyses this will take place through the medium of a strangely broken, perforated, and internally disseminated and disseminating language.

It is this latter reality of language that may be under-theorized in psychoanalysis. In "Short Shadows (II)" (1933*a*/1999) Benjamin describes such a conception of language in an image both wistful and haunting:

> *The Tree and Language.* I climbed up an embankment and lay down under a tree. The tree was a poplar or an alder. Why have I not remembered which? Because while I was gazing up into the foliage, following its movements with my eyes, I suddenly found that, within me, language was so gripped by it that momentarily the age-old marriage with the tree was suddenly reenacted once again in my presence. The branches and the treetop swayed to and from reflectively, or leaned over in rejection; the twigs bent down toward me or leaped upward; the foliage braced itself against a sharp gust of wind, shuddered, or met it halfway; the trunk was firmly planted in the solid ground; and one leaf cast its shadow over another. A gentle breeze signaled the start of a wedding and soon carried throughout the world the children who had quickly sprung from this bed, like an image speech. (1933*a*/1999, 699–700)

The thought-image (*Denkbild*) describes a confusion in names ("Why have I not remembered which?") in the speaker brought about by the language of "overnaming" (Benjamin 1916/1996), even as "the trunk . . . firmly planted in the solid ground" points to the truth of the language of names. The confusion is productive of a sort of internal bursting of language, an "overnaming" in a positive sense, whose task it may be to restore a static idea of "origin" of language with a fluid and endless one. The moment of confusion leads to a mimetic moment in which "language" and "tree" are "married." With this recognition the speaker immerses himself in the contemplation of the language-tree that is in perpetual movement: "leaning," it procreates by way of association and displacement (metonymy); "leaping," it itself attempts to immerse itself in "origin" ("upward"); "one leaf cast its shadow over another" in the act of condensation (metaphor), and thus the language-tree generates dissemination "throughout the world." The language-tree's "children"—the creative distortions that alone can dig into the earth to retrieve what has been forgotten—recall the "newborn" of "The Mimetic Faculty" (Benjamin 1933e, 721), just as they also refer to the general presence of the redemptive world of children in Benjamin's thought. As we will see in the case of Susan in Chapter 6, images, signs, and marks in writing and drawing have histories, too; like language-children, they transform and evolve and enable sparks of non-sensuous similarity between present, past, and future in the analytic space and thus a "reading" of the patient's "mental space." Like the field of contemplation in Benjamin's "The Tree and Language," the analytic space is a site of observation, immersion, attentiveness to the tiniest nuances of PS explosions of D, and of verbal, corporeal, and literal "writing" and "drawing."

Richter makes an important observation regarding the passage from "A Berlin Chronicle" that I quoted earlier: "The contents of memory," he writes, "those crusty layers and hardened sedimentations, Benjamin continues, need to be *umgewühlt* (ploughed through, churned, rototilled) in order to yield mnemonic images" (Richter 2002, 44). The *Umwühlen* that Richter refers to goes on constantly in Benjamin, most explicitly, perhaps in *Berlin Childhood around 1900*; it also goes on in the analytic space.[21] All of these images repeat an original act of "writing."

5. Origin and Mimesis: Benjamin's "Agesilaus Santander"

Benjamin's work, more so than Bion's, is always also literary. Here I will read Benjamin's autobiographical piece "Agesilaus Santander" (1933g/1999) as a poem into which the phenomena I have been discussing are folded. I will follow this reading with a more theoretical description of Benjaminian graphology, which will then act as a bridge into Chapter 6, where I read Susan's drawings graphologically.

Mimesis and transformation, that is, Benjaminian "distortion," are the two processes and practices constituting the Benjaminian tasks of mimetic retrieval and preservation of what had been rendered imperceptible. They emerge from the "eddy" of origin, and they lie at the core of the ethics of Lacanian and Bionian psychoanalysis. "Agesilaus Santander," the enigmatic name Benjamin gives himself in the eponymous autobiographical text (in two versions) of 1933, one of his most esoteric pieces, is driven by them as well: self-naming, which is its topic, is an identificatory and mimetic gesture, a return to the original act of being named. Benjamin takes on the name given to him by his parents, which is not Jewish, thus concealing an utterly unspoken Jewish name. The act of re-writing the name (which is no "true" name) has a protective function—most immediately, to conceal the bearer's Jewishness in the face of the rise of Nazism. The same act that recalls traditions—"he followed the Jewish custom of keeping [the names] secret" (714)—and is thus restorative is also an act of distortion. Benjamin writes that it is possible to reach manhood—that is, to come to know an original name—more than once, where manhood for him, who is not pious, marks a return to origin for the sake of transformation: "because the secret name can remain the same and untransformed only for the pious, the man who is not pious may experience its transformation at a stroke with his new manhood." At this juncture Scholem's guess regarding the key to the name becomes important: "Agesilaus Santander" is an anagram, a re-configuration, of "Der Engel Satanas" (Scholem 1983). This introduces the text's and its images' preoccupation with destructiveness, fallenness, transformation, even heresy (as the *sinthome* is for Lacan and "O" is for Bion) in the context of self-preservation.

This first vague allusion of destructiveness is furthered when one reads that the name ceases to be an "enrichment," that its "image falls away when the name is heard." An emptying out occurs. This loss alludes to the fall of the language of names into the language of judgment and also to the fall into catastrophic history, as "that person"—whom Benjamin now dissociatively distinguishes from the first "I" who "occupied" "my room" "in Berlin"—who emerges from the name as soon as it is spoken does not "appear[...] human" but is "fully armored and accoutered from my name." He "fixes his [own] image to the wall: New Angel." We witness a de-fusion of the strands of subjectivity, a projected identification of "the person" emerging out of the name with the New Angel (Klee's *Angelus Novus*), and an accelerated destructiveness that takes the shape of the perishing angels of the kabbalah of which the New Angel is also one. Their perishing is as constant as their "sing[ing of] His praises." Subjectivity undergoes the falling and the emptying out that characterizes the Baroque. But it also recollects its origin of the name: out of its destructive-and-transformative "eddy" emerge transformations of new selves, even if they are destined to disappear again. Except that the speaker holds fast to the image of the New Angel and keeps him "excessively long." We do not know how exactly he does so, but it seems that his gaze keeps him, as that is also the method used by the Angel to escape Benjamin's thrall: by enthralling Benjamin in turn with his, the Angel's, "feminine aspect,"[22] which will "hold him stationary in the face of the woman whom he was determined not to abandon." The bearer of the "feminine aspect" is still the Angelus Novus, the

horrified contemplator of history, whose hymn-singing and perishing rep
resent redemptive moments that are dependent on both the mimetic and
unfolding reading of the past and the catastrophic "return" into the naught
of the origin. All are mimetic acts. Benjamin, though, as "I," is not privy to
any transcendental sphere of origin and end, but merely exerts his power
in "his ability to wait," held in thrall by his encounter with the "feminine
aspect": "nothing could overcome the man's patience." In fact, he has most
powerfully identified with the angel's "pinions," which enable him to interrupt the constancy of the perishing, even if only for an instant, and "in
translation," so to speak, in love, as the pinions allow him to enthrall "the
woman." "Love" interrupts the perishing, in waiting, and in a moment of
preservation.

The figure of the angel, a force of the mimetic, is persecuted ever
more clearly by loss, dissolution, and evanescence: "But the angel resem-
bles everything from which I have had to part: the people, and especially
the things. He dwells in the things I no longer possess." Nevertheless, he
also teaches the "doctrine of the similar": "He makes [the things] transparent, and behind each of them appears the figure of the person for whom
they are intended." Mimesis is non-sensuous in this pairing of object with
the object's intended; the mimetic relation is defined literally by insight
rather than sensuous similarity. And now "I" and "the angel" are once
more closely identified: in terms of their propensity to "go[. . .] away
empty-handed," which describes their desire not for fusion but for similarity in difference, the center punched out of an enclosing mimetic act to
make room for the new. Pervading all of this is the power of fascination. It
is the fascination of reading, in Benjamin's expanded sense. Through the
"face," the gaze points to origin and future simultaneously:

> [The angel] looks [whomever he has his eye on] steadily in the eye, for a long
> time, and then retreats—in a series of spasms, but inexorably. Why? To draw
> him after himself on that road to the future along which he came, and which
> he knows so well that he can traverse it without turning round and letting
> him whom he has chosen out of his sight.

The "road to the future" is the messianic cessation of time that happens in
the *caesura* ("spasms") and the detour, in the acting out of which the angel
now seems to imitate—or confirm?—the "I." In this interruption recollection, self-destructive reflection, intersubjectivity, and writing and reading
processes occur even as the destructions of the written, of the image, of the
angel himself, refer to the messianic cessation—Bion's positive catastrophe.
The "space" that is described here, the "detour" of reading and writing

history, and of love, is a space in history that is aware of the messianic: "happiness," which recapitulates "origin."

> He wants happiness—that is to say, the conflict in which the rapture of the unique, the new, the yet unborn is combined with that bliss of experiencing something once more, or possessing once again, or having lived. This is why he has nothing new to hope for on any road other than the road home, when he takes a new person with him.

Retrieving experience and renewal by the movement of *retreat*, an act in which the "I" and the angel identify most closely: this retreat is the "edge" and the line of the Other where unfolding and transformation take place, where the self rebuilds herself in dialogue with the Other.

6. *Reading and Drawing Mental Topographies (Thinking)*

In "Doctrine of the Similar," Benjamin writes,

> . . . the literal text of the script is the sole basis from which something similar can form itself. Thus, the nexus of meaning which resides in the sounds of the sentence is the basis from which something similar can become apparent out of a sound, flashing up in an instant. Since this nonsensuous similarity, however, exerts its effects in all reading, at this deep level access opens to a peculiar ambiguity of the word "reading," in both its profane and magical senses. (1933*b*/1999, 697)

Mimetic practice and thought are founded on the ability to read similarity as well as produce it—whether consciously or unconsciously. Overall, Benjamin's "nonsensuous" means not so much "immaterial" as it means "non-visual." Gleaning (*herauslesen*) similarity, perceiving it as it flits past in an instant, means accessing "origins," most immediately in the corporeal substance. The individual wishing to recover his or her own history may attempt to access the original structures of emergent subjectivity. For example, body-memories may emerge from registering and identifying with one's body's unconscious gestures through immersion into the "hand-writing," the unconscious dimension of script or drawing, or by contemplating the deep structures of art works, gestures, or faces, all of which, according to Benjamin, "are similar." In his graphological essays, Benjamin looks at the imagistic dimension that the physical act of writing produces alongside, or within, the letters. These are all immersive and mimetic reading acts that lead to readers identifying unconsciously, then consciously, with their "physiognomies," their lines and their traits. *Herauslesen* thus means making thinkable what was at first unthought. It relies both on the reader's immersion into his or her own corporeal substance, her interlocutor's, and both of their bodies' "writing," thus interrupting their everyday functioning, like freezing a film to bring a particular image into conscious contemplation. This Benjaminian reading process is both an attempt to read "folds"—sudden interruptions in abstract meaning—and an "unfolding" process, which can never fully "know" the fold. Consequently, Benjaminian reading is a process of being attentive to and re-encountering folds.[23] The fold introduces body-experience into script. In these anomic folds what Caygill calls "the absolute" breaks through the "surface" (1998, 4).

Similarly, as far as meaning goes, for Benjamin the ideal manner of reading involves "interruptions of linearity," taking the shape, for example, of exploding individual signifiers out of the sequence of a sentence, and placing them into new constellations, through "strange points of connection between words" (Menke 1991, 127). The new constellations produced by every new "reading" exclude other possibilities as other elements are thereby rendered invisible but continue to wait, alive, in the background, only to break open again the newly emergent constellation, and then to disappear again. The process is contained in his kabbalistic image of the "perishing angels" in "Agesilaus Santander," as we saw. At all times, any text to be read is alive with tension between manifest and latent, with explosive power, like Bion's uncontainable O as the uncontainable that explodes knowledge that thinks of itself as whole and contained. Menke too notes this tension between manifest and fixed and, on the other hand, latent and fluid instances of signification. This tension and the resulting crisis in meaning underlie Benjamin's references to "ornament": ornament is "structure and inscription which cannot be definitively determined" (1991, 123), a floating signifier, as far as meaning goes, indeterminate supplement as far as handwriting goes. Reading and perception of "ornament" is destabilizing and kaleidoscopic. Moreover, such reading is mimetic and both shapes and confirms the structure of subjectivity. In the early 1930s Benjamin attributes such reading to children (including himself as a child), and he prescribes it to the modern "subject in crisis," as Richter puts it (2002, 41), who has lost the illusion of stable meaning and must therefore re-think himself. This form of reading embodies the "coming philosophy."

In the analytic context this means enabling interruptions of a patient's empty experience and time. Incursions by corporeal substance effects a re-drawing of the lines and configurations of the subject-subject relationship. It is not only the process, proper to the Benjaminian and the psychoanalytic method, of reading the materialization of language—in handwriting, drawing, and non-sensuous configurations of the analyst-analysand encounter—in attempts to ease the modern subject's plight that is remarkable. Equally interruptive, as far as understanding "knowledge" goes, are the ways in which Benjamin and (post)-Kleinian psychoanalysis both come to regard certain forms of inscription and their readings as the mimetic expressions of radical changes taking place in a subject's relation to "self," other, and the "material community." While "mimesis" in the form of inscription is a material record of such transformations of mental space, the redeemed self-other relationship, also immersive and "catastrophic," comes into being inter-subjectively and in a more non-sensuous evolved way in the analytic relation. All of these new configurations of mental space topography that Benjamin alludes to in his esoteric mimesis and graphology essays can be understood better by looking more carefully at the analytic relation through Milner's case history of Susan. At stake everywhere here is thinking about "thinking."

We know that such image-reading for Benjamin is always historical. It is always also a rescue of "marginal" elements of the past that are threatening to disappear forever. "Thinking" is for Benjamin and psychoanalysis recovery of the past. Both collective and individual histories require a constant and simultaneous process of recovery and explosion. Thus graphology is to be an "archaeological excavation" (Weigel 1996, 110). The best example of Benjamin digging out semantic and material traces from within signifiers is his *Berlin Childhood around 1900* (1932–34/2006), where these traces are fully understood only when the author follows the chains of associations that are wrought out of the reading process I have described.

Through the analytic relation and its Benjaminian analogue of dialogic reading a subject comes into being who has been mortified in his sovereignty, whose "crown" has slipped into the "creaturely." This subject has passed through an abjection and has constructed—through the "artifice" of material and mental writing and drawing—a new ego, a Lacanian *sinthome*, a dialogical self. I will continue looking at the role played of lines, points, and circles in writing and graphology, as these are the similar ways in which mental space (*Denkraum, Denkbild*) represents its own reconfigurations in Benjaminian graphology and post-Freudian psychoanalysis.

PART 3

Benjaminian Psychoanalysis

Introduction to Part 3

In Chapter 6, I correlate Benjamin's theory of mimesis and its corporeal and graphological manifestations with the 1950s era psychoanalytic case history recounted by British psychoanalyst Marion Milner in her book, *The Hands of the Living God.* Milner was an analyst associated with the British Psychoanalytic Society, influenced by Bion, and friendly with Winnicott. She was essentially a Kleinian and had been analyzed by Sylvia Payne and D. W. Winnicott. I present her analysis of Susan as an unwitting Benjaminian re-construction of a catastrophically damaged personal history and a subsequent series of acts of retrieval and preservation of mental space. The latter occurred by way of a therapy that I view essentially as an enactment of Benjaminian mimetic graphology (Benjamin 1928/1999; 1930/1999). The case came alive only when it veered away from traditional verbal analysis and transformed into a collaborative graphological reading of the 4,000+ doodles and drawings made by Milner's patient Susan.

Susan, whom Milner and Milner's analyst Winnicott diagnosed as schizoid, arrived in Milner's office one day, complaining of loss of the ability to experience and "saying three things: that she had lost her soul; that the world was no longer outside her; and that all this had happened since she received ECT [Electroconvulsive Therapy] in hospital, three weeks before coming to [Milner]" (Milner 1969, xix). Susan's complaints suggest profound alienation from a capacity for experience, which, if already pathological before the ECT, had been greatly enhanced afterwards. In defense against her sense of psychic disintegration and acute psychic agoraphobia she had engineered her psychic withdrawal from the world. During the course of her analysis Susan refers to her withdrawn state as a "cocoon," a containment and envelopment defending against the threat of total

psychic disintegration that she has partially experienced. Susan's main initial complaints regard modern psychiatric technology. Milner was later to
comment on these early days:

> Not only does she say there is something missing that she did have before
> and that she does not care any more, nothing makes any difference . . . When
> she tries to describe further what is missing she talks of her loss of power to
> appreciate, particularly music which meant so very much to her and is now
> just a "jingle of sound"; also that her fingers are now all thumbs, whereas
> before, skilled work with her hands was her greatest comfort; also that she
> feels that she has lost her background, is "shot forward," and no longer
> behind her eyes. (17)

We will see how, in the analysis that followed over the course of many
years, it is really only when Milner begins to engage in a Benjaminian
graphology of Susan's doodle drawings that change occurs. Much of the
reading process undertaken by the analytic pair, Susan and Milner, has to
do, as we shall see, with coming awake and emerging from a cocoon-like
schizoid enclosure.

My juxtaposition of Benjamin's mimetic texts of the 1930s and this case
history of Susan opens up questions regarding the relationship between
individual and collective recovery (of memory and history) and what
Benjamin often refers to as historical "awakening." One of the main sites
for the development of such a dialectic between individual and collective,
this chapter shows, is the site of the body—more specifically, the site of
those bodily perceptions and experiences that ultimately have the power
directly and indirectly to affect individual as well as public spheres. In
Richter's words, the body is "the site in which traditional distinctions
between a self's private history and the public history in which it is embedded break down" (2002, 73).[1] Sigrid Weigel, whose reading of Benjamin's
work of the 1930s is also psychoanalytically inflected (1996), makes a case
for the individual-collective dialectic as well, in particular insofar as she
reads this corpus as a "psychoanalytical reformulation of the Messianic"
(1996, xv). So does the work of W. R. Bion link the individual and collective by way of his clinical work with groups and his theory of group
psychology. He extrapolates even further when he suggests that "the mac-
roscopic vertex of group observation can be correlated and complemented
with the microscopic vertex of psychoanalytic observation" (Pistiner de
Cortiñas, 2003, 226). In this sense I read the case of Susan as both an individual case history and as emblematic of collective phenomena.

Chapter 6

Benjamin and Susan: Drawing, Writing, and *Schriftbild*

In psycho-analytic work, the problems [of communication] . . . are uncharted; difficulties become more marked still when the material to be communicated is pre- or non-verbal. . . . The ability to use points, lines, and space becomes important for understanding "emotional space" for the continuance of the work and avoidance of a situation in which two inarticulate personalities are unable to release themselves from the bondage of inarticulation.

(*Bion 1978, 15*)

Marion Milner's patient Susan came to her complaining, among other things, of having been shot out of her own history by ECT (electroconvulsive therapy) and placed into a vacuum from which to stare, horror-struck, at the catastrophe of her own state. Reminiscent of Benjamin's Angel of History, whose "eyes are staring [and his] mouth . . . open, . . . wings spread" (Benjamin 1940/1969, 257), towards the middle of her analysis Susan produces a drawing in which Milner sees "a look almost of complete disaster in the helplessly staring eyes of the central sun-face" (177) [Figure 2].

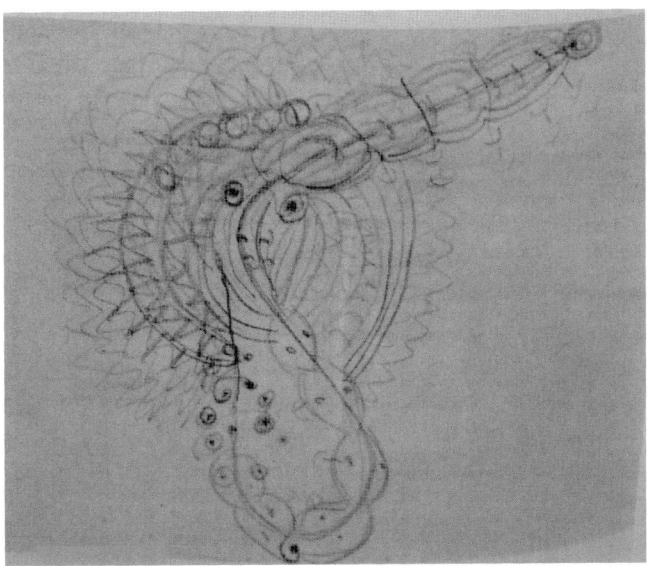

Figure 2 Partition of the Sun. *Source:* Milner 1969, 178.

Milner first reads in the drawing the pangs of a birth, but then finds its effect to be more shattering:

> I found myself calling it "The Dissolution of the Sun" because of the dread in the staring eyes; but . . . this was not quite right, perhaps "Partition of the Sun" would be better, because it is clearly dividing into two, an upthrusting, outgoing force and a primitive container—what I have called the base. (177–9)

As the "container" bursts, this image, like Benjamin's image of the angel, condenses processes of destruction and reconfiguration. Eventually coming to define the first thrust of Susan's analysis, the explosion of rigid containers and of the shells of an "ego" impoverished in experience and without a history, is similar to Benjamin's study of children's watercolors: the "infinite range of nuances" (Benjamin, 1914–15*a*/1996, 50) of color communicates its own intensity and bursts through the law of form. Such color carries what Caygill refers to as an "immanent absolute," and it "dissolves both the gazing self and the gazed-upon world" (Caygill 1998, 84). Susan's drawings, too, together with Milner's readings of them, preserve the constancy of the processes of "perishing," destroying, and emerging. Both the "Sun-face" and Benjamin's Angel of History depict the gaze at catastrophe. For Benjamin the look of horror expresses, as Weigel has put it, the "tension and incompatibility of a philosophy of history [historicism] and Jewish messianism," which could eventually lead "to a different way of writing"(1996, 162) and a different way of thinking. The gazes in "Agesilaus Santander" which are less horror-struck and more mixed with fascination and love may be translated into the "state in which both [analyst and analysand] contemplate the irreducible minimum that is the patient" as Bion puts it (1978, 59).

Throughout this book I have referred to different and opposing kinds of catastrophe: on the one hand, a catastrophic loss of experience (shock, petrification, paralysis, emptiness, muteness), on the other, catastrophic explosions (divine violence, explosive "O" experiences, demolitions of malignant rigid ego defenses) along the lines of the "Partition of the Sun" drawing in which a useless container opens up into a face of horror. Bion's theory, Milner's clinical practice, and Benjamin's theories of impoverished experience and of phantasmagoria are all concerned with redeeming experience and deflating the potentially lethal forms of narcissism inherent in subjective sovereignty. In Chapters 1 and 2 I traced two major divergent responses to impoverishment of experience, loss of history, and consequently an almost total disappearance of the other: on the one hand, escape into false auratic experiences, phantasmagoria, misrecognition of self and other, and on the other, retrieval of experience and the transformation of grandiose "splitting" and omnipotent subject-object relationships into first immersive, then dialogic subject-subject relationships. This is achieved by learning a "modality of imagining a second chance, the hope of sidetracking a catastrophic history," and instead releasing an "imagination that plays games" (Hansen 1999, 324).

Benjamin's analysis of the shock produced by modern experience and Susan's traumatizing experience with ECT relate to each other as macro- to micro-level. The latter is emblematic of the former and shares with it its symptomatology. As Buck-Morss says, in modernity, and this is also Susan's observation concerning her own private experience, "being 'cheated out of experience' has become the general state": "Thus the simultaneity of over-stimulation and numbness is characteristic of the new synaesthetic organization as anaesthetics. . . . [A]esthetics changes from a cognitive mode of being 'in touch' with reality to a way of blocking out reality" (1992, 18). There is partial congruence and potential for mutual enrichment between the ways in which Susan and Milner undo shock and schizoid fragmentation in their analysis and Benjamin's task, in his "Work of Art" essay, of redeeming modern subjectivity from its totalitarian masochism and sadism, and pitting "constant innovation in the subject" (Caygill 1998, 103) against a typically modern frozen monumentality. Susan's case history can in this sense make a statement about technological civilization, and it does so in strongly Benjaminian terms.

As analysis of the drawings becomes dominant, Susan and Milner find themselves in the position of readers of constellations. In the act of gazing at and reading Susan's drawings (the *mene, mene tekel . . .*) something else—traditional analysis, in this case—is brought to a stop:

> The gaze that gleans and thereby perceives the constellation is and sets down a *caesura* that interrupts, limits, and fixes what is "instantaneous"; it figures as differentiation which inscribes a trace into what is undifferentiated and limitlessly different and as an arrest—vis-à-vis the image which it [the arrest] sets off against the background. (Menke, 1991, 121, my translation)

Susan's analysis comes to life only when the analytic pair begins to read Susan's drawings: as if this act of reading itself set a caesura to an unproductive use of language which had characterized the analysis until then. Gaze and caesura enable reading, which in turn interrupts the empty time of catastrophe. In a sense, they interrupt the master signifiers that had overwhelmed the difference within themselves so that it can be read. Everything, if it desires recognition and redemption, must lose its own self-identity by being torn out of its context. This entire process is primordially mimetic. It is similar to what in "A Little History of Photography" Benjamin says photography can do: bring to the surface the "optical unconscious," revealing "image worlds, which dwell in the smallest things" (Benjamin 1931*a*/1999, 512). By reading and interpreting Susan's drawings in words, Milner creates *Denkbilder* ("thought-images"), written constellations out of which thinking can regenerate itself.[1] I will show how, by way of the evocation of body sensations and of linguistic elaborations, these psychoanalytic Benjaminian *Denkbilder* approximate evoking new "mental spaces" (for Susan primarily, but perhaps also for Milner) by way of a backward glance at a catastrophic history in the style of Benjamin's Angelus Novus.

Milner's translations of Susan's drawings, themselves translations of a horrified psyche (or "creature") that has gone mute, open themselves up to even further translation. Just as "Benjamin interprets the Fall in terms of the descent from truth as transformation to knowledge as judgment" (Caygill 1998, 20), opening psychic energies, in particular the modalities of perception, up again in the reverse direction is the manner in which the disfigured and silenced "creature" may once again breathe and speak.

1. Susan and Benjamin

Milner tells us early on that the ECT experience had likely robbed Susan of her unconscious memories of "her mother's hands and arms, holding her, sustaining her, protecting her" (52), which the mother had probably done despite her otherwise inadequate mothering. ECT had also robbed Susan of the sense of "background" that she had so laboriously reacquired, after years of vacuous and psychically disconnected living, by working for four years on a farm (52–3).

Susan's early drawings are full of missile-like "turds" that easily transform also into "devils." They shoot around on almost all of the early drawings, things-in-themselves, the fragments of a panicked, expelled, and defended-against fear of annihilation [Figures 3, 4]. In their disconnectedness they bear some resemblance to the heaps of meaningless material things, ruined and discarded, that grow "skyward" in the *Trauerspiel* landscape, the "heaped up crassness of . . . material . . ., the dominance of the material" (Caygill 1998, 72). They differ, however, in that they themselves are primarily persecutory rather than persecuted, though there is much evidence that Benjamin's baroque man is persecuted by the things that surround him. Some of these turds are more representational and therefore less primitive [Figures 5, 6] than others and come to express, with their

FIGURE 3 Turd-devils. *Source:* Milner 1969, 80.

FIGURE 4 Turd-devils. *Source:* Milner 1969, 89.

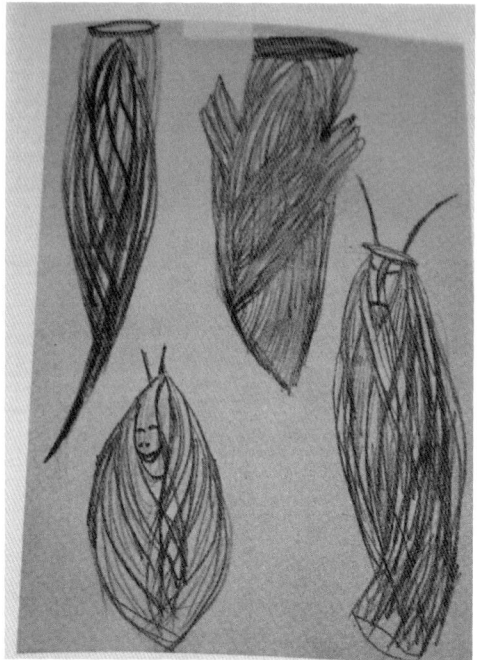

Figure 5 Turd-devils. *Source:* Milner 1969, 105.

"tight haloes" and prissy horns, a smug self-envelopment whose tyrannical power lies precisely in their expulsion and rejection of vulnerability and otherness:

> . . . is she trying to depict her sense of the power and the glory in her infantile acts of defecation? But also, since she has added horns, is there a hint of knowledge that this is devilish, that if she clings onto it she becomes the devil who has to feel she does it all herself and so mocks at, and rejects, any help from me? (107)

"[W]hen you are a devil things cannot come into you," Susan says (147).

On the other hand, also pervading her drawings are images of heads, faces, and bodies that are deeply asleep. The mesh-pattern covering faces and the frequency of closed eyes come to symbolize this loss of relation to the outside world [Figures 7, 8] as well as other forms of schizoid closures [Figure 9].

It is into such configurations of smug self-sufficiency, deluded grandiosity, and total withdrawal that an "explosive discharge of tension" (116) must enter if there is to be change. Premonitions of such discharges appear

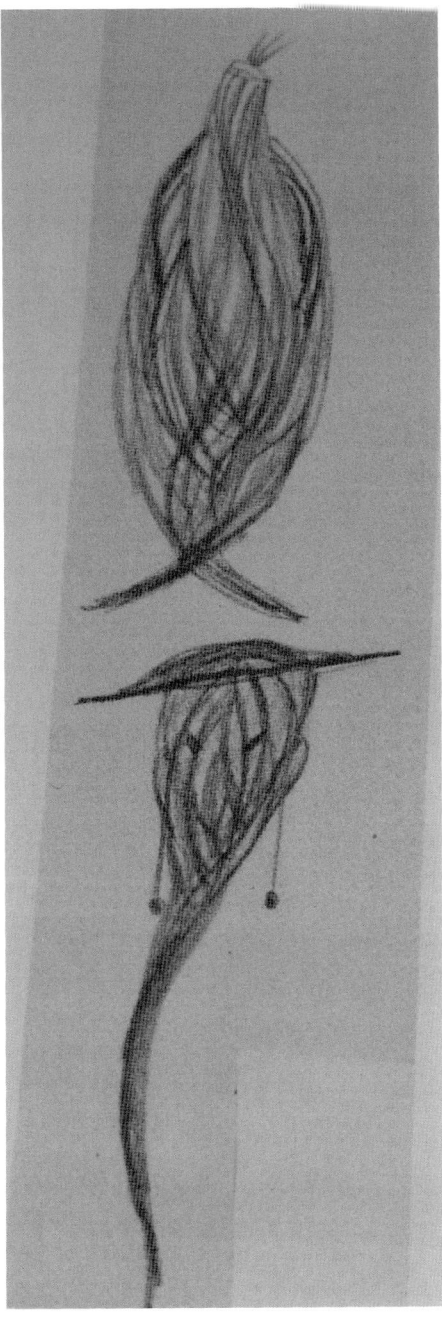

FIGURE 6 Turd-devils. "At its top is the flattened circle (now very small), again apparently meant to indicate a beheading, this time by the use of three little lines which look like spouting blood . . ." *Source*: Milner 1969, 107.

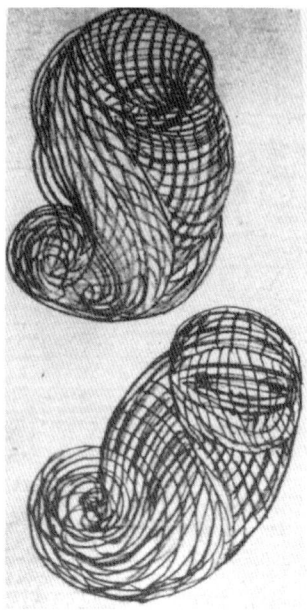

FIGURE 7 Deeply asleep. *Source:* Milner 1969, 135.

FIGURE 8 Deeply asleep. *Source:* Milner 1969, 136.

FIGURE 9 "I note that on this same page there is a drawing of a head swathed in hair with the face featureless and covered with a barred grid. I ask myself, is this her symbol for her denial of the feelings that should show in her face, are they all totally imprisoned?" (76)

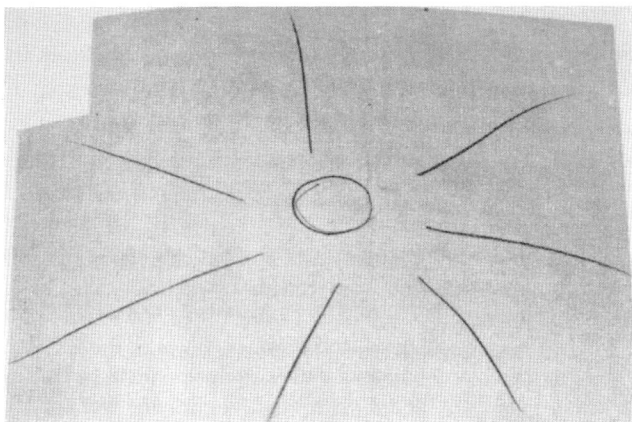

FIGURE 10 Blast. *Source:* Milner 1969, 287.

even early on in lines and circles that suggest explosiveness originating from a bodily orifice [Figures 10, 11].

Thus Susan draws motionlessness and explosive movement, both as negations in ways that recall both Benjamin's horrified, fixed gaze of the angel of history and the explosion of images out of the continuum of a catastrophic historical "progress."

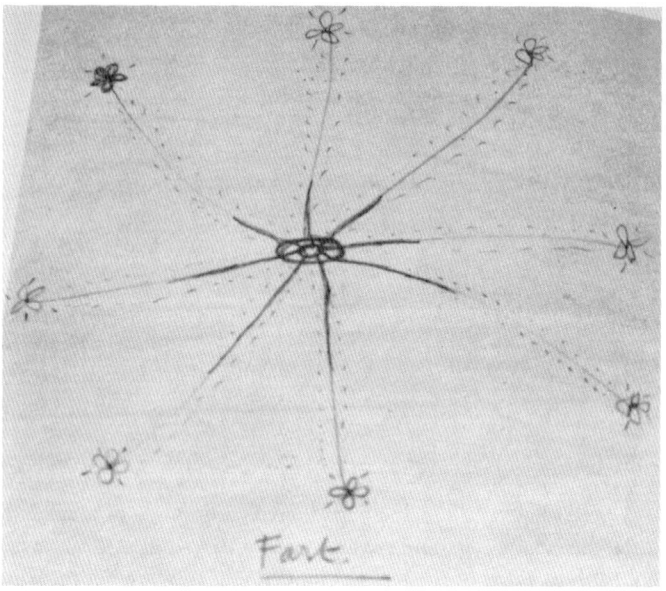

FIGURE 11 Fart. *Source:* Milner 1969, 290.

An example of Susan's semi-conscious need for explosion and shattering as a clearing gesture readying an immobilized mental space for transformation and thinking is an image that functions both synecdochically
and metonymically [Figure 12]. The text complementing this *Denkbild*
reads,

> She had called [the image] a horse's tail or a switch and had associated [it]
> with the story of the medicine woman whose switch was used to select the
> negro who was to die. . . . [G]radually I came to see how highly meaningful
> for the whole of Susan's analysis, and also her choice of the E.C.T., was the
> story about the medicine woman with the switch who picks out the man who
> must be torn to pieces. . . . I am obviously the medicine woman containing
> the projection of her own urge to tear to pieces. But it is also she, whose rigid
> conventional clinging, like Pentheus, to the idea of her rational self-conscious
> ego being all there is of her, must somehow be torn to pieces, by her own urge
> to fuller life . . . (93–4)

It is immediately following this drawing that Susan says that some of
the devil-turds of her drawings are really chrysalises (94); simultaneously,
the first drawing featuring "alternating profiles"—that is, ambiguity and
incompleteness—comes into being [Figure 13] (96). In a similar drawing,
faeces, beta-elements associated with the paranoid-schizoid position,

FIGURE 12 Horse's tail. *Source:* Milner 1969, 92.

transform into *faces*, an image closely associated with the depressive position: the face is a constellation, a re-collection of singularities; additionally, the mother's face represents the mother as whole object:

> On one of these pages there is another "man"... apparently feeling after his buttocks, and just below is a drawing of a large circle containing faces looking out of it. [Figure 14] Bearing in mind her association to the switch form as also being a horse's tail, I could not help seeing in this a picture of that fascinating sight to children, the opening of a horse's anus and seeing it full of emerging faeces—but she has turned the faeces into faces, as if to re-state her claim that faeces are babies—or feelings. (96)

Throughout this chapter I will be linking Susan's drawings to Benjaminian mimesis and read them as *Denkbilder* narrating the constitution of a new but "catastrophized" subjectivity. In the beginning Susan communicates by way of the raw emotions and sense data, the turd-beta-elements. A Benjaminian melancholy-cum-allegorical mode has the psychological effect of breaking down smug self-presence and enabling the rise of the alpha-element—thought. The allegorical mode is a "dispersal of allegorical

FIGURE 13 Alternating profiles. *Source:* Milner 1969, 202.

FIGURE 14 Faces-Faeces. *Source:* Milner 1969, 95.

idea and representation—that is, of the imaginary structure which bridges the gap between image and meaning" (Weigel 1996, 104). Fixed meaning, containment, and representation—but also simply blank thoughtlessness—are all broken up.

During the course of her analysis Susan begins to include cuts in the shape of "beheadings" in her drawings (see Figure 6): "[S]he is saying that some part of her does know the acceptance of 'beheading,' of what feels like a psychically mortal wound, is the price of growth," Milner writes, and continues: "not only [. . .] the dismemberment wound aspect of the circle is important, but also its emptiness" (107–8). Susan enters the psychic equivalent of the Benjaminian melancholic and dismemberment process of the martyr-allegorist. This will eventually be followed by indications that perhaps there could be what Milner calls "a new achievement of the ego" (108). But first her drawings seem to mime the "baroque" processes of stoppage, emptying out, and petrification so central in baroque allegory, together with the sense, which I have been arguing is specific to Benjamin's "martyric" notion of allegory, that "something" is leaking out, getting exposed. Susan's own body seems mimetically to "read" and reflect this sequence:

> . . . she does guess that the rigid muscular contraction, which she always says is centred in the back of her neck, does prevent the inner movements of excitement in her "bottom" and her vagina from rising to her head, and there "giving herself away" by a change in the expression on her mask-like barred face. Yet of course something does get through the neck-barrier—the blushing; and in a few weeks time she was to bring me drawings of faces with great intensity of expression. (108)

As Susan's drawings enter into a mimetic relationship with her bodily sensations and fantasms, they too begin to include "caesuric moments"—the two-pronged act of allegorical and *sinthomatic* writing as I defined and described it in Chapter 2: first an "emptying out," and then compensation for and reconfiguration of the deadened, deflated, and eventually dissolved ("old") ego in the new writing ego. A relative of the Joycean *sinthome*, Susan's psychic cutting-and-reconfiguring processes are reflected and enacted in the "artifice" of her *image*-writings. Her drawings are part reflection of psychic processes and part their enactment. Simultaneously, in her "lines, points, and spaces" (Bion 1978, 15) Susan's experiences, history and reality become thinkable by way of Benjaminian *Schriftbilder*.

The Benjaminian *Schriftbild*'s transformative powers are evoked in Benjamin's essay on Surrealism in a way that emphasizes Surrealism's roots in psychoanalysis: it emerges, then, that the Surrealists' "magical experiments with words" are not just "artistic dabbling[s]"; their "passionate phonetic and graphical transformational games" (Benjamin 1929*a*/1999, 184) are rather to be understood as concrete transformative interventions into real human and social relations. Benjamin himself engages in such transformational playfulness in *Berlin Childhood Around 1900*, for example in the piece "The Mummerehlen":

> There is an old nursery rhyme that tells of Muhme Rehlen. Because the word *Muhme* meant nothing to me, this creature became for me a spirit: the mummerehlen. The misunderstanding disarranged the world for me. But in a good way: it lit up paths to the world's interior. The cue could come from anywhere. (Benjamin 1932–34/2006, 130–1)

The word becomes an image, a distorted one, and thus conventional arrangements within the world (as they are perceived by the child Walter) become fair game for change by way of a play with words. This is surrealist "disarrangement." With such a "disarrangement," the child distorts the world or itself in such a way as to (re-)inscribe itself within the world in its own manner. It re-writes the world to make a space for its particular self: "If, in this way, I distorted both myself and the word, I did only what I had to do to gain a foothold in life" (1932–34/2006, 131). This process is the opposite of the mimicry of assimilation. The word "mummerehlen," lacking clear referential meaning, is the carrier of transformative powers in child Walter's (linguistically constituted) relation to the world. Acting as a distorting force, it becomes a transformative image whose function is to burst through the outlines that seemed to contain its much more complex and evolving reality. It is in fact a "mimetic faculty" at work. Digging into the word "mummerehlen," brings out an alterity that cannot be contained but instead leads to an immersiveness into things, words, and images. These images in turn dissolve existing clear ego-outlines. For Benjamin this word without clear reference marks the entry of an absence and half-knowledge that enables thought as such and a snake-like conjoining of images to emerge:

> ... [mummerehlen] contains the whole distorted world of childhood. Muhme Rehlen, who used to have her place in line, was already gone when I heard it recited for the first time. But it was even harder to find a trace of the mummerehlen. Sometimes I suspected it was lurking in the monkey that swam in the steam of barley groats or tapioca at the bottom of my dish. I ate the soup to bring out the mummerehlen's image. It was at home, one might think, in the Mummelsee, whose sluggish waters enveloped it like a gray cape. *Whatever stories used to be told about it—or whatever someone may have only wished to tell me—I do not know. Mute, porous, flaky, it formed a cloud at the core of things, like the snow flurry in a glass paperweight. From time*

to time, I was whirled around in it. This would happen as I sat painting with watercolors. The colors I mixed would color me. *Even before I applied them to the drawing, I found myself disguised by them.* [my emphases] (1932–34/2006, 133–4)

Similarly, Susan's doodles constitute inscriptions of spaces that open up new spaces for transformed topographies of self. In many of Susan's drawings Milner reads the inscriptions as trying to reach "at the core" of her mental space (in the process of being constructed) a "porous, flaky . . . cloud," a nothingness and nonsense. This is the intangible "snowstorm" in a "glass paperweight," an opaque spot at the "core" of self. Susan begins to inscribe "herself" as a point at the center of a circle, and reaches this point by developing a series of drawings of snakes as coiled circles moving inward, "whirling," as Benjamin says, toward an "undifferentiated state of being, where there is neither subject nor object" as Milner puts it (157) [Figure 15]. Fascinating here, however, is that this snake (which, Milner says, can also very well be read as a coil of faeces that is "very much alive" [156]) is "beheaded." The closing-in-on-itself is interrupted in Susan's drawing by a caesura. At least one possible reading of this line as "cut" would be that at this moment something undecidable enters. Imposing stoppage on the vortical drive of the snake could be the first sign of "something else" and thus of transformation overtaking persisting recursive sameness.

The "stroke" of the snake's beheading, that particular mark of writing, undercuts, then, smug self-presence, self-sufficiency, and omnipotence, and in that sense represents the beginning of O and thought. The cut—castration—marks the appearance of alpha-elements. Cutting, however, is also

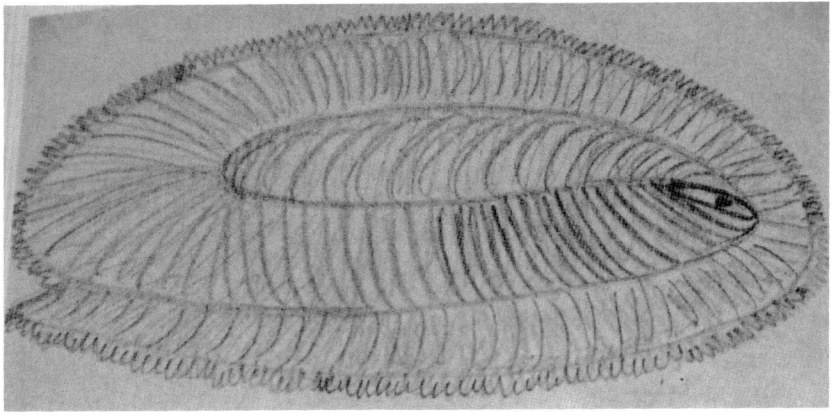

FIGURE 15 Circling inward. *Source:* Milner 1969, 156.

sadistic and at work in PS. Thus it is important to differentiate the schizoid cut from the redemptive one, just as the sadism of Benjamin's allegorist is transformed by the melancholia of the martyr in the combination figure "martyr-allegorist" that, I have argued, comes closest to describing Benjamin's "answer" for modern subjectivity. In this connection, it seems to me that for Susan the birth of the mark actually originated in the field of sound: at one point Susan tells Milner that "while practicing [the piano], three of the notes seemed to exist quite separately from the piano and from her, and she dared not come back to that bit of music for fear she would play it over and over again and not be able to stop" (Milner, 1969, 59). Like the beheading of the snake, these notes, cut out of their context from the piano and Susan "herself," in their insistence ("fear she would play it over and over again") combine the jouissance of the sadistic element in cutting while at the same time binding it and providing a containable form—that is, by protecting the user (*and* possibly an other) from that same jouissance in what Klein calls the depressive position. The notes, then, have the same function letters do (see Chapter 2 this volume). The cutting of the snake, in its origin sadistic, allows for the construction of a mental space that is not dominated by manic, hyperreal, self-sufficient, and murderous turd-snakes, but marked by a Benjaminian origin.

During the course of her analysis and struggle against dissociation, Susan's drawings evolve toward the establishment of diagonal lines (which become increasingly more perforated and permeable) drawn through the page, that, like her use of strokes and lines, signal difference and change, and a growing tendency toward ornamentation and playfulness. The diagonal line represents phenomena of separation: the images that Milner suggests have to do with giving birth to a new idea of herself are symbolized in this dialectical interplay between separation and union embodied in the diagonal lines. The latter also signal the birth of a new subject-object relationship. Giving birth to herself means also, says Milner, giving birth to the idea of her own skin and face, in interface with the Other and thus alive to issues of limitation, interruption, and transgression:

> So it seemed to me now that the idea of a boundary that marks off two differences was coming in, in various ways: whether in the idea of her skin dividing herself from the world, and her face as a meeting place; or in the idea of an interface within herself, between what is conscious and what is unconscious; or, finally, an idea of the differences between what is subjective and objective, thoughts and things, fantasies and actions. (335)

With this clear indication that what Bion termed alpha-function—in place of beta-elements—begins to make a structural appearance, the stage is set for the emergence of the many "birth" drawings in which it is the cut of writing that represents a "birth"—not only of linguistic transformations but also of the sense that the body too revives once language and writing are reborn. A clear manifestation of this idea of rebirth-through-inscription occurs in Figure 16 where the "X-woman" quite literally lives through the letter ("X") as her limbs are also the limbs (and "feelers") of the letter. And then Milner notices something else about this drawing. It can also be read differently, namely as two faces, seen in profile, pressed together:

> ... here the alternation ... is between seeing the whole insect like an X figure and two faces pressed tightly against each other, so that they in fact seem to merge; so here I begin to wonder whether this is not a highly original attempt to portray the sensuous memories of her face, in infancy, pressed against her mother's breast. (111)

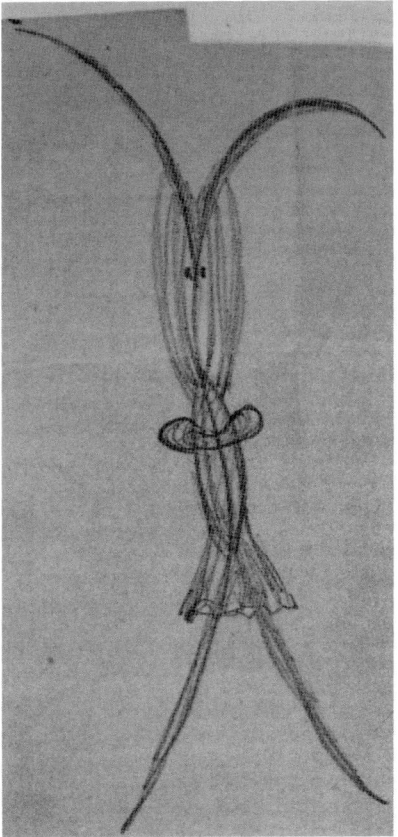

FIGURE 16 X-Woman. *Source:* Milner 1969, 110.

Circles are the shapes in Susan's drawings that are the most fraught; generally, they tend to have to do with constituting a mental space. They appear early in the series and undergo many transformations. For a significant period of time they form the "tight haloes" [Figures 17 and 9] around the "turd-devils" and denote self-conscious and deluded plenitude and restrictive ideals. Circles are also bodily orifices that signify expulsion, murder (67), or terror—as, for example, when Susan expresses terror at "entering" the circle for fear that at its center she might find "the wish to kill her mother" (90)—surely a Kleinian PS scenario before the establishment of the depressive position. Then they come to be a part of the "beheadings," while almost simultaneously they also point to that opaque center of states of undifferentiation, states of O. Later they come to contain that same point (the "nothing") that depicts the soul. [Figures 18, 19, 20] Just as the empty circle can take the shape of a mouth, the circle as bodily orifice can also refer to the ear and with it to openness and exchange, to listening [Figure 21].

While the evolutions of the circle (Bionian "evolutions in O") move toward signifying and enacting the infinite point[2] (of the soul)—Benjamin's origin, Bion's O—and the empty circle as a tolerated absence and thinking

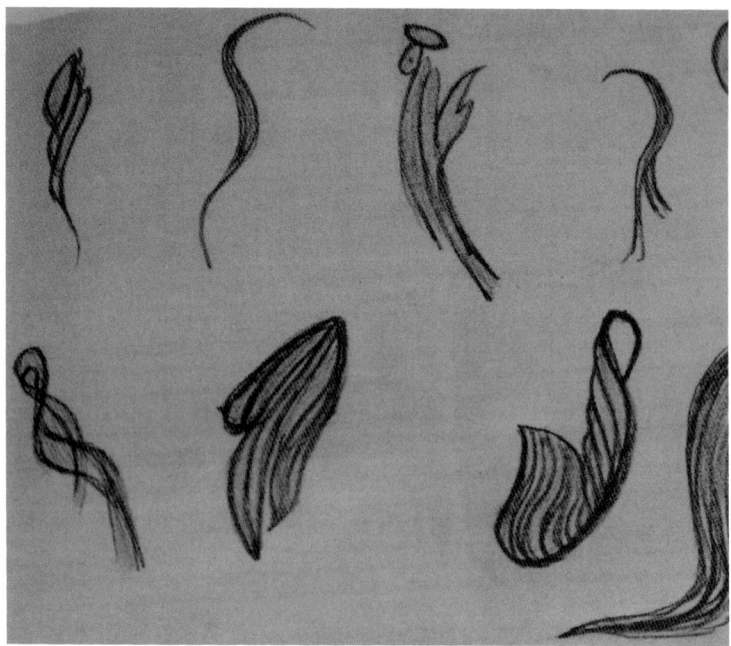

FIGURE 17 Tight haloes. *Source:* Milner 1969, 73.

FIGURE 18 Soul-Circles. *Source:* Milner 1969, 97.

FIGURE 19 Soul-Circles. *Source:* Milner 1969, 126.

FIGURE 20 Soul-Circles. *Source:* Milner 1969, 127.

FIGURE 21 "She brings an outline full-face drawing, with the mouth wide open to form an empty circle . . . This is the first open mouth she has drawn and it is interesting that she has also drawn a musical stave with a series of notes and linked this by a line down from the treble clef to another head which has a black ring circling the head". (124)

space (Warburg's *Denkraum*), another fascinating shape begins to evolve: the "whorl." It often takes the place of breasts, feet, and shoulders in Susan's drawings [Figures 22, 23]. Regarding Figure 23 Milner writes:

> I see the five whorls, which are the same shape as she sometimes uses for breasts, or feet, or even shoulders as standing for my supporting role in the five sessions. But these five whorls are also linked with the eyes, that have this dawning look of recognition; could she not be saying that she has a gleam of hope that something good and supporting is beginning to be really there, outside her? And also, since the whorls are shown as growing out of her own hair, could not this symbol also be expressing the thought that the idea of something that will support her and feed her comes from inside herself, it is felt first of all to be her own creation, something growing out of her own substance, as hair does, or faeces. (139–40)

Since the whorls, in this reading, tend to stand in for body parts that offer or receive support (breasts, feet, the shoulders where babies are lifted), they may also be signs for the *sinthome*, that act examined in Chapter 2

FIGURE 22 Whorls. *Source:* Milner 1969, 138.

FIGURE 23 Whorls. *Source:* Milner 1969, 140.

in which the son shoulders the father, instead of the Name-of-the-Father supporting the son.

In some cases the circle, that crucial empty space (like the Lacanian *vide*), breaks open into "wavy, hair-like forms [like Warburg's *Pathos-formeln*], which then develop into a cowl of hair enclosing a face" (122). This, for Milner, comes to express Susan's newly but precariously recovered sense of background, of corporeality and Benjaminian "corporeal substance," without which the self or the subject becomes a totally managed one, "treated" and, in this case, shocked:

> I begin to wonder . . . whether these really could be an attempt to represent the dark rhythmic heaving currents and pressures of internal awareness from which the "face" of ego-consciousness recurrently emerges, like a flower out of a dark "earth" or background, or a baby out of a dark womb. (122)

This "background" consists originally of the mother's heartbeat and breathing, that "corporeal substance" that the infant "acquires," so to speak for its own background. This "background," particularly when understood

Figure 24 Inside of the mouth. *Source:* Milner 1969, 306.

as the sound of the mother's breathing, is another manifestation of Benjamin's "origin."

The most evolved drawing-writings Susan produces combine signs of a renewed life of the body, a new "'body-attention' or 'concentration of the body'" (48), an acceptance of cutting, absence, and boundaries (and thus the birth of thought), and the development of an empty space for thinking, where this space has permeable boundaries between inside and outside, and where the subject can also recognize the other. So, for example, in the year before "coming out" into the world, Susan begins to make drawings that "prepare a concept of a baseline for 'being in the world'" (304) by exploring the inside of the mouth:

> Soon (7 May) she did a drawing [Figure 24] to which her association was explicitly "Water and land". . . There are also eyes, and I feel, on looking back, that it is something to do with a growing consciousness of differences, probably within the mouth, since the lower curve suggests a jaw and the inner shape a coiled tongue; if so, then the water of her title is likely to be also the saliva in her mouth. (305)

For years Susan had deadened her own perceptions, in particular perceptions of what was occurring internally; her loss of background (feeling she had been "shot forward") had also meant a loss of body-sensations. Early on in the book Milner writes that in order for Susan to gain a "self-presentation" rather than a dissociated "self-representation" (like Benjamin's "name-tags," "too much *din*"), she would have to attempt to encounter a "thought" "before it has become 'bound' by images from the outside world" (45), to tolerate, to put it in Bionian terms, not-knowing, in Lacanian terms, "half-knowing." Additionally, Milner writes, "her capacity for being in the world must have as baseline an undifferentiated sense of loss, a sea of tears, just as she had said that, at N.I. [the psychiatric hospital], it was because she had the heart pains that she could be 'in the world'" (305). In [Figure 25] Susan has drawn a sea that seems to consist of tears, possibly tear drops, strung together—that is, linked, reconfigured—and up above are, as Milner calls them, "beautiful egg-like shapes" and the "hills of her mother's body" (304–5), that is now relinquished, represented and given a basis of mourning acceptance.

Her new-found ability for mourning, which defies Susan's "denial of her own urge to become nothing" (301) as well as the temptation to remain omnipotent and cruel, places her reawakening psychic life-world into a strangely "baroque" landscape. The empty circle in the duck's hind part from which a phoenix emerges [Figure 26] is the psychic and subjective equivalent of the "empty balcony" at the end of Benjamin's *Trauerspiel* book:

> . . . I feel the phoenix, even if it is only emerging from her tail, does express some sort of growing belief in the renewal of life, something to do with spirit, consciousness, that will emerge from the empty circle if she learns how to pray to that. (298)

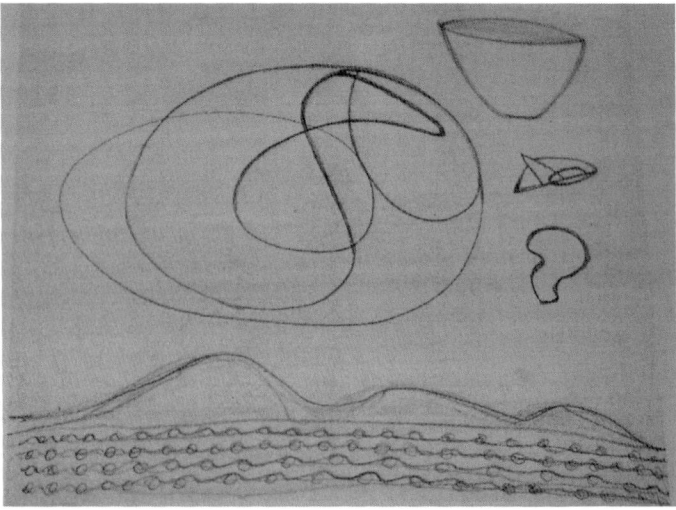

FIGURE 25 Being in the world. *Source:* Milner 1969, 304.

Figure 26 Emerging phoenix. *Source:* Milner 1969, 297.

2. Graphology and "Thinking"

Susan's drawings contain a whole array of "images," some representational, others not. The drawings are consistently a mix of lines, circles, and points of abstract, but also physical intensity and are pictorial representations of emotion and body-feeling. Another example of a drawing that emphasizes body-feeling is the very moving "Post-ECT" drawing in which Susan seems to be struggling with issues of containment ("an arm which both holds the baby and is itself the baby") [Figure 27]. Milner writes:

> . . . it also seemed to me to show many other things, for instance, the circle theme again, made by the enclosing arms that are also womb-like, with the baby as the foetus. And when I did allow myself to go down deep through the first impact of it I found there was somewhere in it, surely, a faint glimmer of hope. Was it a hope that she would somehow be able to find a psychic equivalent of the encircling arms . . .? (251)

Other drawings make manifest the processes of a body-feeling returning to life, such as Figure 24, and fall into the more abstract, non-representational, "writerly" category.

Anthropologist André Leroi-Gourhan argues against the notion that writing originated in pictorial representation and thus in mimesis in its traditional sense (Menke 1991, 131n13). He would presumably not disagree so much with the notion that writing is mimetic in the archaic sense,

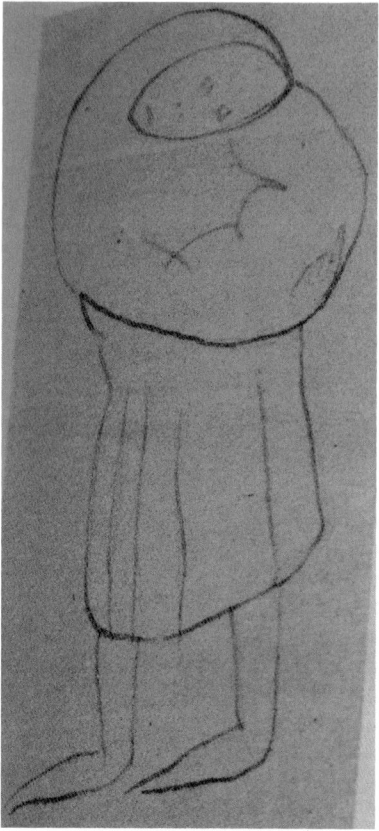

FIGURE 27 Post-ECT. *Source:* Milner 1969, 251.

that it is a translation of physical gesture, of drive intensities. Benjamin's notion of graphology extrapolates the graphic, visual, element that lies beyond graphical and intentional linearity, in fact reads *all* writing as non-linear and as *Schriftbild* and *Schriftkonstellation* (Benjamin 1928/1999, 133) following different spatial principles. In Benjaminian graphology the linear conceptual meanings of signs, regarded sequentially, give way to, as Menke puts it, the "dispersal of writing into drifts of letters" (Menke 1991, 129, my translation) and thus becomes a pulsating surface, an oscillating structure of surfaces. Such configurations and their readings have the power to transform the reading subject by way of "drifts" with the power to reawaken body-language.

In "Graphology Old and New" (1930/1999) and his "Review of the Mendelssohns' *Der Mensch in der Handschrift*" (1928/1999) Benjamin attempts to free the art of graphology from the right-wing life philosophy of Ludwig Klages ("[Graphology's] ability to free itself from sectarianism of every kind is a question of life and death at the present time" (1928/1999, 133) and other attempts to make graphology the playground of irrationalist and mystical expressiveness and interpretation of character. He wishes to recast it as a mimetic faculty, capable of bringing to light unconscious images, and as a semiotics of the body. While Klages had attempted to wrench vague manifestations of expressiveness and "character" from handwriting, the Mendelssohns wanted their analyses to liberate unconscious body-images (1928/1999, 133). Other authors on graphology, like Max Pulver and Robert Saudek, focused, in a precise and, compared to Klages's subjectivism, more objective manner on "the unconscious graphic elements, the unconscious image fantasies" (1930/1999, 399). The Mendelssohns' object is what Benjamin calls "the integral riddle of mankind," the secret that is never given up (1928/1999, 131). Their work is mimetic in the Benjaminian sense in that through a "reading" of handwriting, treated like "a set of hieroglyphs," "the authors have managed to preserve contact with the world of images to a hitherto unprecedented degree" (132). This world of images, that a more psychoanalytically oriented graphology can rescue from oblivion and preserve, is the repressed world of the body—and of the "creature." The "gesture" of handwriting, says Benjamin, "is determined by the *inner* image" (132–3). The latter does not offer information about the writer's character or "morality," just as a deciphering of morality should not be what is at work in physiognomy. Writing and graphology open up—for who is ready to perceive it—a "space behind the writing plane" (134), a "copy in microcosm of a clairvoyant space." Contemplation of this space translates into a reading of *mental space*, both individual and collective:

> Anyone able to share [the Mendelssohns] way of seeing would be able to take any scrap of paper covered with writing and discover in it a free ticket to the great *theatrum mundi*. It would reveal to him the pantomime of the entire nature and existence of mankind, in microcosmic form. (134)

This space is *Denkraum* for Benjamin, Bion, and Milner. For Bion the true thought, standing in a mimetic relationship to creative mental space, precedes the specific individual; it is found by, and irrupts into, this thinker who, by recognizing this thought, must have the ability to withstand the anxiety catastrophic change generates. She must be able to admit its "persecution" and, eventually, through alpha-function, to carry it forward. Thinking is the establishment of links or constellations between mental contents with the aim of constructing a mental space. Its proto-type is the infant-mother relation where the mother's reverie has the capacity to generate the rhythm of true thought in the infant by miming it for him and returning his dread and anxiety in tolerable form. Drawings and their reading in the Susan-Milner relation do the same thing. In general, this same thinking should appear—most artificially but also most transformatively—in the analytic space. The analytic space is artificial just like the *sinthome* is, but that does not hinder its efficiency. Milner says toward the end of her case history that Susan's "struggle [was] to find a symbol for, a way of thinking about, the capacity for reflective thought itself" (361). It seems fitting to me to conjoin these thoughts on thinking and the expeditions into uncharted territory undertaken by these analysts (and certainly their patients) with Benjamin's reception, in his review of Willy Haas's book, *Gestalten der Zeit*, of Haas's definition of "thinking":

> Haas walks this tightrope with dizzying assurance. Nevertheless, the sight might trigger anxiety in spectators, were there not present here a more reliable and higher-grade safety element: the art of knowing how to fall. "To be able to stake one's entire life on an expedition—an expedition that can't be precisely calculated in advance—against some minor detail of this world: this and nothing else is what is meant by 'thinking.'" Is it only by chance that this profound definition which we encounter on the last page of the book is that of a man in free fall? (1931*b*/1999, 430)

3. Benjamin and Susan

Aura

As I bring Susan and Benjamin together in a constellation, it is necessary to look more carefully at the role shock, aura, and phantasmagoria play in Susan's analytic experience since these are the phenomena central to Benjamin's theory of impoverished experience and the fate of the individual in modernity. Susan produced a drawing that she entitled "Aura" [Figure 28]. The drawing emanates elation and ecstasy, and, even though the body is "thin and wooden-looking," it conveys the sense of a well-defended fortress primarily by way of its "spiked breasts." But then Milner tries out an alternative reading:

> The spiked breasts might really be intended to convey a direction of movement, rather than sadistic attacks, a polarity of expansion and contraction which could even be related to breathing; much later we came to consider how far her phrase 'It's in the air and there for everybody' to describe what she surrendered to, did not perhaps mean the rhythm of her breathing. If so, then is the dark shape at the bottom that points downwards pointing to the grave? For if she fully accepts the function of her own breathing she will have to accept the fact that one day she will stop breathing. (167)

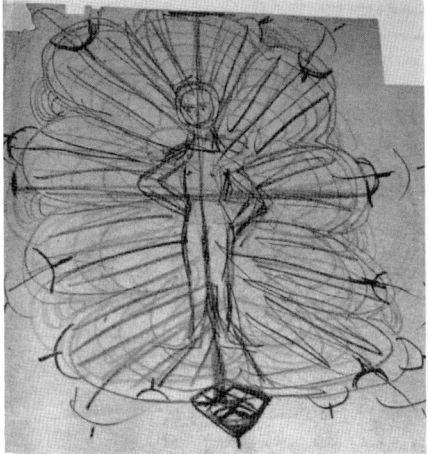

FIGURE 28 "My first impression was that the figure is crucified, but then I notice that the cross is in front, not behind, and centered on the diaphragm, while the arms are not outstretched or nailed up, but placed akimbo, and the hands hidden behind the back ... At the base of the cross is another blackened spiked breast-like shape, now pointing downwards ... Again there seems to be something like a helmet over the head and neck ... Also in the lines of the surrounding aura I see some hint of a spider's web; but there is, at the same time, a sense of tremendous energy, mostly directed outwards ... the body itself is thin and rather wood-looking ..." (165)

The drawing "Aura" itself includes the points and spikes that puncture its own narcissistic aura, that characterized the many "devil" and "turd" drawings, defenses against the self's fragmentations and against acknowledging pain; they had provided something like what Buck-Morss describes as fascist aesthetics: "illusion of invulnerability" (1992, 38).[3] Following the production of "Aura," whenever defensive "aura" appears in Susan's drawings, it does so tongue-in-cheek. This strategy of breaking aura open is repeatedly expressed in Susan's use of the diagonal line, which makes its appearance late in the analysis. Caygill's summary of the fascistic use of aura and the Benjaminian critique of it applies also to this new element in Susan's drawings:

> Fascism makes the negative, repressive response to the dissolution of unique-
> ness and the permeability of borders, one which seeks to monumentalize the
> phantasm of a present and authentic identity and model of experience, while
> communism, for Benjamin, affirms the flux of identity and the permanent
> revolution of the organization of experience. (1998, 102)

Susan's use of the diagonal indicates first of all acknowledgement of "dividing a primary wholeness" (Milner 1969, 324), which signals also the possibility of suffering and the necessity of tolerating separation. An additional step for Susan was to undermine the absoluteness of the separation itself: in later drawings Susan breaks the diagonal, making it "permeable," and adds imagistic signifiers that, almost emblem-like, "comment" on this new topography of mental space [Figure 29]:

> I noted, also, that the eight-pointed star of this 7 October drawing is made from two crosses superimposed; so I come to ask myself, is she not perhaps here expressing her intuition of how two people, having both become aware of being separate through the acceptance of the crucifixion of their birth, can then come together again, in a rediscovered unity . . . in many . . . forms of shared experience? (328)

The broken diagonal connecting the star and the little person points to the positive element in aura, as Benjamin understood it. In Benjamin's famous definition of aura, one of its aspects is the ability of a phenomenon to "return the gaze" (Benjamin 1931*a*/1999, 1936/2002, 1939/1969), which provides "a potentially destabilizing encounter with otherness" (Hansen 1999, 311), as Hansen puts it. The breaks in Susan's lines would seem to indicate an encounter of this sort, or at least to make it possible. The "permeable diagonal" drawings, then, describe the topography of the analytic space in which each subjectivity is put in question by the other.

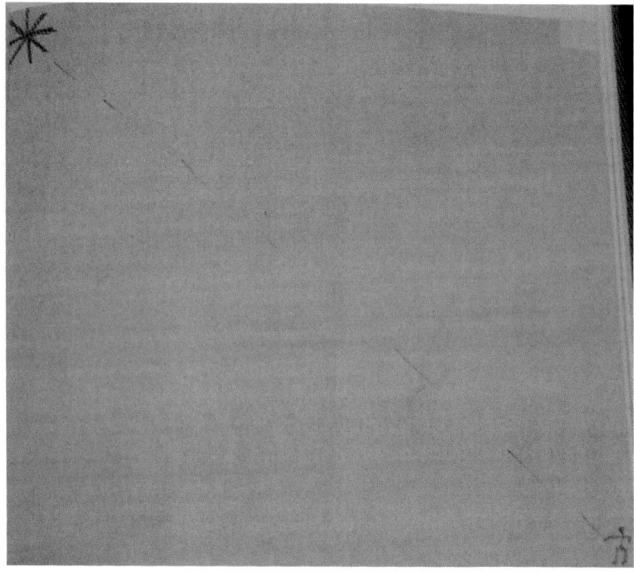

FIGURE 29 Broken diagonal. *Source:* Milner 1969, 329.

The recovery of breathing space and distance is thus a recovery of "good" aura—in Susan's case, of the space of which the traumatic ECT experience had robbed her—necessary for the very possibility of "perceiv[ing] or respect[ing] the uniqueness, difference or distance of *any* objects of experience whatsoever—including that of other persons," as Costello writes in "Aura, Face, Photography" (177).

The original model for gazing at an object and reading its returning gaze and for aura is the gaze between mother and infant. The other's face and its relationship to aura is a big topic among readers of Benjamin. Costello's argument, namely that in Benjamin's mature conception of aura it "pertains to the *subject* rather than the *object* of perception, namely to a particular modality of experience on the part of a perceiving subject" (166), is close to my understanding: aura is something the subject must be able to experience in order to evade the psychological and ethical pitfalls of making the perceiving self a buttressed ego rather than a dialogic subjectivity. Second, Costello writes, "the human face serv[es] as the 'ultimate retrenchment of aura'" (166). I would suggest that rather than determining whether aura "pertains" to "subject" or "object" it may be more precise to say that aura exists—as *anomie*, origin, and O—in the subject-object interchange; and that when there is aura in that space of exchange, when the space between the two is perceived as inhabited by a "broken up diagonal line," by the breath of language,[4] the subject-object relation becomes a "subject-subject" relation. Similarly, in an auratic subject-subject face-to-face subjects would open themselves up to "persecution" by the other without either passively mimicking the other or assimilating the other into the self. In this sense the gaze experience is not about totalizing, and alterity remains uncontained.

Acknowledging alterity in the other means not being able to draw the other's face without holes in the line's containment. Reading faces includes an active element in the process of perceiving them, that is, in tracing the face's lines. The manner in which such "tracings"—complex psychological processes—occur will determine the degree of openness, creativity, and freedom in a relationship. A negatively auratic face-to-face will be one in which one engulfs and petrifies the other. In "*Facies Hippocratica*" (1995), Rebecca Comay shows how photography, according, to Benjamin, has the potential to "write" faces in such a way that their "sacralization"—that is, their totality, their closure—is broken without, however, altogether extinguishing their aura:

As its name suggests, photography would be the supreme instance of writing . . .; the displacement of original "expression" by "copies, signs and images," self-attestation by representation *in absentia*, enigma by phenomenon, "revelation" by the "disclosure" characteristic of a visibilized world. . . . but photography does not violate an aura somehow pristine in its proximity. The camera's violence supervenes only on a previously occluded violence—initiating the "violent shattering". . . of a tradition characterized by exclusivity or domination—such that this prior coercion comes to light. (1995, 226)

The shattering of aura enacted by photography throws light on the domination—the schizoid closures—that had previously enthralled these faces: "For photography exposes the aura to have been already implicated in its own self-betrayal, figuring in its own disfigurement: what is defaced is a face already defaced in having entered the regime of prestige and power" (226). The decay of aura, as I read Comay, is the mortification of an always already constructed prior aura that had set itself up as "originary" and "authentic"—as "contained," in Bion's terminology, and thus deluded and deluding. In response to Comay I would point out that the "proximity" of photography originates (in Benjamin's terms) a space of proximity in which a writing and simultaneous "un-writing" occur. The face is a surface on which the subject-subject encounter is inscribed and read and a space of dual "reverie" in which mental spaces are written and transformed. It is in gazing at and tracing the mother's face that the infant comes to shape itself via recognition of and by the other; still, the other is never wholly assimilable or even wholly recognizable. Something else intervenes to block such plenitude and to introduce both a *caesura* and an opacity that in the best of circumstances leads to creative transcriptions of experience, and in the worst, to a wholesale closing down of that space of exchange, of reading and writing. "Good" aura designates the space of reading, writing, thinking, and transforming that is opened up between two subjects into a third space of language, and "bad" aura designates the sacralization and consequent petrification of that space.

The latter is what Comay says Benjamin describes having occurred in modernity:

> Baudelaire' daily changes of mask, ephemeral as those of a "ham actor"; the fashionable hairdos designed to be seen in silhouette; the vacant stares of Simmel's streetcar passengers; the mirror-eyes of Baudelaire's prostitutes . . . such eyes fascinate because, in reflecting everything, they simultaneously crowd and evacuate the space of proximity, substituting for the distanced nearness of desire the claustrophobic remoteness that Benjamin calls "sex." (226)

To compensate for this unconsciously perceived loss of experience—which includes the *Denkraum* necessary for "good" aura—the "happy face" is plastered all over the modern public spaces as a "compensatory phantasm" (226). In order to evade such idolatry—the delusion that such faces are in fact faces—Benjamin, according to Comay, advocates a sort of "self"-concealment, a becoming-invisible (*ausdruckslos*), an "'unmaking' of the face" in order to rescue it (227). Thus the death mask becomes a sign of refusal of the phantasmagoria of the happy face, of compensatory, empathic identification (228).

Comay's discussion of Benjamin's *topos* of the death-mask, the hidden face, fits in well with my reading of Benjamin's *Ponderación Misteriosa* (Chapter 2). It is, I would add, also dialectical: "the face" is sustained by its very negation, and it is sustained as the face-to-face. Comay concludes that Benjamin's thought is an act of absolute negation: "This nonencounter attests not only to the failure of resuscitation—the mask speaks the impossibility of the dead regaining voice, breath, spiritus—but equally to a failure to have securely died" (233). Comay is talking about the question of *survival*: "The apparition of the face as death mask, resisting all idealization, means, for the survivors, an incessant wake. Perhaps 'attention.' Perhaps insomnia" (233). Equally, of course, it is a question of memory, in particular memory of the other within the self. Susan's painting entitled "My Mother" is such a dialectical expression: the painting is simultaneously a representation and preservation of a face and an attack on its wholeness. Moreover, precisely because of Susan's re-presentation of the face as broken, suffering, but also, in an almost radiant way, living, by the holes opening up ways into "other" places, the painting represented a moment of reawakening in Susan's analysis [Figure 30].

Survival begins with, as Milner writes, "fashioning a kind of psychic sphere or new womb out of one's own body image" (273). The lines of the "Post-ECT" drawing had indicated the modality of Susan's re-writing of her own mental space as an "originary" process in its ambiguating use of containers (as themselves contained, etc.). Milner's reading of Susan's late drawings leads her to conclude that in this process of self-reconstruction it is essential to reach an "undifferentiated and indeterminate state," an *Ausdruckslosigkeit* and "empty circle," "at times identified with death, since it is a wiping-out of all images of the self, an achieved darkness that can feel like being nothing," achieved by a "deliberate stilling . . . [where] one stops thinking and simply waits and watches" (253–4). This "waiting and watching" corresponds to the "attentiveness" that Benjamin ascribes to Kafka: "Kafka . . . possessed in the highest degree what Malebranche called 'the natural prayer of the soul': attentiveness. And in this attentiveness he included all living creatures, as saints include them in their prayers"

FIGURE 30 My mother. *Source:* Milner 1969, 194.

(Benjamin 1934, 812). Milner feels charged with the task of undoing "knowing": "I came to be increasingly sure that she needed me, recurrently, to put into words the fact that I did not, could not, know the total reality of what she was trying to express" (255). This "not-knowing," like Lacan's "half-saying," moves alongside the significance of a series of drawings in which "figures or faces show[ed] multiple or indeterminate boundaries of the skin" (259n1). The supreme significance of these drawings is their conception of subjectivity as permeable and immersive with regard to its relation with the "material community." Susan inscribes this psychic transformation in the difference between the early "turd" drawings and the broken diagonal line drawings.

Such drawings undermine aura and open up and infinitize mental space. This is "writing" that is born of and is indistinguishable from distortions out of "origin." Benjaminian distortion interrupts language and is a subsequent elaboration of the primal Fall. The Fall has turned the individual and his fallen language, which nevertheless "remembers" the language of names, into writing, rescuing the language of names from oblivion and assimilation.[5] Susan's drawings and handwriting are examples of Benjamin's "exciting writing"; they are also elaborations of Warburg's *Pathosformeln*.

When Susan, almost performing an originary act, cuts through the paper with a diagonal she creates an originary fold and an edge that enables subsequent inscriptions into new territory for the elaborations of her self-construction. The diagonal's caesura marks the first move into *das Gedichtete* (Chapter 3, this volume) for Susan. Her marks, lines, and strokes are re-inscriptions and thus "distortions" of origin. The diagonal marks the crack, the in-between of the various possible images that also mark their decline and transformation into something else. This *edge* is, like the instant in which one language crosses into another in Benjamin's theory of translation, a threshold into pure language. In this way the diagonal functions as origin for the florescence of writing.

In the penultimate aphorism of "Short Shadows (I)" (1929*b*/1999) Benjamin describes the experience individuals have, when they have their fortunes read, of suddenly feeling the excitement of being offered various images of themselves—in the past and present, but primarily in the future:

> . . . the impoverished and desolate human being seeks out the image as a disguise within himself. For we are generally lacking in internal resources. This is why it makes us so happy when someone approaches us with a whole boxful of exotic masks, offering us more unusual kinds, such as the mask of the murderer, the magnate, or the round-the-world sailor. We are fascinated . . . [F]ortunetellers and palm-readers and astrologers . . . know how to transport us into those silent pauses of fate that only subsequently turn out to have possessed the seed for quite a different lot in life from the one given us. (1929*b*/1999, 271–2)

The "silent pauses" away from the homogeneously inscribed image of the self and the moment in between "masks" are like the caesura of writing that moves the self elsewhere by way of the "distorted images of ourselves that the charlatan holds out to us," and to the edge of the known that also inaugurates the unknown, the Other. This is the meaning of the "sharp, black edges at the feet of things, preparing to retreat silently, unnoticed, into their burrow, their secret being" (1929*b*/1999, 272) of the "short shadows" of these Benjaminian pieces. They originate images that generate thought-images in the same way that writing (as "distortion") does. The edges of writing open up the crack.

4. Awakening

Through the subtle developments of line, contour, breakages, and shadings in her drawings, Susan becomes increasingly aware of the boundaries of

FIGURE 31 Awakening. "It shows a little duck inside a big one, the little duck wearing a hat. What she says is, 'It's got a hat on; that means it's ready to come out.'" *Source*: Milner 1969, 302.

the skin, the edges of the bodies of subject and object, and of marks of difference. Awareness of boundaries and edges and initiation into a world of differences, oscillations, translations, and exchanges that Milner now notes in Susan have as much to do with the "handwriting" that makes strokes on the page as they do with skin touching and "stroking" skin. Commenting on [Figure 32], Milner writes:

> I even wondered whether the slight curve indicated that the part of her that could be seeking a mutuality of touch was here her cheek, the addition of the nose suggesting also the memories of the smell of what she touched with her cheek. (334)

Growing awareness of skin, surfaces, and transformation of the annihilating threat of the "no-thing" into a thinkable "absence of a thing" and thus the establishment of O, one day enables Susan to write (to Milner): "I am in the world for the first time for sixteen years" [Figure 31] followed by the Benjaminian observation, "The shock of the realization that one could have been unconscious for so long a time seems almost to send one into unconsciousness again" (375). The dialectic of "inside" and "outside" reawakens for Susan as well. The perception of an outside world comes, for Susan, side by side with a reestablished sense of a "mental space," a *Denkraum*, of absent-mindedness, thought, and play (as, for example, the diagonals in Susan's late drawings begin to be ornamented and take on more playful shapes). This is also the space of the body, and the space traversed by the originary leap, the *Ur-sprung*. It is the space that I am calling

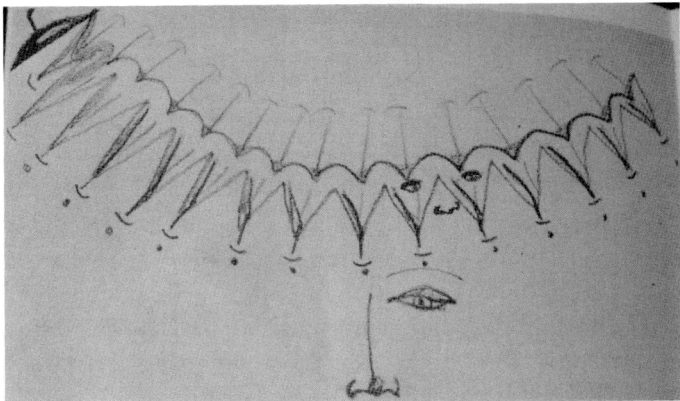

FIGURE 32 Touch of the cheek. *Source:* Milner 1969, 334.

the "space of writing" necessary for the construction of constellations among subjects and objects, subjects and subjects, subjects and their own thoughts and perceptions, that allow for play and transformations of meanings. This is a Benjaminian theory of mimesis.

Conclusion

Rilke's 1900 poem, "Die Blinde," develops many of the phenomena and motifs constituting this book. The "catastrophe" and "survival" that I have described concern the mental space, the *Denkraum*, of the modern individual, encroached upon by the "too much" of modern existence—the traumas of the Real of the twentieth century and impoverishment of experience. Benjamin's work and the "tasks" (for everyone) that he sets are, together with psychoanalysis, ultimately about re-configuring the topographies of mental space and thus also of the self-other relationship. I have attempted to convey the graphic and "non-sensuous" nature of such mental space. "Non-sensuous" has been a difficult term both to imagine and to convey, as, I believe, it combines the meanings of "*ausdruckslos*," but also material and corporeal; non-visual, but also readable. The nature of the mental space that emerges from my constellation of texts in this book, and the obliquely presented (for those who wish to read it) theory of the modern subject I ascribe to Benjamin, is the non-sovereign, forever unfinished, and uncanny space in between subject and object, and between subject and subject that is co-written, is being co-written, and will continue to be co-written. At the same time, the reading-and-writing that weaves the text between subject and object and between subjects, this dialogical structure, is also a theory of reading (and writing, which relies on prior reading) proper; it is simultaneously intensely psychoanalytic and Benjaminian.

It is also the space of literature. One can describe such a theory of reading as a theory of reception as well: a reception of the Other. The Other is received when the receiving subject withdraws and abjects itself momentarily to make space: we have seen this dynamic at work in all of the scenarios I have described. At the same time, such a subject does not subjugate itself to the other: it is not just martyr. Instead, it subverts all grandiosity, not just its own. Mental space continuously engages in *Umwühlen*: rototilling. *Umwühlen* in language and "rummaging" in words are acts that have the power to change a subject's experience in time as well as its relationship to memory, to its own body, and to what Benjamin called "the material community."

"Die Blinde" provides a concrete representation of the relationship between traumatically collapsed psychic structures (catastrophe), absence of mental space, loss of distance, and a new deployment of lines of writing that originate structures leading toward the outside, the open, the Other.

The poem also narrates an increasing diminution of the visual and growth of the aural. Vision is lost suddenly and catastrophically:

Doch es war schrecklich in den ersten Tagen.	But it was terrible in the first days.
Am ganzen Leibe war ich wund. Die Welt,	My whole body was wounded. The world,
die in den Dingen blüht und reift,	that blooms and ripens in the things,
war mit den Wurzeln aus mir ausgerissen,	had been torn out of me by the roots,
mit meinem Herzen (schien mir), und ich lag	together with my heart (it seemed to me), and I lay
wie aufgewühlte Erde offen da und trank	there like dug up earth, and drank
den kalten Regen meiner Tränen,	the cold rain of my tears,
der aus den toten Augen unaufhörlich	that incessantly and quietly flowed from
und leise strömte, wie aus leeren Himmeln,	my dead eyes, like from empty skies,
wenn Gott gestorben ist, die Wolken fallen.	when God has died, and the clouds fall.

But the next line immediately counters this imagery: with the line, "Und mein Gehör war groß und allem offen" ["And my hearing was great and open to everything"], implosion, deadness, and emptiness are countered. This is expectant space, and it is "groß"—a truly "big" and positive word in Rilke. Note that the "world," here identified with sight, is figured as a torn out and absconded tree, and that the void that it leaves makes the skies collapse ("die Wolken fallen" ["the clouds fall"]) onto the blind woman. The tree reminds us of Benjamin's language-tree of "Short Shadows (II)." Loss of sight leads to a new kind of sensory perception in which vision not only disappears but also becomes irrelevant. A visceral perception of an indeterminate presence takes its place, that uncanny sense of the curtains' heaviness, for example, in Mallarmé's "Igitur": "Aber sprech ich zu dir, Mutter?/Oder zu wem denn? Wer ist denn dahinter?/ Wer ist denn hinter dem Vorhang? – Winter?" ("Am I speaking to you, Mother?/ Or to whom? Who is back there?/ Who is behind the curtain? – Winter?"). Such a form of perception concerns the viscerally physical, the formless, the intractable remnant (Kafka's Odradek); it subverts the totalizing grandiosity of vision. "Mother" still finds herself in this illusory realm: "Um dein Gesicht sind noch alle Dinge bemüht,/ ihm wohlzutun" ["All things are still concerned to please your sight (or face)"]. The Blind Woman's eyes, in contrast, seem at first to become petrified and mute in a post-traumatic way:

Wenn deine Augen ruhn	When your eyes rest
und wenn sie noch so müd waren,	no matter how tired they were
sie können wieder steigen.	they can rise again.
. . . Meine schweigen.	. . . Mine are silent.
Meine Blumen werden die Farbe verlieren.	My flowers will lose their colors.
Meine Spiegel werden zufrieren.	My mirrors will freeze shut.
In meinen Büchern werden die Zeilen	In my books the lines will grow
verwachsen.	together.
Meine Vögel werden in den Gassen	My birds will flutter around in the alleyways and wound
herumflattern und sich an fremden Fenstern	themselves on strangers'
verwunden.	windows.
Nichts ist mehr mit mir verbunden.	Nothing remains connected with me.

There is dissociation at work here again, in the repetition of the traumatic wounding, the birds having lost direction, and the loss of all connection. One line sticks out: that of the "lines" in the "book" having become "verwachsen"—overgrown and grown or woven together. The image alludes to a tree, and we remember the uprooted tree as the image for the descent of blindness. "Verwachsen" has more than one meaning: on the one hand, entangled, like branches or roots; it can also mean "deformed," and clearly this meaning is at work in the line as well. But it can refer to a wholly positive sort of growth as well: the growing over and healing of a wound, which operates exactly like written texts, reaching out from the subject's incompleteness.

This meaning helps us in the poem's next few lines: the blind woman now identifies herself as an island, disconnected as she is: "Ich bin eine Insel." At this instant the "FREMDE" responds to her for the first time, connecting to her, as one who is also "disconnected" ("a stranger"):

DER FREMDE:	THE STRANGER:
Und ich bin über das Meer gekommen.	And I have come here across the sea.

DIE BLINDE:
Wie? Auf die Insel? . . .
   Hergekommen?
DER FREMDE:
Ich bin noch im Kahne.
Ich habe ihn leise angelegt—
an dich.

THE BLIND WOMAN:
What? To the island? . . . Come
  here?
THE STRANGER:
I am still in the boat.
I have quietly docked it—
against you.

Imagining the Stranger's boat crossing the water produces more imagery of incision, inscription (the oars slicing through the water's surface and transforming its configurations) and creating movement, like Benjamin's leaves being blown away from the rooted parent tree. The result is motion into the open, which is increasingly identified with the blind woman. She has, as we know, opened her hearing. Her still shaken and dissociated state is now interrupted by the stirring growth of a different sort of structure: something or someone strange who listens to her. The imagery surrounding the "Stranger" is of edges and rims (his boat cuts through the water to reach the island; it edges up to the island's rim) which are associated with the cut the blind woman has experienced: her being cut off from "the world," the tree that has been uprooted. The cuts and edges are transformations and rejections of the illusorily seamless relation to the outside world supplied by vision (which is also the world of the symbol, for Benjamin), and into a partially dissociated state (associated with allegory, for Benjamin) where the sense of hearing takes over, accompanied by a partial sense of boundary dissolution between inside and outside. In other words, like "catastrophe" in this book, images of edges and rims have positive and negative effects. While the Stranger enters into the Blind Woman's dissociated state and *interrupts* it with a presence that cannot be described visually, but only by way of the Blind Woman's description of the alteration in her perceptions, he does not, however, fill her emptiness or stabilize her state: his boat "ist bewegt" ["is agitated"] he says, but "seine Fahne weht landein" ["its flag waves into the [island's] interior"]. The Blind Woman repeats: "Ich bin eine Insel und allein" ["I am an island and alone"]. But now she adds: "Ich bin reich.—" ["I am rich.-"]. As long as she had insisted on her visual relation to the world and protested its destruction she had stood still ("Alle meine verführten Gefühle . . ./ Ich weiß nicht ob sie Jahre so standen, . . ." ["All of my seduced senses . . ./ I don't know if they stood so for years, . . ."]), but "Dann wuchs der Weg zu den Augen zu" ["Then the pathway to the eyes closed up," that is, "grew together"].

Ich weiß ihn nicht mehr.
Jetzt geht alles in mir umher,

sicher und sorglos; wie Genesende

gehn die Gefühle, genießend das
  Gehen,
durch meines Leibes dunkles Haus.

I don't know it any more.
Now everything walks around
  within me,
securely and carefree; like
  convalescents
the feelings move, enjoying their
  walk,
through my body's dark house.

It seems that a different way of "seeing" and "reading," a different relation to walls and edges, as well as a translation in perception and a wholly changed relation to the body have brought about this change. Edges remain edges and cuts even as they do not end all connections. Things are not transcended, but invite the "convalescent" to identify with them:

meine Stimme nimmt jeder Vogel mit

aus den täglichen Wänden.

my voice is transported by every
  bird
from the daily walls.

And here we are once again reminded of Benjamin's "Short Shadows (II)": the tree's "children," its leaves whirling through the world, the "whirling leaves" of this book's cover, the words.

NOTES

Introduction

1. In "Critique of Violence" (1921) Benjamin had engaged with Schmitt's ideas as well.
2. Herzog (2003), of whose essay I became aware only as this book had already gone to press, also focuses on the notion of "catastrophe" in the work of Benjamin. Our emphases in unfolding it differ significantly, however.
3. See Mikkel Borch-Jacobsen (1993), Judith Butler (1991), in particular the "Psychic Mimesis" section of her essay, as well as Jacques Derrida (1981), "The Double Session" on Mallarmé's "Mimique."
4. See, among others, Beatrice Hanssen (2000), Samuel Weber (1991), Rainer Nägele (1991), Bettine Menke (1991), Sigrid Weigel (1996), Bainard Cowan (1981), Susan Buck-Morss (1989), Timothy Bahti (1992), John Pizer (1987), Max Pensky (1996).
5. Pizer (1987) emphasizes both the contradictoriness and the succinctness bordering on esotericism of the main interpretations of Benjamin's "origin." See his summary of scholarship on Benjamin's notion of "origin."
6. Like the perishing angels of the kabbalah that Benjamin mentions in "Agesilaus Santander" (see Chapter 5).
7. Kabbalistically, the *Ein-Sof*. The two certainly work together: see Howard Caygill (1998), "Introduction."
8. Benjamin's contemporary, art historian Aby Warburg, established the term *Denkraum*, thinking space, as a realm in which a viewer's primitive destructive urges could find both cathartic (and mimetic) release and be thought through. See Chapter 3, Warburg (1999), and Brosius (1997).

Chapter 1

1. Hanssen (1995) explains Benjamin's notion of origin by way of his theory of translation and translatability: translation combines restoration with difference and intractable unfinishedness (any translation can be further translated).
2. See also Pensky (2001).
3. This is one context in which Hanssen's (2000) reference to the realm of "the mothers" and her invocation of Bachofen are most helpful.
4. See Fenves (2001) on the influence on Benjamin's thinking of the Husserlian notion of *epochē*, which involves the sort of radical "withdrawal" I find to be at work in the undoing of a constitution—be it legal or psychic.
5. At first in the breakdown of language as communication that takes place in the *Trauerspiel*, there is "contemplative paralysis" and a "deadening of emotions . . . [that] can increase the distance between the self and the surrounding world to the point of alienation from the body," which, however, also has antithetical effects: "As soon as this symptom of depersonalization was seen as an intense degree of mournfulness, the concept of the pathological state, in which the

most simple object appears to be the symbol of some enigmatic wisdom because it lacks any natural, creative relationship to us, was set in an incomparably productive context" (1928/1998, 140).

6. In "Agesilaus Santander" (1933*g*/1999) a text esoterically about *Ursprung*, recollection, memory, and exile at a moment of danger (August 1933), Benjamin identifies himself closely with this baroque melancholy and with Saturn. Scholem (1983) confirms the significance of this connection when he claims to solve the name-anagram: "Agesilaus Santander" is a transformation of "Angelus Satanas," and thus related to the abysmal fascinations of the Baroque.

7. In a strange but suggestive way this phrase, "a new-born object," resonates with the "newborn" in Benjamin's 1933 essays, "Doctrine of the Similar" and "The Mimetic Faculty" which carries the significance of a remnant of a mimetic faculty—that is, how being immersed in the ways in which the various languages, verbal and non-, create community—that has now been lost, but of which the "newborn" reminds us.

8. See also Bolz (2002), 122.

9. See Samuel Weber (1991) and Nina Zimnik (1997), for example.

10. That is, he embodies the fundamental split that inhabits human language; he acts as caesura. As such, and perhaps somewhat surprisingly so, the allegorist acts out *Ursprung*. The typical allegorist (who wishes to forget about his martyr-trait) does not exploit his activity in order to break out of convention.

11. On the whole, Steinberg reads Benjamin as a Kantian, which, again, is and is not the case.

12. Some truly moving embodiments of what Benjamin is talking about here are the stunning outdoor life-size "scenes" of the Monti Sacri in Orta and Varallo.

13. Makropoulos (1989) claims that Benjamin attempts to construct transcendence from within immanence as a form of redemption (20). I agree more with Weber who claims that at the end of the *Trauerspiel* book we are left with radical ambiguity and ambivalence. The latter may not be total, however. I agree with Norbert Bolz (2002) that the theological paradigm is the most constant one in Benjamin; it remains to be seen, however, what an immanent theology might be. As Bolz says, according to Benjamin, history has to be understood theologically, but must not be represented in theological terms (117).

Chapter 2

1. A master signifier is a signifier which stops the slippage of meaning and establishes the symbolic order by way of this fixed meaning. The choice of specific signifier is random; once it is set in place, however, it provides a stable signifying—symbolic—order. It is functional and thus an "empty signifier."

2. "[T]he symptom is a mode of treatment" (Gault 2007, 73).

3. All citations refer to the French publication of Lacan's Seminar XXIII. The English translations are by Luke Thurston (unpublished).

4. Lacan (1975–76) says Joyce perceived this slipping of the Borromean knot in the shape of "original sin" (13) (the "sin" here another source for the

neologism "sinthome"); the same guilt pervades Baroque culture in Benjamin's view.

5. See also Menninghaus (1980, 218).

6. My summary of the three orders that structure human life and subjectivity is very cursory and formulated specifically for my purposes here. For an excellent introduction to Lacanian terminology, see Evans (1996).

7. Lacan says in the Seminar on the *sinthome* (1975–76) that the subject/knot without *sinthome* is "paranoiac" (12). In the trinity knot all three "have one and the same consistence. And this is what paranoiac psychosis consists of" (13). The ramifications of this for aesthetic theory are very rich.

8. The *objet a* is "the object which can never be attained, which is really the cause of desire rather than that toward which desire tends . . . It is the object of desire insofar as the subject compulsively strives toward it. It is the cause of desire in its phylogenetic persistence in the psyche as a trace of that lost plenitude toward which desire tends" (Ross 2002).

9. See Bowie, quoted in Ross (2002).

10. "Let us illustrate this with the incident that interrupted my class: a bomb scare. The bomb did not exist. However, we had the proof that, without existing, it produces its effect. . . . at the very moment when this object crops up via the signifier 'Bomb!' the Other is emptied, disappears. Only the object remains, the object in a desert" (Miller 1994, 81).

11. See also Metzger (1997, 162).

12. "the jouissance of the phallus . . . is located at the conjunction of the symbolic and the real, and is experienced as a parasite by the subject supported by the speaking-being, in the sense of what I designate as the unconscious. I mark it in balance over against meaning. This is the site consciously designated as power by the speaking-being" (Lacan 1975–76/1999, 56).

13. The "lamella" in Lacan's terminology is the placenta, that part of the primordial body from which the subject must separate in order to exist.

14. See Beckett's *Not I*, where such a "third person" is embodied by the "Auditor," who simply listens to the monologue of "Mouth" who, seemingly telling her own story, insists on doing so in third person, thus establishing "three" participants to the narrative, which never succeeds in separating itself from the "Mouth" as long as it refuses to say "I."

15. We also see it at work in Benjamin's (1932–34/2006) appropriations of this element of baroque *and* modernist relationship to language, as for example in the "Mummerehlen" segment in his *Berlin Childhood Around 1900.*

16. Even as allegorical writing may also stand in a mimetic relationship to creation. One might ask whether the martyr-allegorist in Benjamin's *Trauerspiel* book functions as a sort of analyst for us as we face violent demands for apotheosis all around us in a re-theocratizing twenty-first century.

17. See also Warburg's "Denkraum" (Chapter 3) and Bion's rescue of the idea of "thinking" in Chapter 5.

18. Apollon refers to a specific case in which the end of the treatment manifests an at least partial slipping away of the imaginary and the establishment of a *sinthome:* "There is, however, a remnant, one that Marguerite recognizes as essential and that no satisfaction reduces. Here she finally recognizes the source of all her misfortune and of her greatest madness. She hangs on to this remnant . . . And to do that she will take any risk. In not wanting to make any

concession on this remnant, her life may now take an unpredictable turn" (139–40).

19. In part the theory of the *sinthome* arose in response to the problem of the perseverance—the remnants—of symptoms upon completion of analysis. It was to offer an answer to the question of the "meaning" of these leftover ruins of symptoms, after they had been translated into verbal communiqués. There is precisely no question of meaning in the *sinthome;* rather, it is a question of being.

20. See also Susan Buck-Morss (1992).

21. See also Makropoulos (1989, 22).

22. See also Nägele (1991): "[t]he rise of allegory in modernity indicates a fundamental shift in the experience and concept of subjectivity" (82).

23. For a detailed discussion of "*Ponderación Misteriosa*" and a summary of its reception, see Pensky (2001), chapter 3.

24. Zimnik (1997, 297) interprets the empty balcony as an image for the potential for true democracy.

25. The extent of Benjamin's familiarity with kabbalistic thought is a contested subject. I am guided by the few references Benjamin makes to kabbalah (1933g and 1916). It seems likely that Benjamin was or would have been interested in the *Zohar*'s presentation of *God*'s relationship to the signifier as well as to the origin of writing. The kabbalistic idea most relevant to my understanding of writing and the consequent structure of subjectivity in Benjamin and by extension to a significant extent in Lacan as well is that of *tsim-tsum* (Scholem 1961, 260), a key moment in the act of creation that would seem to undermine and negate the act itself in that its main function is an act of subtraction and withdrawal (261). The deity's *tsim-tsum* is self-eclipse, a "banishing Himself from His totality" (261), a strange moment of self-deconstruction on the part of God about to engage in the act of creation. The act of "withdrawing" something to make room for what will be in that space is followed by the material manipulation of letters. It is originary: creation through the speech act cannot take place without the writing. *Tsim-tsum* as withdrawal is analogous to the *act* of the *sinthome* that withdraws the Name-of-the-Father to begin the process of writing. It can but must not be an act of violence. Nevertheless, it may be an act of "divine violence" as Benjamin conceives of it in "Critique of Violence," and thus also related to martyrdom.

Introduction to Part 2

1. In particular Beatrice Hanssen (2000) and Eric Santner (2006) and their interpretations of "the creaturely"; Peter Fenves (2001), in his interpretation of the relationship between the messianic, "silence," and the infinitesimal site of the body, and Sigrid Weigel and Gerhard Richter, in their psychoanalytic readings of Benjamin's mimetic "corpus."

2. See also Susan Buck-Morss (1992) and Margaret Cohen (1995) on Benjamin's "phantasmagoria"; Winfried Menninghaus (1980) and Bernd Witte (2007) on Benjamin's theories of language, mimesis, and "rescue"; Howard Caygill (1998) on the importance to Benjamin of color, in particular, children's use of

watercolors; of Rainer Nägele (1991) on the psycho-philosophical importance of *caesura* in Benjamin's work, and Norbert Bolz (2002) on Benjamin's messianism.

Chapter 3

1. Franz Rosenzweig was to make a similar argument, for example, in "Das neue Denken" (Rosenzweig 1984).
2. See also Caygill (1998).
3. "There is at least one spot in every dream at which it is unplumbable—a navel, as it were, that is its point of contact with the unknown" (Freud 1965, 143n.).
4. "What I saw in her throat: a white patch and turbinal bones with scabs on them" (Freud 1965, 143).
5. "Wagner's *Gesamtkunstwerk*, 'intimately related to the disenchantment of the world' [Adorno], is an attempt to produce a totalizing metaphysics instrumentally, by means of every technological means at its disposal" (Buck-Morss 1992, 25).
6. See Chapter 5.
7. See Sandler (2003). In his memories of his war experiences Bion recognized phantasmagoric mental functioning as having been produced by trauma: "value judgments constantly conjoined with feelings of possessing what can be called 'the absolute truth'"; delusion of omnipotence, as well as "the persistence of a hallucination, ever-repeating, reproducing" (64).
8. "Kafka . . . divests the human gesture of its traditional supports and then has a subject for reflection without end . . . But do we have the doctrine which Kafka's parables interpret and which K.'s postures and the gestures of his animals clarify? It does not exist; all we can say is that here and there we have an allusion to it. . . ." (Benjamin 1934a, 122) *and*: "No other writer has obeyed the commandment 'Thou shalt not make unto thee a graven image' so faithfully" (129).
9. Benjamin's second major emphasis in his reading of Kafka, the theatricality of modern subjectivity as it finds expression in writing and *gesture*, is intimately related to the martyrdom-allegory-innervation sequence as it emerges in the *Trauerspiel*. In his Kafka essay Benjamin writes, "'Often the official dictates in such a low voice that that the scribe cannot even hear it sitting down; then he has to jump up, catch the dictation, quickly sit down again and write it down, then jump up again and so forth. How strange that is! It is almost incomprehensible!' It may be easier to understand this if one thinks of the actors in the Nature Theater. Actors have to catch their cues in a flash, and they resemble those assiduous people in other ways as well. Truly, for them 'hammering is real hammering and at the same time nothing'—provided that this is part of their role. They study this role, and only a bad actor would forget a word or a movement. For the members of the Oklahoma troupe, however, the role is their earlier life; hence the 'nature' in this Nature Theater" (1934, 137).
10. "The true, creative overcoming of religious illumination certainly does not lie in narcotics. It resides in a *profane illumination*, a materialistic, anthropological inspiration" (Benjamin 1929a, 209),
11. See also Caygill 1998, 120.

12. The compulsive repetition or echoing of a verbal utterance made by another person.
13. The abnormal imitation of another's physical actions, often seen in schizophrenia.
14. The metaphor here is physical, though what I am describing is psychophysical. The more physiological version of the metaphoric tumble is the phenomenon of "the bends," nitrogen narcosis, in which a diver who ascends too quickly to the surface from a deep dive is overcome with decompression sickness. Inert gases come out of their solution in the body's tissues via abnormal channels, causing life-threatening symptoms. Bion offers a strikingly similar scenario of a body-mind reacting to the sudden explosions of psychic containers: "The ensuing state can be most easily expressed by using surgical shock as a model: in this the dilatation of the capillaries throughout the body so increases the space in which blood can circulate that the patient may bleed to death in his own tissues" (see Chapter 5).
15. In his "The Double Session" (1981), Derrida writes of Mallarmé's acts of mimesis as a sort of performance of the original out of nothing, making his poetic word creative in its most archaic sense. In Mallarmé's "Mimique," he "represents nothing, imitates nothing, does not have to conform to any prior referent with the aim of achieving adequation or verisimilitude. One can here foresee an objection: since the mime imitates nothing, reproduces nothing, opens up in its origin the very thing he is tracing out, presenting or producing, he must be the very movement of truth. Not, of course, truth in the form of adequation between the representation and the present of the thing itself, or between imitator and imitated, but truth as the present unveiling of the present ... but this is not the case ... We are faced then with mimicry imitating nothing: faced, so to speak, with the double that couples no simple, a double that nothing anticipates, nothing at least, that is not itself already double. There is no simple reference ... this speculum reflects no reality: it produces mere 'reality-effects' ... in this speculum with no reality, in this mirror of a mirror, a difference or dyad does exist, since there are mimes and phantoms. But it is a difference without reference, or rather reference without a referent, without any first or last unit, a ghost that is the phantom of no flesh ..." (206). I prefer to read "Igitur" as a sort of prayer to the original hole and less of a performance of Creation.
16. The parallel here with Daniel Paul Schreber who also attained his freedom by demonstrating his mental acuity in his book, *Memoirs of My Nervous Illness*, is striking, especially considering some of the thematic overlap between the two texts. Schreber's text is quite psychotic, of course, while Warburg's is not.

Chapter 4

1. See also Menke (1991), 111.
2. See Evans (1996): "As well as the object of language, *das Ding* is the object of desire. It is the lost object which must be continually refound, it is the prehistoric, unforgettable Other ... The Thing is thus presented to the subject as his

Sovereign Good, but if the subject transgresses the pleasure principle and attains this Good, it is experienced as suffering/evil . . ." (205).

3. See also Gebauer and Wulf (1996): "[Nonsensuous] designates similarities that are not directly legible but must be decoded, which suggests that the whole cosmos is permeated by similarities, the sense of which is always there to be exposed to minds capable of decoding it in an act of reading" (270).

4. While Caygill holds that montage—the compilation of constellations that do justice to alterity—replaces mimesis, I would prefer to say that the two continue to work side by side in the mimetic processes.

5. Throughout this text, childhood mimesis is mediated by language (131).

6. What Levinas (1996) calls "contraction" and "absolute passivity." It is also the kabbalistic *tsim-tsum*, as Gerschom Scholem (1961) describes it.

7. "By the detour of world-annihilation, which radicalizes the Cohenian method of annihilation by revealing its 'content,' consciousness is entirely removed from the causal schemata through which the world as a whole has been held together. In the terms Benjamin uses in 'The Program for the Coming Philosophy' and 'On Perception,' phenomenology transforms the concept of knowledge, and by so doing it makes possible a transformation of the concept of experience" (Fenves 2001, 193).

8. See also Lacan (1968, 201).

Chapter 5

1. The works by Klein I draw on (1987) in this section are some of her most influential: "The Psychological Principles of Infant Analysis" (1926/1987), "Infantile Anxiety Situations Reflected in a Work of Art and in the Creative Impulse" (1929/1987), "The Importance of Symbol Formation in the Development of the Ego" (1930/1987), "A Contribution to the Psychogenesis of Manic-Depressive States" (1935/1987), "Mourning and Its Relation to Manic-Depressive States" (1940/1987), "Notes on Some Schizoid Mechanisms" (1946/1987).

2. ". . . [B]ecause we cannot be certain of the identities that describe the archaic link between the ego and the Other, it may be more helpful to speak of an *abject* rather than of an ego of an object already there. The future subject is founded upon a dynamic of abjection whose optimal quality is fascination. And if this future subject readily grants himself a 'presence' of other people that he internalizes as much as it expels, he is not facing an object but, in fact, an *ab-ject*, with this *a* understood in the privative sense of the prefix, that is, as vitiating the object as well as the emerging subject" (Kristeva 2002, 72–3).

3. Klein 1935/1987, 143–4.

4. See Grotstein (2006, 114).

5. "What to my view is quite specific for mania is the utilization of the sense of omnipotence for the purpose of controlling and mastering objects. This is necessary for two reasons: (a) in order to deny the dread of them which is being experienced, and (b) so that the mechanism . . . of making reparation to the object may be carried through" (Klein 1935/1987, 133).

6. Sandler (2003) notes that often a consequence of PS processes is that while at first "aspects of the mind" are expelled, later it is "the mind itself that suffers this fate" (66). Elizabeth Bott Spillius writes: "Gradually this capacity evolves into an ability to imagine that the bad feeling of being frustrated is actually occurring because there is a good object which is absent and which may or may not return. If, however, capacity for frustration is low, the 'no-breast' experience does not develop into the thought of a 'good breast absent'; it exists as a 'bad breast present'; it is felt to be a bad concrete object which must be got rid of by evacuation, that is, by omnipotent projection. If this process becomes entrenched, true symbols and thinking cannot develop" (1994).

7. "In the words of Aristotle, 'catastrophe' is an action bringing ruin and pain on stage, where corpses are seen and wounds and other similar sufferings are performed" (Aristotle, *Poetics*, XI, 10) (Sportelli 1988, 126).

8. Adorno's discussion of poetic language is all in one way or another related to his famous pronouncement about "poetry after Auschwitz." It regards the historical fact of the language of instrumentality, rationality, and efficiency having been irreparably discredited in view of its collusion with the "event" Auschwitz. Yet Adorno also pointed out that this saying was to be understood dialectically: true art should resist this saying and not fall to cynicism; instead, it should retrieve language, confront the horrors that still cling to it, and use it differently, self-consciously, as *other*. Such art, conscious of where language "has been," so to speak, is art that remains "true to suffering," even as it makes language "suffer." In "Commitment" (1962) Adorno writes: "The abundance of real suffering tolerates no forgetting . . . Yet this suffering, what Hegel called consciousness of adversity, also demands the continued existence of art while it prohibits it; it is now virtually in art alone that suffering can still find its own voice, consolation, without immediately being betrayed by it" (312).

9. The founder of the Tavistock Clinic, in 1920, was Hugh Crichton-Miller. Aside from Bion, other notable psychiatrists and psychoanalysts associated with it were R. D. Laing, John Bowlby, and Michael Fordham.

10. Beckett's novel *Murphy* (1938) dramatizes this entirely.

11. There are many other Benjaminian images about how to envision history redemptively that may be relevant to the individual analytic situation: for example, in Thesis III, Benjamin writes,

> A chronicler who recites events without distinguishing between major and minor ones acts in accordance with the following truth: nothing that has ever happened should be regarded as lost for history. To be sure, only a redeemed mankind receives the fullness of its past—which is to say, only for a redeemed mankind has its past become citable in all its moments. (Benjamin 1940/1969, 254).

Recording everything "that has ever happened," an obvious impossibility, is Bion's thought without a thinker, the open system of "O," as we will see. The narrative transformations that are possible within this stance before the past make the past both readable and useful for the present. The relationship of past moments to moments occurring now is refined in Thesis IV with this metaphor: "As flowers turn toward the sun, by dint of a secret heliotropism the past strives to turn toward that sun which is rising in the sky of history. A historical materialist must be aware of this most inconspicuous of all transformations" (1940/1969, 255).

Projective identification, which enables the infant to gain distance from "himself" by contemplating what he "sees" in the mother, or the analysand to contemplate in what he has projected onto the analyst, may have a counterpart in what the historical materialist does in the present when he contemplates the "catastrophes" of the "past" (which are also his own); those moments of the past, however, whether catastrophic or not, do not remain static but are always on the verge of disappearing. Benjamin's theory of experience, a way of being in the world that is not guided primarily by instrumental reason but that learns to engage with the past in a way that is not dominated by ideas of conquest and a progress that depends on a view of the past as conquered as well, has, in my opinion, enough affinity with Bion's way of thinking and difference from what is primarily an individualist focus, to have something to offer to Bionian psychoanalysis.

12. They are psychotic mechanisms that destroy links established by interpretation in analysis, the analytic couple linked in a common effort, as well as the capacity for understanding itself (Bion 1959, 309). Attacks on linking, says Bion, come into being when the most primitive form of communication, projective identification primarily of fear of death into the mother who processes it without too much dread and makes it available for re-introjection, fails too many times. This failure makes the external object appear hostile to communication and to curiosity, leading to arrested development.

13. In this particular vocabulary we catch a glimpse of the thought of Levinas, to whose thought Bion's is anything but foreign.

14. Benjamin, of course, too flirts with Platonism in his *Trauerspiel* book.

15. Weigel (1996) too insists that it is in distortion that Benjamin seeks "truth."

16. See also Hansen (1999): "Benjamin seeks to reactivate the abilities of the body as a medium in the service of imagining new forms of subjectivity" (321).

17. See also Weigel (1996): "The fact that an image in the form of a bodily expressive gesture becomes engraved in memory, the so-called 'pathos formula' (*Pathosformel*), is attributed to an excitation compared with the leaving of a trace; that is entirely analogous with the psychoanalytical description of the mnemic or memory trace (see Wind 1983, 30–1)" (1996, 151).

18. See Fenves (2001) and Caygill (1998) on Benjamin's "Dialogue on the Rainbow."

19. While Caygill (1998) refers to "folds" in Benjamin's thinking and language several times and in suggestive ways, he does not take the thought any further.

20. In her 1929 essay, "Infantile Anxiety-Situations Reflected in a Work of Art and the Creative Impulse," Klein originated the creative impulse in the transition from PS (destruction) to D (reparation) by way of her reading of Ravel's opera *L'enfant et les sortileges*. She implies that the destructions, violences, and terrors of PS form the "black hole," so to speak, without which no art work—or any reparation, including healthy object relations—can come into being.

21. Possibly Benjamin's reference to language's "age-old marriage with the tree" is also a reference to the Tree of Life of the Lurianic kabbalah, the ten *sefirot*,

products of the "catastrophe creation," the explosive exile of creation from the center of its Creator. To what extent Benjamin was consciously influenced by the kabbalistic symbolism that was being unearthed (and *umgewühlt*) by his close friend Gershom Scholem remains an open question.

22. Undoubtedly, Benjamin is also referring to the *Shekhinah*.
23. "[U]nfolding [i]s the continuation of the script's texture, the script-surface . . . the constant postponement of the end in meaning" (Menke 1991, 128, my translation).

Introduction to Part 3

1. See Santner (1996) where he bridges the divide between individual and collective when he has Schreber's physical symptoms and delusions tell, in "translation," so to speak, the story of the "state of emergency," when "at moments of heightened social antagonism, what is 'rotten in the law' begins to leak through from its normally circumscribed spaces" (16), as he writes.

Chapter 6

1. See also Weigel (1996), 51.
2. See Peter Fenves (2001) on infinity.
3. Caygill (1998) refers to such "bad" aura as denial of finitude (93).
4. The theological version of this original face-to-face could be the *imitatio dei* (see Chapter 3), where the mimetic origin of the human face is followed by the bestowal of language upon the human.
5. See also Weigel (1996), 130.

Works Cited

Adorno, Theodor W. 1961/2005. Trying to Understand Endgame. In *Modernism: An Anthology*, ed. Lawrence Rainey, 1119–39. Hoboken & London: Wiley-Blackwell.

—. 1962. Commitment. *New Left Review* I: 87–8, September-December 1974.

—. 1983. *Prisms*, ed. and trans. Shierry Weber Nicholsen and Samuel Weber. Cambridge, MA: MIT Press.

Agamben, Giorgio. 2005. *State of Exception*, trans. Kevin Attell. Chicago: The University of Chicago Press.

American Psychiatric Association. 1994. *Diagnostic and Statistical Manual of Mental Disorders*, 4th edition.

Andre, Chris. 1998. Aphrodite's Children: Hopeless Love, Historiography, and Benjamin's Dialectical Image. *SubStance* 27, no.1, 85: 105–28.

Apollon, Willy. 2002a. The Letter of the Body. In *After Lacan: Clinical Practice and the Subject of the Unconscious*, by Willy Apollon, Danielle Bergeron, and Lucie Cantin, ed. Robert Hughes and Kareen Ror Malone, 103–15. New York: State University of New York Press.

—. 2002b. The Symptom. In *After Lacan: Clinical Practice and the Subject of the Unconscious*, by Willy Apollon, Danielle Bergeron, and Lucie Cantin, ed. Hughes and Ror Malone, 117–26.

—. 2002c. From Symptom to Fantasy. In *After Lacan: Clinical Practice and the Subject of the Unconscious*, by Willy Apollon, Danielle Bergeron, and Lucie Cantin, ed. Hughes and Ror Malone, 127–40.

Badiou, Alain. 2007. *The Century*, trans. Alberto Toscano. Malden, MA: Polity Press.

Bahti, Timothy. 1992. *Allegories of History: Literary Historiography after Hegel*. Baltimore, MD: The Johns Hopkins University Press.

Beckett, Samuel. 1938/1994. *Murphy*. New York: Grove Press.

—. 1953/2009. *The Unnameable*. In *Three Novels: Molloy, Malone Dies, The Unnameable*. New York: Grove Press.

—. 1957/1994. *Endgame*. In *Endgame and Act Without Words*. New York: Grove Press.

—. 1972/1973. *Not I*. London: Faber and Faber.

—. 1982/1994. *Catastrophe*. In *Collected Shorter Plays of Samuel Beckett: All That Fall, Act Without Words, Krapp's Last Tape, Cascando, Eh Joe, Footfall, Rockaby and others*. New York: Grove Press.

Benjamin, Walter. 1913–14/1996. The Metaphysics of Youth: "The Conversation." In *Walter Benjamin. Selected Writings. Volume 1. 1913–1926*, ed. Marcus Bullock and Michael W. Jennings, 6–17. Cambridge, MA & London, England: The Belknap Press of Harvard University Press.

—. 1914–15a/1996. A Child's View of Color. In *Walter Benjamin. Selected Writings. Volume 1*, ed. Bullock and Jennings, 50–51.

—. 1914–15b/1996. The Life of Students. In *Walter Benjamin. Selected Writings. Volume 1*, ed. Bullock and Jennings, 37–47.

—. 1914–15c/1996. Two Poems by Friedrich Hölderlin. In *Walter Benjamin. Selected Writings. Volume 1*, ed. Bullock and Jennings, 18–36.

—. 1916/1996. On Language as Such and on the Language of Man. In *Walter Benjamin. Selected Writings. Volume 1*, ed. Bullock and Jennings, 62–74.

—. 1916a. The Role of Language in *Trauerspiel* and Tragedy. In *Walter Benjamin. Selected Writings. Volume 1*, ed. Bullock and Jennings, 59–61.

—. 1918/1996. On the Program of the Coming Philosophy. In *Walter Benjamin. Selected Writings. Volume 1*, ed. Bullock and Jennings, 100–10.

—. 1919–22/1996. Goethe's Elective Affinities. In *Walter Benjamin. Selected Writings. Volume 1*, ed. Bullock and Jennings, 297–360.

—. 1920/1996. The Concept of Criticism in German Romanticism. In *Walter Benjamin. Selected Writings. Volume 1*, ed. Bullock and Jennings, 116–200.

—. 1921–23/1996. The Task of the Translator. In *Walter Benjamin. Selected Writings. Volume 1*, ed. Bullock and Jennings, 253–63.

—. 1921/1996. Critique of Violence. In *Walter Benjamin. Selected Writings. Volume 1*, ed. Bullock and Jennings, 236–52.

—. 1922–23/1996. Outline of the Psychophysical Problem. In *Walter Benjamin. Selected Writings. Volume 1*, ed. Bullock and Jennings, 393–401.

—. 1925/1996. Naples. In *Walter Benjamin. Selected Writings. Volume 1*, ed. Bullock and Jennings, 414–21.

—. 1927/1999. Moscow. In *Walter Benjamin. Selected Writings. Volume 2. 1927–34*, trans. Rodney Livingstone and Others, ed. Michael W. Jennings, Howard Eiland, and Gary Smith, 22–46. Cambridge, MA & London, England: The Belknap Press of Harvard University Press.

—. 1928/1998. *The Origin of German Tragic Drama*. New York & London: Verso.

—. 1928/1999. Review of the Mendelssohns' *Der Mensch in der Handschrift*. In *Walter Benjamin. Selected Writings. Volume 2*, ed. Jennings, 131–4.

—. 1929a/1999. Surrealism: The Last Snapshot of the European Intelligentsia. In *Walter Benjamin. Selected Writings. Volume 2*, ed. Jennings, 207–21.

—. 1929b/1999. Short Shadows (I). In *Walter Benjamin. Selected Writings. Volume 2*, ed. Jennings, 268–72.

—. 1930/1999. Graphology Old and New. In *Walter Benjamin. Selected Writings. Volume 2*, ed. Jennings, 398–400.

—. 1931a/1999. Little History of Photography. In *Walter Benjamin. Selected Writings. Volume 2*, ed. Jennings, 507–30.

—. 1931b/1999. Theological Criticism. In *Walter Benjamin. Selected Writings. Volume 2*, ed. Jennings, 428–32.

—. 1931 or 1932/1999. Experience. In *Walter Benjamin. Selected Writings. Volume 2*. ed. Jennings, 553.

—. 1932–34/2006. *Berlin Childhood around 1900*, trans. Howard Eiland. Cambridge & London: The Belknap Press of Harvard University Press.

—. 1933a/1999. Short Shadows (II). In *Walter Benjamin. Selected Writings. Volume 2*, ed. Jennings, 699–702.

—. 1933b/1999. Doctrine of the Similar. In *Walter Benjamin. Selected Writings. Volume 2*, ed. Jennings, 694–8.

—. 1933c/1999. Experience and Poverty. In *Walter Benjamin. Selected Writings. Volume 2*, ed. Jennings, 731–6.

—. 1933d/1999. The Mimetic Faculty. In *Walter Benjamin. Selected Writings. Volume 2*, ed. Jennings, 720–2.

—. 1933*e*/1999. The Lamp. In *Walter Benjamin. Selected Writings. Volume 2*, ed Jennings, 691–3.

—. 1933*f*/1978. Berlin Chronicle. In *Reflections: Essays, Aphorisms, Autobiographical Writings*, by Walter Benjamin. New York: Harvest/HBJ.

—. 1933*g*/1999. Agesilaus Santander (II). In *Walter Benjamin. Selected Writings. Volume 2*, ed. Jennings, 714–16.

—. 1934/2002. Problems in the Sociology of Language. In *Walter Benjamin. Selected Writings. Volume 3, 1935–1938*, trans. Edmund Jephcott, Howard Eiland, and Others, ed. Howard Eiland and Michael W. Jennings, 68–93. Cambridge, MA & London, England: The Belknap Press of Harvard University Press.

—. 1934*a* /1999. Franz Kafka: On the Tenth Anniversary of His Death. In *Walter Benjamin. Selected Writings. Volume 2*, ed. Jennings, 794–818.

—. 1934*b*. Franz Kafka: On the Tenth Anniversary of His Death. In *Illuminations: Essays and Reflections*, ed. Hannah Arendt, 111–40. New York: Schocken Books.

—. 1936/2002. The Work of Art in the Age of Its Reproducibility. *Walter Benjamin. Selected Writings. Volume 3*, ed. Eiland, 101–33.

—. 1920–21 or 1937–38/2002. Theological-Political Fragment. *Walter Benjamin. Selected Writings. Volume 3*, ed. Eiland, 305–6.

—. 1939/1969. On Some Motifs in Baudelaire. In *Illuminations: Essays and Reflections*, ed. Hannah Arendt, 155–200. New York: Schocken Books.

—. 1940/1969. Theses on the Philosophy of History. *Illuminations*, 253–64.

—. 1974. *Gesammelte Schriften vol. 3*. ed. Rolf Tiedemann and Hermann Schweppenhäuser. Frankfurt am Main: Suhrkamp Verlag.

—. 1994. *The Correspondence of Walter Benjamin 1910–1940*, ed. Gershom Scholem and Theodor W. Adorno. Chicago & London: The University of Chicago Press.

Bierce, Ambrose. 1911. *Devil's Dictionary*. Online Etymology Dictionary. http://www.etymonline.com.

Bion, W. R. 1959. Attacks on Linking. *International Journal of Psycho-Analysis* 40: 308–15.

—. 1962. *Learning from Experience*. New York: Basic Books.

—. 1965/1977. *Transformations*. In *Seven Servants: Four Works*, by W. R. Bion. Lanham, MD: Jason Aronson, Inc.

—. 1970/1977. Attention and Interpretation. In *Seven Servants: Four Works*, by W. R. Bion. Lanham, MD: Jason Aronson, Inc.

Bloom, Harold. 1991. Freud: Frontier Concepts, Jewishness, and Interpretation. *American Imago* 48, no.1: 135–52.

Bolz, Norbert. 2002. *Heilsversprechen*. München: Fink Verlag.

Bonnefoy, Yves. 1999. Igitur and the Photographer. Part I, trans. Mary Ann Caws. In *Stéphane Mallarmé: Painter among the Poets*. New York: Hunter College Art Galleries.

Borch-Jacobsen, Mikkel. 1993. *The Emotional Tie*. Palo Alto, CA: Stanford University Press.

Bott Spillius, Elizabeth. 1994. Developments in Kleinian Thought: Overview and Personal View. *Psychoanalytic Inquiry* 14, no. 3, Contemporary Kleinian Psychoanalysis: 324–64.

Bowie, Malcolm. 1991. *Lacan.* Cambridge, MA: Harvard University Press.

Brosius, Christiane. 1997. *Kunst als Denkraum: Zum Bildungsbegriff von Aby Warburg.* Herbolzheim: Centaurus.

Buck-Morss, Susan. 1989. *The Dialectics of Seeing: Walter Benjamin and the Arcades Project.* Cambridge: The MIT Press.

—. 1992. Aesthetics and Anaesthetics: Walter Benjamin's Art Work Essay Reconsidered. *October* 62: 3–41.

Butler, Judith. 1991. Imitation and Gender Insubordination. In *Inside/Out: Lesbian Theories, Gay Theories,* ed. Diana Fuss, 13–31. New York: Routledge.

Caillois, Roger. 1938. Mimicry and Legendary Psychasthenia. *October* 31: 17–32.

—. 1964. *The Mask of Medusa.* UK: Northumberland Press.

Caygill, Howard. 1998. *Walter Benjamin: The Colour of Experience.* New York & London: Routledge.

Cohen, Margaret. 1995. *Profane Illumination: Walter Benjamin and the Paris of Surrealist Revolution.* Berkeley, CA: University of California Press.

Comay, Rebecca. 1995. *Facies Hippocratica.* In *Ethics as First Philosophy: The Significance of Emmanuel Levinas for Philosophy, Literature and Religion,* ed. Adriaan Theodoor Peperzak, 223–34. New York: Routledge.

Costello, Diarmuid. 2005. Aura, Face, Photography: Re-reading Benjamin Today. In *Walter Benjamin and Art,* ed. Andrew Benjamin, 164–84. London & New York: Continuum Books.

Cowan, Bainard. 1981. Walter Benjamin's Theory of Allegory. *New German Critique* 22: 109–22.

Derrida, Jacques. 1981. *Dissemination,* trans. Barbara Johnson. Chicago: The University of Chicago Press.

Dravers, Philip. 2005. Joyce & the Sinthome: Aiming at the Fourth Term of the Knot. *Psychoanalytical Notebooks of the LSNLS 13, Lacan with Joyce,* 6. http://www.londonsociety-nls.org.uk/pdfs/Joyce&sinthome.pdf (accessed July 10, 2008).

Evans, Dylan. 1996. *An Introductory Dictionary of Lacanian Psychoanalysis.* London & New York: Routledge.

Fenves, Peter. 2001. *Arresting Language: From Leibniz to Benjamin.* Berkeley, CA: Stanford University Press.

Ferenczi, Sándor. 1921/1926. Psycho-Analytical Observations on Tic. In *Further Contributions to the Theory and Technique of Psycho-Analysis,* trans. Jane Isabel Suttie et al. London: Hogarth Press and The Institute of Psycho-Analysis.

Freud, Sigmund. 1920/1961. *Beyond the Pleasure Principle.* London: Hogarth Press.

—. 1921/1990. *Group Psychology and the Analysis of the Ego.* New York: W.W. Norton & Co.

—. 1930/1989. *Civilization and Its Discontents.* W.W. Norton & Co.

—. 1933/1960. Why War? In *Einstein on Peace,* ed. Otto Nathan and Heinz Norden, 186–203. New York: Schocken Books.

—. 1965. *The Interpretation of Dreams,* trans. James Strachey. New York: Avon Books.

Früchtl, Josef. 1986. *Mimesis: Konstellation eines Zentralbegriffs bei Adorno.* Königshausen: Neumann.

Gault, Jean-Luis. 2007. Two Statuses of the Symptom: 'Let Us Turn to Finn Again.' In *The Later Lacan: An Introduction,* ed. Véronique Voruz and Bogdan Wolf, 73–82. Albany: State University of New York Press.

Gebauer, Gunter and Christoph Wulf. 1996. *Mimesis: Culture—Art Society.* Berkeley, CA: University of California Press.

Glover, Nicola. Psychoanalytic Aesthetics: The British School. http://www.human-nature.com/free-associations/glover/chap4.html

Goldstein, Kurt. 1933. L'analyse de l'aphasie et l'étude de l'essence du langage. In *Psychologie du langage, Numéro Exceptionnel du Journal de Psychologie normale et pathologique,* by Delacroix et al., 495–6.

Gombrich, E. H. 1986. *Aby Warburg: An Intellectual Biography.* Chicago: The University of Chicago Press.

Grotstein, James. 2006. Klein's Theory of the Positions Revisited. In *Other Banalities: Melanie Klein Revisited.* ed. Jon Mills. London & New York: Routledge.

Grotstein, James. 2007. *A Beam of Intense Darkness: Wilfred Bion's Legacy to Psychoanalysis.* London: Karnac Books.

Haas, Willy. 1930. *Gestalten der Zeit.* Berlin: G. Kiepenheuer.

Hansen, Miriam Bratu. 1999. Benjamin and Cinema: Not a One-Way Street. *Critical Inquiry* 25 (2): 306–43.

Hanssen, Beatrice. 1995. Philosophy at Its Origin: Walter Benjamin's Prologue to the *Ursprung des deutschen Trauerspiels. MLN* 110 (4): 809–33.

—. (2000). *Walter Benjamin's Other History: Of Stones, Animals, Human Beings, and Angels.* Berkeley, CA: University of California Press.

Healy, Patrick. Joyce: Through the Lacan Glass. In *Lacanian ink 11,* ed. Jacques-Alain Miller. http://www.lacan.com/frameXI3.htm (accessed July 14, 2008).

Herzog, Annabel. 2003. Levinas, Benjamin, and the Oppressed. *The Journal of Jewish Thought and Philosophy* 12 (2): 123–38.

Heschel, Abraham Joshua. 1998. *Man's Quest for God.* Santa Fe: Aurora Press.

The Internet Encyclopedia of Philosophy. http://www.iep.utm.edu/l/lacweb.htm#SH4a.

Jay, Martin. 2006. *Songs of Experience: Modern American and European Variations on a Universal Theme.* Berkeley, CA: University of California Press.

Klein, Melanie. 1935/1987. *The Selected Melanie Klein,* ed. Juliet Mitchell. New York: Free Press.

Koepnick, Lutz P. 1996. The Spectacle, the *Trauerspiel,* and the Politics of Resolution: Benjamin Reading the Baroque Reading Weimar. *Critical Inquiry* 22: 268–91.

Kristeva, Julia. 2001. *Melanie Klein,* trans. Ross Guberman. New York: Columbia University Press.

Lacan, Jacques. 1966. *Écrits.* Paris: Seuil.

—. 1968. *Speech and Language in Psychoanalysis,* trans. Anthony Wilden. Baltimore, MD and London: The Johns Hopkins University Press.

—. 1975. Seminar 22: R.S.I., 1974–75. *Ornicar?* Nos. 2–5.

—. 1975–76/1999. *Le Séminaire livre XXIII. Le sinthome.* Texte établi par Jacques-Alain Miller. Paris: Seuil.

—. 1998. The Rat in the Maze. *Encore 1972–73. The Seminar of Jacques Lacan. Book XX,* ed. Jacques-Alain Miller, trans. Bruce Fink, 137–46. New York & London: W.W. Norton & Co.

Levinas, Emmanuel. 1996. Substitution. In *Emmanuel Levinas: Basic Philosophical Writings,* ed. Adriaan Theodoor Peperzak, Simon Critchley, Robert Bernasconi, 79–96. Bloomington: Indiana University Press.

Lupton, Julia R. 1996. *Afterlives of the Saints: Hagiography, Typology, and Renaissance Literature*. Palo Alto, CA: Stanford University Press.

Makropoulos, Michael. 1989. *Modernität als ontologischer Ausnahmezustand? Walter Benjamins Theorie der Moderne*. München: Fink Verlag.

Menke, Bettine. 1991. *Sprachfiguren: Name, Allegorie, Bild nach Benjamin*. München: Fink Verlag.

Menninghaus, Winfried. 1980. *Walter Benjamins Theorie der Sprachmagie*. Frankfurt a.M.: Suhrkamp Verlag.

—. 1992. Das Ausdruckslose: Walter Benjamins Kritik des Schönen durch das Erhabene. In *Walter Benjamin. 1892–1940. Zum 100. Geburtstag*. ed. Uwe Steiner, 33–76. Bern/Berlin/Frankfurt a. Main/New York/Paris/Wien: Peter Lang.

Metzger, David. 1997. Freud's Jewish Science and Lacan's *Sinthome*. *American Imago* 54, no. 2: 149–64.

Miller, Jacques-Alain. 1994. Extimité. In *Lacanian Theory of Discourse: Subject, Structure, and Society*, ed. Mark Bracher et al., 74–87. New York and London: New York University Press.

—. 1996. Joyce avec Lacan—Preface. Trans. Josefina Ayerza and Cory Reynolds. In *Lacanian ink 11: Art and the Other*, 3–6, http://www.plexus.org/lacink/lacink11/index.html.

Milner, Marion. 1969. *The Hands of the Living God: An Account of a Psychoanalytic Treatment*. Madison, CT: International Universities Press.

Nägele, Rainer. 1991. *Theater, Theory, Speculation: Walter Benjamin and the Scenes of Modernity*. Baltimore, MD: Johns Hopkins University Press.

Neri, Claudio. 2003. Anthropological Psychoanalysis: Bion's Journeying in Italy. In *Building on Bion. Roots: Origins and Context of Bion's Contributions to Theory and Practice (International Library of Group Analysis*, 20), ed. Robert M. Lipgar and Malcolm Pines, 132–52. London: Jessica Kingsley Publishers.

Pensky, Max. 1996. Tactics of Remembrance: Proust, Surrealism, and the Origin of the *Passagenwerk*. In *Walter Benjamin and the Demands of History*, ed. Michael P. Steinberg, 164–89. Ithaca: Cornell University Press.

—. (2001) *Melancholy Dialectics: Walter Benjamin and the Play of Mourning*. Amherst, MA: University of Massachusetts Press.

Pistiner de Cortiñas, Lia. 2003. Transcending the Caesura: The Road Toward Insight: From *Experiences in Groups* to *A Memoir of the Future*. In *Building on Bion: Branches: Contemporary Developments and Applications of Bion's Contributions to Theory and Practice*, ed. Robert M. Lipgar, 225–52. London & New York: Jessica Kingsley Publishers.

Pizer, John. 1987. History, Genre and "Ursprung" in Benjamin's Early Aesthetics. *The German Quarterly* 60, no. 1: 68–87.

Richter, Gerhard. 2002. *Walter Benjamin and the Corpus of Autobiography*. Detroit, MI: Wayne State University Press.

Rilke, Rainer Maria. 1900/1962. "Die Blinde." In *Gesammelte Gedichte*. Frankfurt am Main: Insel Verlag.

—. 1910/1990. *The Notebooks of Malte Laurids Brigge*, trans. Stephen Mitchell. New York: Vintage Books.

Rosand, David. 1999. Reason's Secrets. *The New Republic* (August 23), http://www.thenewrepublic.com/magazines/tnr/archive/0899/082399/rosand082399.html.

Rosenzweig, Franz. 1984. *Zweistromland: Kleinere Schriften Zu Glauben Und Denken.* The Hague: Martinus Nijhoff.

Ross, Steven. 2002. A Very Brief Introduction to Lacan, http://web.uvic.ca/~saross/lacan.html#Objet_a (accessed July 16, 2008).

Rothberg, Michael. 1997. After Adorno: Culture in the Wake of Catastrophe. *New German Critique* 72: 45–81.

Salecl, Renata. 2001. www.dum-club.si/mateja/medici/medici.html (accessed July 16 2008).

Sandler, Paulo Cesar. 2003. Bion's War Memories: A Psychoanalytical Commentary: Living Experiences and Learning from Them: Some Early Roots of Bion's Contributions to Psychoanalysis. In *Building on Bion. Roots: Origins and Context of Bion's Contributions to Theory and Practice (International Library of Group Analysis, 20),* ed. Robert M. Lipgar and Malcolm Pines, 59–84. London: Jessica Kingsley Publishers.

Santner, Eric. 1996. *My Own Private Germany.* Princeton: Princeton University Press.

—. 2006. *On Creaturely Life: Rilke, Benjamin, Sebald.* Chicago: University of Chicago Press.

Scheffczyk, Leo. 1969. *Der Mensch als Bild Gottes.* Darmstadt: Wissenschaftliche Buchgesellschaft.

Schmitt, Carl. 2005. *Political Theology: Four Chapters on the Concept of Sovereignty.* Chicago: University of Chicago Press.

Scholem, Gershom. 1961. *Major Trends in Jewish Mysticism.* New York: Schocken Books.

—. 1983. *Walter Benjamin und sein Engel: Vierzehn Aufsätze und kleine Beiträge.* Frankfurt a.M.: Suhrkamp Verlag.

Schreber, Daniel Paul. 1988. *Memoirs of My Nervous Illness,* trans. and ed. Ida Macalpine and Richard A. Hunter. Intro. Samuel M. Weber. Cambridge, MA & London, England: Harvard University Press.

Schwarzschild, Steven. 1975. The Legal Foundation of Jewish Aesthetics. *Journal of Aesthetic Education* 9, no. 1: 29–42.

Sportelli, Annamaria. 1988. 'Make Sense Who May,' A Study of *Catastrophe* and *What Where.* In *'Make Sense Who May': Essays on Samuel Beckett's Later Works,* ed. Robin J. Davis and L. Butler, Lance St. J., 120–8. Gerrards Cross: Colin Smythe.

Steinberg, Michael. 1996. Introduction. In *Walter Benjamin and the Demands of History,* ed. Michael P. Steinberg, 1–23. Ithaca: Cornell University Press.

Stirk, Peter M. R. 2005. *Carl Schmitt, Crown Jurist of the Third Reich: On Preemptive War, Military Occupation, and World Empire.* UK: Edwin Mellen Press.

Szondi, Peter. 2006. Hope in the Past: On Walter Benjamin. In *Berlin Childhood around 1900,* by Walter Benjamin, trans. Howard Eiland, 1–33. Cambridge, MA: The Belknap Press of Harvard University Press.

Trakl, Georg. 1917. *Gedichte.* Leipzig: Kurt Wolff Verlag.

Warburg, Aby. 1995. *Images from the Region of the Pueblo Indians of North America,* trans. Michael P. Steinberg. Ithaca and London: Cornell University Press.

—. 1999. *The Renewal of Pagan Antiquity: Contributions to the Cultural History of the European Renaissance.* Los Angeles: Getty Research Institute for the History of Art and the Humanities.

Weber, Samuel. 1991. Genealogy of Modernity: History, Myth and Allegory in Benjamin's *Origin of the German Mourning Play*. *MLN* 106, no. 3: 465–500.

Weidmann, Heiner. 1992. *Flanerie, Sammlung, Spiel. Die Erinnerung des 19. Jahrhunderts bei Walter Benjamin*. München: Wilhelm Fink Verlag.

Weigel, Sigrid. 1996. *Body- and Image-Space: Re-Reading Walter Benjamin*. London: Routledge.

Wind, Edgar. 1983. Warburg's Concept of *Kulturwissenschaft* and Its Meaning for Aesthetics (1931). In Edgar Wind, *The Eloquence of Symbols: Studies in Humanist Art*, ed. J. Anderson. Oxford: Clarendon Press.

Witte, Bernd. 2007. *Jüdische Tradition und literarische Moderne*. München: Carl Hanser Verlag, GmbH & Co.

Zimnik, Nina. 1997. Allegorie und Subjektivität in Walter Benjamins *Ursprung des deutschen Trauerspiels*. *Germanic Review* 72, no. 4: 285–302.

Žižek, Slavoj. 1993. *Tarrying with the Negative: Kant, Hegel and the Critique of Ideology*. Durham: Duke University Press.

INDEX